Praise for *The Jewish Experience*

"Rabbi Mark Wildes has written an extraordinary book. With great clarity, honest self-reflection, and deep wisdom, this master teacher of Jewish texts and values explains what Judaism has to offer the contemporary Jew seeking meaning in today's complex world. In the last three decades, Rabbi Wildes has influenced thousands of Jews – literally – to appreciate the depth and relevance of traditional Judaism, and he has now made his teachings available to novices and veterans alike. Rabbi Wildes's range of sources is impressive – ancient and modern, Jewish and non-Jewish, academic and popular, all presented in an interesting and engaging fashion. Over the years I have learned much from this great teacher as I have now from this important book."

Rabbi Dr. Jacob J. Schacter
University Professor of Jewish History and Jewish Thought
Senior Scholar, RIETS
Yeshiva University

"After October 7th, *The Jewish Experience* is a critical read. Whether you're a skeptic or a believer, this book is for anyone who wants to know Judaism's approach to life's greatest mysteries. While posing difficult questions about faith, tradition, and Jewish life in the twenty-first century, Rabbi Mark Wildes never fails to bring a smile to my face."

Dr. Shai Davidai
Professor, Columbia University

"In a time when so many are searching for meaning and connection, *The Jewish Experience* offers a much-needed invitation into the depth and beauty of Jewish life. Rabbi Mark Wildes has dedicated his life to building new doorways into authentic Jewish thought and practice – doors that welcome seekers with warmth, intelligence, and integrity. This book is a natural extension of his mission, and a vital contribution to the Jewish future."

Rabbi Dr. Ari Berman
President, Yeshiva University

"The most urgent mission for the Jewish people today – is simply to be more Jewish. To know, to learn, to understand – and to practice. Rabbi Mark Wildes, a pioneer in Jewish outreach and education at the renowned Manhattan Jewish Experience (MJE), has authored an extraordinary book which speaks directly to this mission. *The Jewish Experience* gives the novice and the seasoned a powerful resource to grasp the depth and, indeed, the soul of Jewish thought and practice."

Sivan Rahav-Meir

Journalist and Israeli Media Personality

"What a delightful, insightful, accessible, and necessary book! In *The Jewish Experience*, Rabbi Wildes has provided a modern-day Guide for the Perplexed for the great many Jews now seeking a more informed and intimate relationship with Judaism and Jewish life. This book is more than a must – it's a mitzvah."

Dr. Michael Oren

Historian, Diplomat

Former Israeli Ambassador to the United States

Previous Praise for Rabbi Mark Wildes

"Rabbi Wildes... urges young Jews around the world not just to treasure their heritage and history but to recognize why Judaism's timeless values have much to say in today's complex world."

Rabbi Lord Jonathan Sacks

Former Chief Rabbi of the United Hebrew Congregations of the Commonwealth

"...Wildes shows an impressive ability to seamlessly fuse Torah teachings with pop culture in a manner that makes for an accessible, entertaining, and insightful read."

The Algemeiner

THE JEWISH EXPERIENCE
Discovering the Soul of Jewish Thought and Practice

Rabbi Mark Wildes

THE JEWISH EXPERIENCE

DISCOVERING THE SOUL OF JEWISH THOUGHT AND PRACTICE

THE DAHAN FAMILY EDITION

MJE
Maggid Books

The Jewish Experience
Discovering the Soul of Jewish Thought and Practice

First Edition, 2025

Maggid Books
An imprint of Koren Publishers Jerusalem Ltd.

POB 8531, New Milford, CT 06776-8531, USA
& POB 4044, Jerusalem 9104001, Israel
www.korenpub.com

References to Koren Shalem Siddur
are from the *Nusah Ashkenaz* edition of
The Koren Shalem Siddur, The Lobel Edition
(Koren Publishers Jerusalem, 2024)

The publication of this book was made possible
through the generous support of *The Jewish Book Trust.*

ISBN 978-1-59264-712-5, *hardcover*

Printed in ROT

Dedicated by Jackie and Omri Dahan

To our grandparents and parents, who bestowed upon us
an unbroken chain of proud Jewish life…
and to our children, Maya, Ezra, and Jonah
the future links in the chain.

To our beloved friends,

Rabbi Mark and Jill Wildes

for seeing and igniting the spark in all of us.

זֶה דּוֹר דֹּרְשָׁו מְבַקְשֵׁי פָנֶיךָ...

This is the generation of those who seek Him,
those who strive for your Presence…
(Psalms 24:6)

Contents

Introduction xi
Acknowledgments xvii

Chapter 1
Finding God: A Journey Through History, Science, and the Soul 3
Part 1: Finding God from Without 4
Further Reading 23
Part 2: Finding God from Within 24
Part 3: Can You Be Good Without God? 33
Putting Faith into Practice: The *Shema* 43
Further Reading 46
Takeaways 46

Chapter 2
Torah: Reverberations from On High 57
The Written Torah 77
The Oral Torah 78
A Letter in the Scroll 89
Further Reading 93
Takeaways 94

Chapter 3
Prayer: Mindfulness for Anxious Times 101
The Philosophy of Prayer: Four Approaches 102
The "How-Tos" of Prayer 118
The Kabbalah of Prayer..................................151
A Broken Heart..153
It's Not All or Nothing 156
Further Reading.......................................156
Takeaways...157

Chapter 4
Kindness and Charity: Building a World of Compassion ..165
Acts of Kindness....................................... 168
Charity 186
The Kabbalah of Kindness............................... 192
Putting Kindness and Charity into Practice 193
A Parting Word from Elvis.............................. 194
Further Reading...................................... 194
Takeaways...195

Chapter 5
Shabbat: An Island in Time............................. 203
The Meaning of Shabbat..................................204
The "How-Tos" of Shabbat................................212
The Kabbalah of Shabbat 240
Saying No to One Thing Is Saying Yes to Another 241
Developing Your Own Shabbat Experience 244
Keeping Shabbat for Those Who Can't 244
Further Reading.......................................246
Takeaways...246

Chapter 6
Tikkun Olam: Jewish Social Justice 255
Spiritual *Tikkun Olam*................................... 274
Tikkun Olam as a Legal Force 277
The Kabbalah of *Tikkun Olam* 278
My Own Take.. 280
Not a Religion of Its Own 281
The Dawning of Redemption 282
Further Reading...283
Takeaways.. 283

Image Credits 288

Introduction

Year after year, Apple achieves so many more technological breakthroughs than their competition. Apple has access to the same talent pool as all the other technology companies, yet they consistently innovate and outsell all the others. What is their secret?

In a popular TED Talk with over 64 million views, Simon Sinek explains that the most successful organizations, companies, and leaders communicate not only *what* they do or *how* they do it, but also *why* they exist. What is the company or leader's purpose? Why should anyone care about their company or product? If all Apple communicated was that they make beautifully designed computers, they wouldn't outsell their competitors, because telling others *what* you do is simply not inspiring. To motivate others to act, people need to know the *why*. This is the reason Apple's marketing communicates *why* they exist. As Sinek puts it: "People don't buy *what* you do but *why* you do it."

How many of us know the *whys* behind Judaism? How educated are we as to why Judaism exists in the first place – what it is trying to accomplish for our lives and for the world at large? Most of us know Judaism has a lot of whats. It purports a belief in God, has a day of rest called the Sabbath, and mandates certain dietary restrictions. But why? Why do these and the many other Jewish traditions matter? Why choose Judaism over the countless other religions in the first place? Why choose religion at all? The reality is that most of us were never told the whys behind the many whats of Judaism, leaving us unmoved and unmotivated.

As the great Jewish thinker Maimonides wrote: "You can only love God according to the knowledge you have of Him. The amount of love depends on the amount of knowledge. A small amount of knowledge arouses a lesser love, and a greater amount of knowledge arouses a greater love" (Maimonides, *Mishneh Torah,* Laws of Repentance 10:6). This quote captures the intimate relationship between what we know intellectually and what we feel emotionally, between our knowledge of Judaism and the feelings we have for being Jewish.

It's no wonder that so few Jews possess a deep appreciation for their Jewish heritage when they never had the chance to learn the whys behind Judaism's beliefs and practices. Although Jewish people rank high in secular education, most of us finish our Jewish education by the time we turn twelve or thirteen. Bar and bat mitzvahs effectively serve as graduation ceremonies from Jewish learning. So as we enter adolescence and the college years and start asking the big questions about life, Judaism has already become a distant memory relegated to the past. For lots of people, Judaism isn't in the mix of ideas to help us address the hard problems of life. Instead, many turn to other spiritual traditions. Buddhism, yoga, and mindfulness have become alternative religions, but Torah is no longer a source of wisdom to consult. Because we only learned about Judaism when we were children, it doesn't feel sophisticated enough to speak to our complex adult lives. As a result, we remain unaware of the depth of our Jewish heritage and its relevance in the modern world.

That's why I wrote this book. I have spent the last thirty years teaching the fundamentals of Jewish thought and practice, demonstrating their relevance to our lives today. My beloved students come from all backgrounds, primarily men and women with no formal Jewish education but who are smart, well educated, curious, and motivated to learn. The encounter with my students each week has forced me to clarify complicated ideas and articulate *why* the age-old concepts and practices of Judaism are more essential for our lives today than ever before. This book is for bright and inquisitive but Jewishly uneducated people like my students who are seeking more depth in their lives.

But this book is not only for Jews or non-Jews with little or no background in Judaism. It is also for students who went to Jewish schools. It is possible to attend Jewish day school for twelve years, study Torah for a year or two in Israel, and even complete rabbinical school, like I did, and still not learn the reasons behind the mitzvot and the fundamental ideas of

Judaism. Similarly, many of my students have some Jewish education but still feel that they don't know the basics of Judaism. This book is for them too.

It is also for Jewish educators. I get calls and texts all the time from rabbinic colleagues and educators asking me how I teach about belief in God, how we know the Torah was given at Mount Sinai, why God needs our prayers, or the meaning of Shabbat. This book is therefore also for the thousands of rabbis and teachers in the United States and throughout the world who are looking for a ready-made guide to help them present basic topics of Judaism.

In reworking my classes for this book, I made sure to incorporate my students' questions and comments, since my goal is not only to present Judaism's core teachings and the whats of Jewish observance, but also why these ideas and observances are compelling for us today. Besides explaining what classical Judaism has to say about God and Revelation, I will therefore also discuss why these areas of Jewish tradition still matter today.

This includes many deep and fundamental questions: Why does believing in God or in a divinely inspired Torah impact our lives? How should the biblical text be read in modern times: literally or metaphorically? In what way are practices of observant Jews derived from the Torah? How are Shabbat, *kashrut,* and other parts of Jewish tradition meant to transform us as individuals and as a community?

I will also try to answer questions like: Does God really care if we drive a car on Shabbat? What does it matter what I eat? Or my favorite question about prayer: If God already knows what we want, what is the point of praying, and how is it designed to bring about the kind of mindfulness our generation seeks today? We all know that giving to others in need is a good thing, but how does performing acts of kindness or giving charity also bind us to God? Is there a specific *Jewish* responsibility to fix the world's problems and bring about positive change for society at large? What happens after we die? Is there really a Messiah, or was that just a made-up idea to keep oppressed Jews from losing hope? What is the Jewish attitude to sex? Is there religious significance to the modern State of Israel – especially in the wake of October 7, the worst single attack on the Jewish people since the Holocaust? Finally, what is the point of all the Jewish holidays? Why is Yom Kippur, a twenty-four-hour day when we deprive ourselves of food and drink, considered the happiest day of the year? Why is the Jewish New Year so solemn – and does Judaism have an equivalent of New Year's resolutions? In general, what is each holiday all about and, more importantly, what spiritual impact is each one meant to have on us?

Some chapters in this volume lend themselves more to ideas (the whys), such as the chapters on God and Torah, and others to hands-on "how-tos" (the whats), such as those on Shabbat, prayer, and kindness. In addressing the whys, I offer many of the rational explanations offered by the Sages for the mitzvot, as well as deep ideas from the Kabbalah, age-old mystical wisdom that so many people are finding relevant today. In this way, this book serves as both an introduction to Judaism and a hands-on guidebook to Jewish practice.

In writing this book, I struggled between referring to Jews as "they," in the third person, and "we," in the first person. On one hand, this book is for anyone interested in Judaism, Jew and non-Jew alike, and so "they" reflects the inclusive spirit I strived for. At the same time, "we" feels warmer and more personable, a tone I try to achieve in my classes and writing as well. To try to strike a balance, I ultimately decided to alternate between first and third person throughout the book. If you're a non-Jewish reader, please don't be put off – this book is for everyone!

Throughout the book, in addition to the main text, you will see the following additional features:

- **Kabbalah Corner** – Kabbalah, the Jewish mystical tradition, explores the Torah's deeper spiritual dimension. In each chapter, you'll find "Kabbalah Corner" boxes offering inspirational, eye-opening insights from Jewish mysticism that relate to the subject matter. You'll recognize these by the (א) icon. In Kabbala, a letter on fire symbolizes the fusion of divine energy (*ohr*) with form (*tzurah*), expressing how the infinite light of God is channeled through the finite vessels of Hebrew letters. This imagery reflects the dynamic, living nature of Torah, where each letter burns with spiritual vitality and creative power.
- **Quotes** – Classical Jewish works have a remarkable ability to distill Jewish wisdom into pithy, profound teachings. Throughout the book, you'll find "Quotes" boxes featuring direct quotations from essential sources from the Bible and Talmud down to modern texts. You'll recognize these by the shaded background ( ).

- **Stop and Reflect** – Judaism is about more than laws and ideas; it's a path to personal growth and a deeper connection with God and with yourself. In each chapter, you'll find "Stop and Reflect" boxes encouraging you to pause, reflect, and jot down your thoughts. You'll recognize these by the ( ) icon.
- **Takeaways** – Each chapter in this book is chock-full of information. To make sure the forest doesn't get lost for the trees, at the end of each chapter you'll find a set of short, bullet-point "Takeaways" that sum up the chapter's essential points.

Finally, while the book expresses my own take on the different areas of Jewish tradition, I also rely on the profound ideas of my mentors and teachers from whom I have been privileged to learn. In particular, I often cite the teachings of Rabbi Joseph B. Soloveitchik (1903–1993), a brilliant talmudic scholar and philosopher whose teachings have had a profound impact on me. While I never merited to study under this great rabbi directly, most of my teachers were his students. I also went to great lengths to incorporate the teachings of many other rabbinic, contemporary, and classic thinkers, while offering both rational and mystical explanations to ensure this work can be appreciated by as wide an audience as possible. Reading this book is therefore like reading twenty books in one since it incorporates the insights of many different scholars – ideas which not only speak to me, but also have resonated with my many students for the last three decades.

This book offers a reboot for your Judaism. It would be nice to begin with a clean slate, to start without any preconceived assumptions we have about Judaism. But even if you do not approach this book with a clean slate, your starting point is the part of you that seeks answers, that craves purpose and meaning, and feels some connection, however distant, to the Divine. That too is a good place from which to restart your Judaism: from the spark of your Jewish soul.

I write this introduction sitting at the Western Wall in Jerusalem with the hope that the holiness of this place somehow finds its way into this book. My sincere wish is that you find my thoughts and ideas compelling and inspiring. I pray my words arouse a renewed interest in your Jewish heritage and kindle a greater love for Torah, your soul, and their divine source.

Acknowledgments

From a young age I was blessed with extraordinary parents, mentors, colleagues, and friends, who have shaped my life and guided my work. Without them, this work would never have come to be.

First, to my dear friends Jackie and Omri Dahan, who generously sponsored *The Jewish Experience*. The talmudic sage Rabbi Chanina once said: *I have learned much from my teachers and even more of from my friends, but from my students I have learned more than from all of them.* (Talmud Ta'anit 7a). My relationship with Jackie and Omri began as teacher and students at the Manhattan Jewish Experience (MJE is the outreach and educational program I established in 1998 which engages less-affiliated Jewish twenty- and thirty-year-olds in Jewish life), but over time our bond developed into a friendship from which my wife and I have gained immensely. As much as I remain their teacher and mentor, they have become mine, guiding me in my outreach and educational work. I am indebted to them for encouraging me to write this book while providing the means to make it possible. In doing so, Jackie and Omri have ensured that the same wisdom that inspired their own journey is now available to illuminate the paths for others.

To my beloved parents Ruth and Leon Wildes, of blessed memory, who modeled a Judaism I have transmitted to my own children and students. My mother, a woman of deep faith and warmth, was my first genuine source of spiritual inspiration. Her love for Shabbat and the graciousness with which she received guests at her expanding Shabbat table inspired me to establish MJE. This book is a testament to the love she gave me and the model of Judaism she created in our home.

My father was my greatest mentor. From the time I was in elementary school through graduate school, my father would correct all my papers with his notorious red pen. It was sometimes a brutal experience, but he taught me how to write and speak, reviewing my weekly Shabbat sermons for close to three decades. My law school professor and Torah study partner, my father stood behind my every endeavor. When he saw my passion was Jewish outreach and education, he supported my decision to establish MJE and not follow him into the legal field, even after putting me through law school and graduate school. This book stands as a tribute to his unwavering guidance and love.

My wife Jill – my partner for the last twenty-nine years – is my greatest inspiration. Her passion for Jewish life has motivated thousands of others to explore their own spiritual heritage. Jill devotes herself to the myriads of young people in the MJE community, hosting twenty students at our Shabbat table each week and modeling a Judaism which is both open and vibrant. She is the love of my life and my constant source of support, without whom neither MJE nor this book would ever have been possible.

My children, Yosef, Ezra, Yehuda, and Avigayil, are my deepest sources of pride. I am grateful to each of them for their contributions to this book: Yosef and Yehuda for helping me clarify and formulate some of the kabbalistic ideas, Ezra for his help with the teleological argument and the relationship between God and morality, and Avigayil for working with me on the quotes found throughout the work. One of my greatest joys is studying Torah with my children, and so weaving their insights into this work was especially meaningful.

To my brother Michael and sister-in-law Amy, for all their love and support. Amy originated the name "Manhattan Jewish Experience" (MJE), which in turn inspired the title of this book, "The Jewish Experience." Judaism was never meant to be something we just study, but rather an *experience* that is lived and celebrated. That is what we have shared with the participants of MJE these last twenty-six years – a Jewish experience – and it is my sincere hope this book offers the same opportunity.

Special thanks to my beloved teacher and mentor Rabbi Dr. Jacob J. Schacter for encouraging me to write this book. For over twenty years I've sat at the feet of this brilliant scholar, absorbing his wisdom and being the beneficiary of his loving guidance. It was Rabbi Schacter who first invited me to teach a Basic Judaism course at his then-synagogue The Jewish Center in New York City. That class, which developed over the next three decades, is the subject matter for this book.

To Rabbi Joseph Grunblatt, of blessed memory, my childhood rabbi who guided me in my first outreach endeavor at the Queens Jewish Center, and Rabbi Dr. Norman Lamm, of blessed memory – noted scholar and past president of Yeshiva University where my father, myself, and all my children studied. To my rabbinic mentors Rabbi Haskel Lookstein, Rabbi Ephraim Buchwald, Rabbi Jonathan Rosenblatt, Rabbi Johnny Krug, and Rabbi Aaron Bina – your impact is woven into this book and all my work. To my MJE colleagues Rabbi Pinny Rosenthal, Rabbi Ezra Cohen, Rabbi Avi Heller, and the entire MJE team – you make our mission to educate and inspire possible.

To the exceptional team at Koren Publishers – Matthew Miller, Aryeh Grossman, Reuven Ziegler, Caryn Meltz, Taly Hahn, Tani Bayer, Ita Olesker, Nechama Unterman, and Debbie Ismailoff – your dedication and professionalism brought this book to life. Special thanks to Rabbi Tzvi Sinensky for his meticulous review of the manuscript and his invaluable insights which truly enhanced the book.

And finally, to God for granting me life, sustaining me, and enabling me to write this book. I am humbled by the experience of sharing even just a measure of the Torah's timeless wisdom. May these words bring more of His light into the world, enabling others to draw closer to His presence.

CHAPTER 1
Finding God

CHAPTER 1

FINDING GOD

A Journey Through History, Science, and the Soul

I have always considered myself a rationally oriented individual. I was attracted to Judaism's intellectual approach already in my teens and loved to debate my more skeptical friends using the logic and reason I would find in the Talmud. I was drawn to more rational rabbinic figures like Maimonides, and I loved that Judaism did not require me to simply "believe" but instead encouraged logical and reasoned analysis. As I have gotten older, though, I have come to realize the limited ability of logic and reason to answer all of life's questions – including the belief in God. I have found great wisdom and inspiration in Judaism's mystical teachings, and I feel strongly that they also must be studied if one is to gain a true appreciation for the depth of Jewish thought, especially when it comes to God. In the next few sections, I will therefore present both the rational and mystical basis for the Jewish belief in a supernatural God. Perhaps one approach will speak to you more than the other, but both perspectives are necessary to give us a window into arguably the most important contribution Judaism has made to the world: the belief in one God.

I like to call these *finding God from without* and *finding God from within.* Finding God from without involves looking at external and more objective factors – history and science – which strongly suggest the existence of a supernatural creator. Finding God from within signifies a more mystical approach, tapping into a spiritual reality the Jewish Sages believe exists within each of us. According to Judaism, we can use both avenues to develop a belief in, and more importantly, an attachment to God.

We will start with the more rational methodology of *finding God from without* in part 1 and proceed to the more mystical approach of *finding God from within* in part 2. We will then discuss the relationship between God, morality, and kindness in part 3.

PART 1: FINDING GOD FROM WITHOUT

Close your eyes, turn off your brain, and just *believe* away. This is how many people think of faith. While this may be true of other religions, it is generally not true of Judaism.[1] Judaism largely rejects blind faith. Indeed, the great Jewish philosopher Maimonides formulates the biblical command to believe in God as "to know" that there is a God.[2] Judaism demands that we have *knowledge,* an intellectual basis for our belief. But how is that possible? The God of Judaism cannot be seen or experienced by any of the five senses. So how can God's existence be rationally demonstrated?

To answer this question, it is important to recognize that absolute proof, even in the realm of science, simply does not exist. A theory is accepted not because it has been 100 percent proven, but because it *best* explains the cumulative data or phenomena. As Nobel Prize–winning physicist Richard Feynman is often quoted: "It is scientific only to say what is more likely and less likely."

Therefore, our goal is not to demonstrate proof but probability – what makes the most sense. That is also how we make our most important life decisions – not based on complete certainty, but on what is most reasonable.

One of my mentors shared that right before he was about to get married, the officiating rabbi – the great twentieth-century thinker Rabbi Joseph B. Soloveitchik – turned to him and, somewhat in jest, asked: "So, are you sure she is the right one?" My friend, the groom, was stunned by the question and said nothing in response. The rabbi continued: "Good, only a fool could be sure." Rabbi Soloveitchik was trying to assure my friend that there is no such thing as perfect certainty, especially when it comes to matters of the heart, such as the person we marry. On the other hand, that does not mean the groom was being foolish or acting irrationally by getting married. Most brides and grooms believe they are making the right choice. But it is impossible to be 100 percent certain of anything – not in the realm of human relationships and not about the existence of God. My goal in this section is therefore not to establish a definitive proof for God's existence but to articulate a reasonable basis for belief, one that best explains our reality.

There are several external factors which serve as a rational basis for the belief in God, giving us what contemporary author Lawrence Kelemen calls "permission to believe." The two I have found most compelling are the "Argument from Jewish History" and the "Argument from Intelligent Design." Neither proves God's existence, but both make a powerful argument for the existence of a supernatural creator.

THE ARGUMENT FROM JEWISH HISTORY

The story is told of King Louis XIV asking the philosopher Pascal for some proof of a supernatural force in the world. Pascal answered, "The Jews, your majesty. The Jews."

Pascal was far from alone. To me and so many others, the survival of the Jewish people – against all odds – serves as evidence, or at least a reasonable basis, for the belief in a supernatural force responsible for Jewish survival throughout the ages.

> "The Jewish people are eternal. Nothing can destroy the Jew; only his body, never his soul." (The Lubavitcher Rebbe)

Allow me to explain as we take a brief stroll through Jewish history.[3] The Jewish people began as slaves. But unlike other groups who served the ancient Egyptian Pharaohs, the Jews managed to escape into the Sinai Desert in around the year 1300 BCE. Attacked by warring tribes, the Jews wandered in the wilderness but eventually arrived at their promised land. After fighting more battles, the Jews settled peacefully in ancient Israel, building a Temple in Jerusalem under the wise King Solomon. The Temple stood for more than four centuries until 586 BCE, when Nebuchadnezzar, king of Babylon, having first defeated the Assyrian and Egyptian armies, swept into Israel, plundered Jerusalem, destroyed the Temple, and exiled the survivors to Babylon.

BABYLONIA AND PERSIA

For all intents and purposes, Jewish history should have ended at this point, with the remaining Jewish minority assimilating into Babylonian culture. But the Persians toppled the Babylonians, and the Persian King Ahasuerus installed an antisemitic leader named Haman, who attempted to annihilate the entire Diaspora Jewish community. Haman's genocidal attempt was not only foiled, but it reignited a Jewish renaissance, celebrated each year on the Jewish holiday of Purim. Meanwhile, the Persian leader, Cyrus the Great, had allowed the Jews to return to Israel and rebuild their Temple. A small but committed group of Jews did so, becoming the first people ever to regain a land they had lost more than a half a century before.

GREECE AND ROME

Under Alexander the Great, the Greeks defeated the Persians and eventually ruled the Jews of ancient Judea. Following a period of much infighting between Jewish Hellenists and traditionalists, the Greek Seleucids outlawed the practice of Judaism and converted the Jewish Temple into a place of idol worship and paganism. The Jews went underground. Utilizing guerrilla tactics, they revolted against the Greeks, repelling their far superior forces, and ultimately expelled the Greeks – the mightiest military force on the planet – from Jerusalem. The success of the Jewish rebellion and reinstatement of Jewish independence in ancient Israel is celebrated every year on the holiday of Hanukkah.

Meanwhile, Rome expanded its empire and, in 40 BCE, having succeeded Greece as the world power, dispatched tens of thousands of infantry and cavalry to conquer Jerusalem from the Jews. There were several Jewish rebellions against the Romans, but all were suppressed. Thousands of Jews were killed, the Jewish Temple was razed to the ground, and, once again, the Jewish survivors fled into the Diaspora.

TWO THOUSAND LONG YEARS

In the Diaspora, the Jews, no longer in their land and without a Temple, were more vulnerable than ever. What followed for the next two thousand years were centuries of persecution – crusades, expulsions, inquisitions, pogroms – more and more antisemitism, culminating in the Holocaust. Once again, that should have been the last chapter in the history of the Jews.

But it wasn't. Quite the opposite.

> "Israel is like a lamb surrounded by seventy wolves: It survives only thanks to the protection of the shepherd." (*Midrash Tanchuma*)

COMING HOME

Instead, for the first time in history, a people twice exiled from its land returned to establish an independent state. On May 14, 1948, the State of Israel was created.

The next day, fewer than 45,000 Jews, many of them Holocaust survivors, faced the combined military forces of Egypt, Syria, Iraq, Lebanon, and Transjordan. The secretary-general of the Arab League proclaimed over the airwaves: "This will be a war of extermination and a momentous massacre."[4] Somehow the Jews held out. A month after the war broke out, the United Nations declared a ceasefire, and for the first time in two thousand years the Jews had a state of their own.

KABBALAH CORNER:
The year 1948 corresponds to 5708 in the Jewish calendar. Astonishingly, the 5,708th verse of the Torah, Deuteronomy 30:3, states: "The Lord your God will restore your fortunes and have compassion on you: He will return to collect you from all the peoples to which the Lord your God has scattered you." A kabbalist in the holy city of Tzefat pointed out this connection to my teacher Rabbi Benjamin Blech, noting that this verse is a clear allusion to the ingathering of the exiles, which took place in that very year, marking the establishment of the State of Israel.

IN JUST SIX DAYS

In 1964, the Palestinian Liberation Organization (PLO) and other Arab groups opposed to Israel's existence were created to terrorize the Jewish community from within. The Jews held out until May 1967, when massive numbers of troops began mobilizing along Israel's southern border with Egypt and its northern border with Syria, the Golan Heights. Egypt's President Abdul Nasser ordered the United Nations Emergency Force to withdraw, and on May 18, 1967, the Voice of the Arabs radio station proclaimed: "The sole method we shall apply against Israel is total war, which will result in the extermination of Zionist existence."[5] The Syrian defense minister, Hafez Assad, announced that "the time has come to enter into a battle of annihilation."[6] On

STOP AND REFLECT:
If you had to rate the depth of your connection to Israel on a scale from 1 to 10, with 1 being the weakest connection and 10 being the strongest, what number would you choose and why?

IDF soldiers at the Western Wall, June 7, 1967

May 30, King Hussein of Jordan entered into a defense pact with Egypt, whereupon Nasser announced: "The armies of Egypt, Jordan, Syria, and Lebanon are poised on the border of Israel... while standing behind us are the armies of Iraq, Algeria, Kuwait, Sudan, and the whole Arab nation."[7] On June 4, Iraq joined the military alliance with Egypt, Jordan, and Syria. The president of Iraq declared: "Our goal is clear: to wipe Israel off the map."[8]

A total of 465,000 troops, 2,800 tanks, and 800 aircraft encircled the tiny infant State of Israel.[9] As Middle East policy analyst Mitchell Bard described, "Approximately 180 Israeli tanks faced 1,400 Syrian tanks on the Golan Heights, while fewer than 500 defenders with only three tanks were attacked by 600,000 Egyptian soldiers backed by 2,000 tanks and 550 aircraft along the Suez Canal."[10]

Rather than wait to be attacked, Israel struck preemptively. On June 5, 1967, virtually the entire Israeli air force took off at 7:14 a.m. In less than two hours, three hundred Egyptian aircraft were destroyed. Israeli fighters attacked Jordanian and Syrian planes and an airfield in Iraq. By the end of the first day, almost the entire Egyptian and Jordanian air force – and half of the Syrian's – had been destroyed on the ground.

While most of the Israel Defense Forces (IDF) were fighting the Egyptians and Jordanians, a small group of soldiers were left to defend the northern border against the Syrians. It was not until the Jordanian and Egyptian forces were defeated that the IDF was able to send reinforcements to the Golan Heights, where Syrian gunners held control of the strategic high ground. On June 9, after two days of heavy air bombardment, Israeli forces succeeded in breaking through Syrian lines.

It took only three days for the Israeli forces to defeat the reputable Jordanian legions. So on the morning of June 7, the order was given to recapture the Old City of Jerusalem. Israeli paratroopers stormed the city and secured it before Defense Minister Moshe Dayan arrived with Chief of Staff Yitzhak Rabin to formally mark the Jewish people's return to their historic capital and their holiest site.

In just six days, Israel went from defending herself from complete annihilation to reunifying Jerusalem and capturing the Sinai Peninsula, the Golan Heights, the Gaza Strip, and the West Bank. The world was stunned. Israeli troops marched to the Western Wall, the last remaining wall of those encircling the ancient Jewish Temple Mount, and Chief Rabbi Shlomo Goren blew a shofar to celebrate the return of the people of Israel to the heart of the Land of Israel – to Jerusalem.

The victory of the Six-Day War bordered on the miraculous. David Ben-Gurion, the first prime minister of the State of Israel, summed it up best when he said: "In Israel, in order to be a realist, you must believe in miracles."[11]

> "The Six-Day War was a miracle. It was as if the heavens themselves opened up to defend the people of Israel." (Golda Meir, third prime minister of Israel)

To me, that is Jewish history in a nutshell.

JEWISH IMMORTALITY

In 1892, the great American writer and poet Mark Twain famously asked: "The Jews constitute but one percent of the human race. It suggests the nebulous dim puff of stardust lost in the blaze of the Milky Way. Properly the Jew ought hardly to be heard of.... The Egyptian, the Babylonian, and the Persian rose, filled the planet with sound and splendor, then faded to dream-stuff and passed away; the Greek and the Roman followed, and made a vast noise, and they are gone; other peoples have sprung up and held their torch high for a time, but it burned out, and they sit in twilight now, or have vanished. The Jew saw them all, beat them all, and is now what he always was, exhibiting no decadence, no infirmities of age, no weakening of his parts, no slowing of his energies, no dulling of his alert and aggressive mind. All things are mortal but the Jew; all other forces pass, but he remains. What is the secret of his immortality?"[12]

If I may be so bold as to offer an answer to Mark Twain's question, *What is the secret of his immortality?*, my simple response is "God." To me, it is all but impossible to explain Jewish history without believing in a higher force ensuring Jewish survival throughout the ages. To be sure, we can rationally explain any one of the above-mentioned instances of Jewish survival, be it the expulsion of Greek forces from ancient Judea or the salvation of Persian Jewry, without having to acknowledge a supernatural force. But to explain the *totality* of Jewish history – how one nation could survive *all* these attempts at its destruction – one has little choice but to concede that some other force is at work.

The Jewish belief in God is a belief not merely in a God of creation but also in a God of history – that God is actively involved in the affairs of the world.

KABBALAH CORNER:
God is *sovev kol almin*, meaning that He surrounds the universe. But since God is infinite, He is not bound by the changes that occur within the finite laws of nature, such as changes between seasons. Simultaneously, He is *memalei kol almin*, filling the world so He can establish an intimate relationship with each of His creations. (Rabbi Shneur Zalman of Liadi, founder of Chabad Chasidism)

The continued survival of the Jewish people against all odds demonstrates God's involvement, for as history attests, time and again, when a minority group lives within a different majority culture, the minority people eventually vanish, due to either physical annihilation or cultural assimilation. For over two thousand years, the Jewish people lived as a miniscule, counter-cultural minority within dozens of Diaspora countries and came uncomfortably close to both annihilation and assimilation. But neither happened. How? Is the Jewish people's continued survival simply a coincidence, a fluke of history?

AM YISRAEL CHAI: THE JEWISH PEOPLE LIVE!

But the Jews have not simply survived. Despite the years and intensity of persecution, the Jews have contributed to the world in a way vastly disproportionate to their small numbers. Despite the fact that the Jewish people consist of less than one-fifth of 1 percent of the world population, they have won 22 percent of all Nobel Prizes.[13] In virtually every field of human endeavor – science, law, medicine, and philosophy – Jews are consistently at the forefront. Jews have not simply endured; they have excelled. Some joke that three of the four thinkers who most influenced twentieth-century Western thought were Jewish – and the fourth was wrong![14]

You do not need to be a religious person to recognize that some other power is at work – a force which ensured that the Jews escaped Egyptian slavery, repelled the Greeks, and survived the Babylonian, Persian, and Roman Empires and their powerful armies.

Arch of Titus

I was overwhelmed by this thought when I first visited the famous Arch of Titus in Rome. The arch depicts the Roman legionnaires carrying the vessels of the Jewish Temple they had just destroyed, as they marched the defeated Jews into exile and slavery. It was honestly a depressing image to behold. But then I noticed something which made me smile. The Hebrew phrase *Am Yisrael Chai* – "The Jewish people live!" – was spray-painted on the adjacent wall. This phrase, no doubt written by an Israeli tourist with chutzpah, is the Jewish response to millennia of persecution. The Arch of Titus celebrates the power of the ancient Roman Empire and their defeat of the Jewish people. But that was two thousand years ago. Today the Roman Empire is no longer, and the Jewish people live and thrive in Israel and throughout the world.

How can one explain the continued existence of the Jewish people? How does tiny Israel continue to blossom with so many powerful enemies on her borders?

> "Israel is a land the Lord your God cares for; the eyes of the Lord your God are constantly upon it from the beginning of the year to the end." (Deuteronomy 11:12)

How, in six days, did Israel manage to triple its size in a completely defensive war? A war in which soldiers – among them self-avowed secularists – claimed they saw miracles and found themselves praying at the Western Wall when it was all over!

Imagine if we could travel back in time and tell the great Pharaohs of Egypt that thousands of years later it wouldn't be Egypt that would survive, but the people they enslaved.

Imagine if we could tell the Caesars of Rome that their powerful legions would not stand the test of time, but instead it would be the small minority they oppressed and whose Temple they destroyed.

Imagine if Joseph Stalin and Adolf Hitler could see the hundreds of thousands of Jewish children today attending Jewish schools or the many Jews who gather every Friday night to pray at the Western Wall in Jerusalem, while Stalinist Russia and Nazi Germany lie consigned to the dustbin of history.

> "Surveying the breathtaking landscape of Jewish history, we know this: that those who sought to destroy the people of the covenant gather dust in the museums of mankind while *am Yisrael chai,* the people Israel lives." (Rabbi Jonathan Sacks)

BIBLICAL PREDICTIONS COME TRUE

Perhaps most remarkable, the Bible predicted that the Jews would survive for eternity. In describing the covenant God forged with the Jews, the Bible states: "You shall be to me a kingdom of priests and a holy nation."[15] The Italian sage Rabbi Ovadia Sforno understands the phrase "a holy nation" to mean an immortal nation never to disappear from the stage of history.[16] As to the phrase "a kingdom of priests," Sforno explains this too along similar lines: Just as the *kohanim* (the Jewish priests) were selected to be the teachers within the Jewish community, so too, among the nations of the world, the Jewish people were selected to be teachers in regard to monotheism and its values. In other words, to the extent that the Jewish people fulfill their mission to be "a kingdom of priests," their survival is guaranteed.

Later in the Bible, the prophet Jeremiah, in expressing God's vision, declares: "For I will bring annihilation upon all the nations among whom I have dispersed you, but upon you I will not bring annihilation."[17] Jeremiah continues: "If these laws [of nature] should ever be annulled by Me – declares the Lord – only then would the offspring of Israel cease to be a nation before Me for all time."[18] Finally, Malachi, the last prophet of the Bible, declared: "For I am the Lord – I have not changed; and you are the children of Jacob – you have not ceased to be."[19] The biblical commentator Radak explains this verse to mean that the Jewish people will not be destroyed "like the other nations" even though they may be "exiled and driven to every corner of the world."[20]

Nor does the Bible foretell that the Jews will survive because they will increase in numbers and build a great empire. Precisely the opposite is true. Moses tells the people: "It is not because you are the most numerous of peoples that the Lord grew attached to you and chose you – indeed, you are the smallest of peoples."[21] Moses, the greatest prophet, anticipates that the Jews will survive not because of their size but despite their small numbers.

WHAT IS THE JEW?

These biblical prophecies were confirmed by many modern thinkers, including the great Russian writer Leo Tolstoy, who declared: "What is the Jew? … What kind of unique creature is this whom all the rulers of all the nations of the world have disgraced and crushed and expelled and destroyed; persecuted, burned and drowned, and who, despite their anger and their fury, continues to live and to flourish? The Jew – is the symbol of eternity. … He is the one who for so long had guarded the prophetic message and transmitted it to all mankind. A people such as this can never disappear. The Jew is eternal. He is the embodiment of eternity."[22] Russian philosopher Nikolai Berdyaev also believed Jewish survival throughout the ages could be explained only in supernatural terms: "The Jews have played an all-important role in history. Their destiny is too imbued with the 'metaphysical' to be explained either in material or positive historical terms…. Its survival is a mysterious and wonderful phenomenon demonstrating that the life of this people is governed by special predetermination."[23]

We have answered Mark Twain's question: God is the secret to Jewish immortality.

THE ARGUMENT FROM INTELLIGENT DESIGN

Intelligent Design, or what some call the teleological argument, posits that one can develop a belief in God by observing the orderly and sophisticated design of the universe. Advocates of this approach argue that the extraordinary complexity of the world strongly implies the existence of a deliberate creator, and that the sheer improbability that such complexity can occur on its own makes the alternative implausible. This approach dates back to the ancient Greek philosophers, including Socrates, Plato, and Aristotle, and has been argued by Christian, Islamic, and Jewish[24] thinkers alike.

With the advent of modern scientific discoveries, the teleological argument has become even more compelling. For example, in 1953 James Watson and Francis Crick discovered DNA, a molecule found in every human cell which contains an exact blueprint of the body's every physical detail, from our fingerprints to the size and shape of our heart and the color of our eyes. This discovery has become even more fascinating in the computer age because DNA surpasses the storage efficiency of any modern-day hard drive.[25] In fact, if we were to electronically store the huge amount of information found in a single strip of DNA, it would take up trillions of computer bytes, yet DNA somehow crams all this information into a tiny molecule. The Australian microbiologist Dr. Michael Denton put it memorably when he wrote that "the information necessary to store the design of all the species of organisms which have ever existed on the planet could be held in a teaspoon and there would still be room left for all the information ever written in any book."[26]

MARVELS OF THE HUMAN BODY

The wonders of the design of the universe do not end with DNA. Every part of the human body coded into that DNA strip is incredibly intricate and sophisticated.

> "How great are Your works, O God, how profound Your designs." (Psalms 92:5)

When I was younger, I had difficulties with my eyesight. I had what they call strabismus and was legally blind in my left eye, so I spent a good deal of my childhood in the ophthalmolo-

ANATOMY OF THE HUMAN EYE

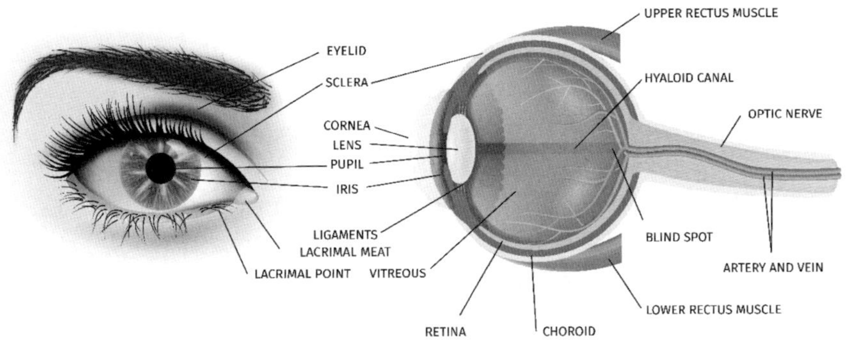

gist's office. I became fascinated with how the eye operates in such an elaborate way as to bring us the clear vision we take for granted. The eye contains millions of color sensors, which produce incredible detail over a vast range of lighting situations. Where there isn't enough light for color vision, millions of black and white sensors automatically switch on. The optic nerve accepts the signals and, as Kelemen writes, "recodes them into more compact signals, and shoots them down the few hundred thousand nerve fibers leading to our brain at about a billion impulses per second."[27] While all this is happening, the pupil adjusts itself to maintain the right lighting, another system in the eye regulates focal lengths for image sharpness, and an image enhancer clarifies distortions caused by motion or darkness. The detail and complexity of the human eye is simply astounding.

And all this is just one part of our anatomy! Aside from our eyes, Kelemen continues, "a perfectly fit ball-in-socket system allows our bones fluid movement; tendons, ligaments, and skin bind our limbs together without compromising flexibility; and muscles drive the whole skeletal system, responding with equal precision to the subtlest and most intense neural messages. Meanwhile, at every moment, the brain and its network of more than a million billion neural connections reach out to supervise all these operations and more... [and] our digestive system removes and restores valuable proteins, carbohydrates, and fats from foods, separating and excreting compounds the body cannot use."[28]

Thousands of years before the discoveries of modern anatomy, the Jewish Sages were acutely aware of the genius of the human digestive system. Numerous times daily we recite the blessing of *Asher Yatzar*, in which we thank God for crafting the human body with countless holes and cavities.[29] In many cases, we declare, if just one of these body parts would break down, the entire body would cease to function. The blessing concludes by recognizing the wonder of human anatomy (see text of prayer on p. 122).

STOP AND REFLECT: Which part of human anatomy do you find most remarkable and why?

What we have said so far, of course, concerns only the human body. There is also immensely sophisticated plant, fish, and bird life. And we haven't even touched on the physical design of the earth, solar system, and galaxies. The more we look at human anatomy and the more we investigate the universe, the more complexity, precision, and order we see. All this begs the obvious question: Who or what is behind all of this?

MONKEYS ON TYPEWRITERS

Nobel laureate Sir Fred Hoyle once remarked: "It was more likely that a tornado sweeping through a junkyard might assemble a Boeing 747" than that a single bacterium – the simplest life form – could have randomly evolved on its own. The probability of a virus or fungus randomly evolving is more unlikely; the complexity of a human being – even more so. This is why Dr. Francis Crick, the Nobel Prize recipient for his work identifying the structure of DNA, acknowledged that life could not have developed randomly. He was joined by other world-renowned scientists including Hoyle and his colleague Dr. Chandra Wickremasinghe, who famously remarked:

"Life cannot have had a random beginning. Troops of monkeys thundering away at random on typewriters could not produce the works of Shakespeare, for the practical reason that the whole observable universe is not large enough to contain the necessary monkey hoards, the necessary typewriters, and certainly the wastepaper baskets necessary for the deposition of wrong attempts. The same they said is true for living material."[30]

Monkey at a typewriter, 1907

The teleological argument is illustrated by a famous Jewish parable. A rabbi was once asked by a king how he knew of God's existence. To answer the question, the rabbi asked the king to leave the room. After the king stepped out, the rabbi composed a beautiful poem with ink and quill. After the king returned, the rabbi handed him the poem. The ink was still wet. The king praised the rabbi for writing such a beautiful poem. The rabbi responded that he had not written the poem but simply poured some ink over the paper, and the letters and words had formed themselves. The king ridiculed the rabbi, arguing that it was impossible for a single letter to arrange itself from an ink spill, let alone a word, a sentence, or a carefully phrased poem. "There is your answer," the rabbi exclaimed. "If ink poured from an inkwell cannot form a poem without the hand of a poet, then certainly the world, which is infinitely more complex than a poem, could not possibly form itself without the hand of a master creator."[31]

SHAKESPEAREAN SONNETS

The teleological argument surely has its critics. The argument can be broken down into its two basic premises: There is ordered complexity evident in the world, and that ordered complexity implies a creator. The Scottish philosopher David Hume rejected the first assumption, arguing that our limited scope of understanding of the world's expanse deprives us of the knowledge necessary to make such a claim. In Hume's *Dialogues,* he depicts a character, a religious skeptic named Philo, who argues for this position: "A very small part of this great system, during a very short time, is very imperfectly discovered to us; and do we thence pronounce decisively concerning the origin of the *whole*?"[32]

But Hume's argument is not persuasive. The small segment of our universe which we do understand, and which Hume concedes *does* display ordered complexity, implies the existence of a creator. Indeed, Sir Isaac Newton, one of the most influential scientists of all time – and a believer in monotheism and the divinity of the Bible[33] – is quoted as having said that "in the absence of any other proof, the thumb alone would convince me of God's existence."[34]

> "Gravity explains the motions of the planets, but it cannot explain who set the planets in motion." (Sir Isaac Newton)

The most popular challenge to the teleological approach, though, is the argument that with the passage of enough time, the complexity of our reality, and even life itself, can develop through the evolutionary processes of random mutation and natural selection. The great physicist Stephen Hawking invoked the infinite monkey theorem – that if you have enough monkeys "hammering away on typewriters," though "much of what they write will be garbage…very occasionally, by pure chance they will type out one of Shakespeare's sonnets."[35]

The question remains: How much time is necessary for all of this to develop *on its own*? At first glance, approximately three and a half billion years ago – the time frame scientists estimate for the origin of life – seems long enough to account for our intricate evolutionary development.[36] In fact, though, noted scientists argue that much more time is needed.[37] MIT physicist and Bible scholar Gerald Schroeder demonstrates that mathematically speaking, random typing by monkeys would require a significantly longer amount of time than cosmologists estimate as the age of the universe[38] for monkeys to produce even a short sonnet of a hundred words, let alone our universe, which is exponentially more complex.[39]

KABBALAH CORNER:
From Aristotle, who believed the world is eternal, to modern scientists, who postulate infinite universes, thinkers for millennia have attributed infinitude to something other than God. However, the Jewish Sages highlight that the letter *samech* (ס), a circle symbolizing infinity, does not appear in the biblical account of creation. For the Torah, infinity belongs solely to God. (Rabbi Akiva Tatz)

THE MULTIVERSE THEORY

For this reason, some scientists subscribe to the Multiverse Theory, which purports that there are multiple, possibly infinite, alternate universes, providing sufficient opportunity to create a uniquely complex world such as our own. MIT Professor Max Tegmark, for example, argues that the unlikely probability that our universe randomly possesses the exact properties necessary for sustaining life requires us to

The Big Bang 

believe that other universes exist. That, he claims, is the only way to provide enough alternatives to allow for a reasonable possibility for at least one of those universes, namely our own, to be sufficiently suited for life.[40]

But many scientists are skeptical. Cosmologist George Ellis notes that the "multiverse idea is provable neither by observation, nor as an implication of well-established physics. It may be true, but it cannot be shown to be true." He quotes the popular mathematics writer Martin Gardner, who put it more sharply: There "is not the slightest shred of reliable evidence that there is any universe other than the one we are in."[41]

These critiques have led significant numbers of contemporary scientists and mathematicians to reject the multiverse theory and instead ascribe the complexity of the universe to God. In the August 1997 edition of *Science,* Gregg Easterbrook published an article entitled "Science and God: A Warming Trend?"[42] in which he remarked: "The fact that the universe exhibits many features that foster organic life – such as precisely those physical constants that result in planets and long-lived stars – also has led some scientists to speculate that some divine influence may be present."[43]

> "Science demonstrates the existence of a Being that is neither a body nor a force in a body. That Being is the ultimate cause of the entire natural order." (Maimonides, *Guide for the Perplexed)*

BEYOND THE BIG BANG

To claim that our complex universe and human anatomy developed randomly, then, requires its own leap of faith – a greater leap, I believe, than the one required to believe in a supernatural creator. Yet even if we were to make this leap, we must still explain how finite matter originally came into existence all on its own. The most popular explanation for the origin of our universe is the Big Bang Theory – that the world exploded into existence – but the question as to what *caused* the explosion remains unclear. Some theorize that quantum fluctuation, a principle of quantum mechanics, allows matter and energy to come into existence on its own, but this remains unproven. And even if we assume that matter can somehow come into existence on its own and that the universe randomly developed the complexity necessary to sustain life, we must also explain how inanimate matter can become more than the sum of its parts, creating consciousness. Scientists continue to lack a full biological account for consciousness.

In the end, the argument from intelligent design or the teleological argument, while not offering definitive proof, remains a compelling basis for the existence of God, providing us with "permission to believe." Arthur Compton, winner of the Nobel Prize in physics, is quoted as having powerfully asserted: "It is not difficult for me to have…faith, for it is incontrovertible that where there is a plan there is intelligence – an orderly, unfolding universe testifies to the truth of the most majestic statement ever uttered – 'In the beginning God.'"[44]

Further Reading

Even if one becomes convinced of God's existence through a study of history and science, many are still bothered by other important issues. The age-old question as to why bad things happen to good people is an obstacle for many people to believe in an all-powerful and benevolent God. Other questions regarding God's existence and how He relates to the world require a deeper dive into Jewish philosophy and Kabbalah (Jewish mysticism). These and other issues are real questions – some with which I personally struggle – that deserve to be answered. The important thing to know is that there are real answers and approaches to these questions, some of which I have taught and incorporated into my classes over the years, but which are beyond the scope of this work. I would urge you to do further reading on these issues from the following books:

STOP AND REFLECT: What is one other area about God or your relationship with God that you would like to learn more about?

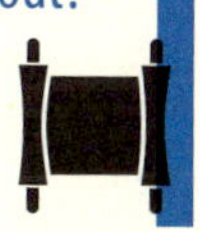

In Good Faith: Questioning Religion and Atheism
Scott A. Shay

If God Is Good, Why Is the World So Bad?
Benjamin Blech

God and Evil: A Unified Theodicy
David Birnbaum

God According to God
Gerald L. Schroeder, PhD

The Secret Life of God
Rabbi David Aaron

The Challenge of Creation: Judaism's Encounter with Science, Cosmology, and Evolution
Natan Slifkin

PART 2: FINDING GOD FROM WITHIN

Thus far, we have looked at the Jewish belief in God based on external factors – either by observing the intelligent design inherent in creation or by looking at the miracle of Jewish history. Another Jewish approach posits that God can be discovered by simply looking within. Many students I have mentored throughout the years have reported that they intuit a deep sense of spiritual connection, even though they have not been taught about God or spirituality. They discern a part of their makeup connected to something beyond the physical. Judaism strongly believes we are not simply bodies but also souls – that we possess a deeply metaphysical part to our composition as human beings.

BREATH AND THE SOUL

The Hebrew word for the highest perceived part of the soul is *neshamah* – a variation of the word *neshimah* or breath –

since, according to the Bible, God endowed the first man with a soul by breathing into him: "And God formed man out of the dust of the ground and breathed into his nostrils a breath of life."[45] God created the other parts of the physical world through speech[46] but used breath to create humankind. Breath implies a more intimate level of connection[47] between creator and creation because when one breathes into another, they are sharing a part of themselves with another. Hence, the soul, with which we are created, is more of a pure and direct aspect of divinity than the rest of creation. It is therefore not surprising that so many people, unschooled in religion or spiritual practices, experience an innate spiritual connection. Judaism strongly endorses the notion that we enter the world with a deep spiritual component.

STOP AND REFLECT: When have you most deeply experienced a sense of your own soul?

TORAH IN UTERO

Several important Jewish sources point to this belief. The Talmud teaches that we are created with a preexisting sense of God: "A fetus is taught the entire Torah while in the womb.... And once the fetus emerges into the airspace of the world, an angel comes and slaps it on its mouth, causing it to forget the entire Torah."[48]

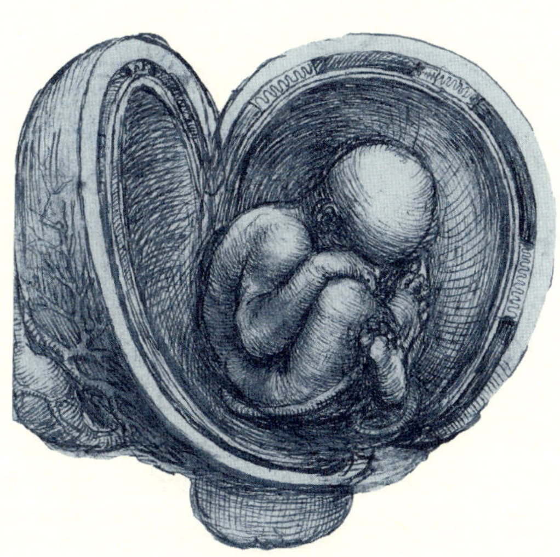

Baby in Utero by Leonardo da Vinci, 1510

Whether this passage is meant to be read literally – that there is an actual angel teaching Torah to a fetus – or metaphorically, the question arises: If a child is forced to forget his learning upon birth, why was the child taught the Torah in utero in the first place? Rabbi Joseph B. Soloveitchik suggests that it is to teach us how the soul comes into the world: "Learning is the recollection of something familiar. The Jew studying Torah is like the amnesia victim who tries to reconstruct from fragments the beautiful world he once experienced. In other words, by learning Torah man returns to his own self; man finds himself."[49]

KABBALAH CORNER:
What does it mean that the angel causes the fetus to forget Torah when it leaves the womb? The kabbalists teach that speech limits our ability to fully experience the world, as words can never fully capture our thoughts and emotions – hence the phrase "there are no words." This suggests that after we learn from the angel in the womb and are born, gaining the ability to communicate orally, our understanding becomes more limited than it was beforehand. In this sense, the newborn is considered to have "forgotten" Torah because it cannot fully articulate what it learns and experiences. (Rabbi Akiva Tatz)

THE BEST TEACHERS

Rabbi Soloveitchik's understanding of this talmudic passage suggests that we are born with an already existing spiritual familiarity, a metaphysical part of us that is already connected to something beyond.

> "Every soul from Adam to the end of the universe was formed during the six days of Creation. All were present in the Garden of Eden and at the time of the giving of the Torah." (*Midrash Tanchuma*)

As such, children and students are not simply blank slates who can only learn and grow by having their parents and teachers impose their knowledge and values upon them. Instead, children enter the world already possessing some spiritual connection or wisdom which a parent or teacher must unearth. One of my esteemed teachers, Rabbi Shlomo Riskin, therefore teaches that the job of a good parent or teacher is not to mold, but to extract – to uncover the greatness that lies within each child. Extracting presupposes that one already possesses something uniquely spiritual. But what is that innate spirituality with which we enter the world? What is this part of one's "own self" to which we can return by studying Torah?

Judaism believes that people possess a Godly soul, one that is either literally a piece of God Himself[50] or a reflection of God. Those scholars who subscribe to the literal understanding, who believe that the soul is literally Godliness, compare the human soul to a piece of sculpted rock, one which a sculptor took from a larger chunk of marble. The constitution of both the smaller piece and larger block is the same. The only difference between them is that one is a segment of the other.[51] Another way of looking at the human soul is like a ray of the sun. In this metaphor, the sun is compared to God and every human being is a reflection or a ray of the sun. One of my teachers, Rabbi David Aaron, who suggested this metaphor,[52] likens someone who negates the existence of God to a ray of the sun denying there is a sun. It is ultimately a denial of one's own existence, of which one is merely a reflection.

THE OLD BEARDED MAN IN THE SKY

Either way, seeing God not as an external foreign power, but as a force within us, is radically different from the view of God with which many of us were raised. We often think of God as some distant bearded man in the sky, sitting on a throne with a huge control panel which he uses to manipulate our lives. This simplistic view has been reinforced by the physical personification of God we read in the Bible (meant only as metaphors to enable us to understand God's actions[53]) and the ties we have with our Christian friends and people of other religions whose conception of God is also more corporeal. God becomes a caricature, a detached figure of physical power too consumed with the bigger, more important things in life to worry about little me or you. Add to the mix all the bad things we see happening to good people (and good things happening to bad people), and we are left perceiving God as removed, distant, and unfeeling – or simply irrelevant to our lives.

Believing there is an aspect of God *within us* is a game changer. By creating humanity with God as an integral part of our internal makeup, God does not remain some power force "out there" but an energy within – a power that partners with mere mortals and provides humankind with the ability to reflect God's spirituality and holiness in the physical world. This in turn helps us accomplish one of Judaism's main goals: infusing the physical world with divine holiness. Unlike other faith systems whose goal is to escape or transcend the material world, Judaism seeks to imbue the material world and our physical lives with spirituality and holiness.[54]

HEAVEN ON EARTH

The goal is therefore not to remove oneself from physicality but to bring some of heaven down to earth. The Torah and its many commandments are the tools through which we are meant to reveal the Godliness within us so we can transform our own physical lives and our material world into a more spiritual place. According to the Jewish mystics this is the very reason for human existence: to create a *dirah batachtonim, a home for God and His spirituality right here on earth.*

> "When the Holy One, blessed be He, created the world, He desired a dwelling place in the lower realms, just as He has in the higher realms." (*Midrash Tanchuma)*

Before the creation of the world, there was just God and His spirituality. God created the physical world so His Infinite Light could illuminate our earthly, finite existence. That's where you and I come in. As physical beings with souls, we are uniquely positioned to introduce God's spirituality into the mundane physical parts of our existence. The Torah's commandments or mitzvot are the instruments through which we accomplish this. Each mitzvah, in one way or another, is a tool to elevate and sanctify some other physical activity. For example, reciting blessings before eating and observing the laws of *kashrut* imbue the physical act of eating with holiness, and the laws of family purity[55] elevate the sexual encounter between husband and wife. Every one of the 613 mitzvot is designed to infuse another physical activity in which we engage with holiness.

> "Man's greatness lies in his ability to elevate the physical world and infuse it with spirituality." (Rabbi Moshe Chaim Luzzatto)

The mitzvot also enable our souls to strengthen their connection to their divine source and achieve what the kabbalists teach is another primary objective of the soul: *devekut,* attachment of the soul to God's Infinite Light, from which the soul is derived. Since the soul is removed from its Godly source and placed into an entirely foreign environment, the physical realm, the soul yearns to return home. During its sojourn in the material world, the soul's focus is its reconnection to its spiritual source, to God Himself.[56]

SOMETHING IS MISSING

The frustration of the soul, having to endure a physical existence not conducive to its spiritual makeup, is a feeling many of us experience. Often when we feel something important in our life is missing, we cannot identify what exactly that thing is, since we are otherwise happy, well-adjusted people. We may have an excellent job and career, good relationships, and a happy family life – but something is still missing.

My wife is a good example. When we first met, she was already pursuing a religious lifestyle, despite not having been raised in an observant home. When I asked her why she felt the need to pursue a spiritual path – she came from a good family, had lots of friends, and was well on her way to accomplishing her career goals – she said there was something missing: "I looked at my life and all was fine, but I just couldn't believe this was everything…there has to be more to life." That phrase, "There has to be more to life," became the tagline on all Manhattan Jewish Experience (MJE) brochures and flyers. The expression captures what so many otherwise happy and successful people feel and confirms what the spiritually sensitive among us intuitively know: We are a composite of body and soul. If we feed the body but ignore the soul, we will feel something significant missing from our lives and, at some point, we will become unhappy. This mysterious feeling of lack burns within, leading many to try different types of physical pleasures, but it is often just the soul crying out to nourish its hunger for spiritual connection.

The existential lack we feel comes from a hidden part of who we are, urging us to pay more attention to our souls and to nurture them.

> KABBALAH CORNER:
> The soul is compared to the elements of fire and air because the soul also naturally rises, constantly seeking to transcend the physical. By contrast, the body is associated with water and earth, which are bound by gravity. This tension between the soul's desire to ascend and the body's grounded nature is at the heart of the feeling of inner lack and longing. (Rabbi Zamir Cohen)

> "The human body is like a musical instrument: We must learn to play it in harmony with our soul." (Rabbi Nachman of Breslov)

With this perspective, we come to another question. As we have explained, a person's soul yearns for its source, for spiritual perfection and the opportunity to bask in the Infinite

Light of its Maker. But how can we achieve such an existence? Judaism's mystical tradition teaches that the Torah was given to connect our souls to our Creator and to shine God's Infinite Light upon us and upon the world around us,[57] but how exactly? How does Torah study and mitzvah performance accomplish such a feat?

REVEALING THE LIGHT WITHIN

The Zohar,[58] one of the primary sources for kabbalistic wisdom, teaches that the 613 commandments of the Torah are not merely restrictions, "dos and don'ts" that govern our daily behavior. Rather, the commandments are the means to attain spiritual growth and return to our true essence, to that Godly part within. This is based on another teaching of the Zohar that "the Torah and God are totally one."[59] Rabbi Shneur Zalman of Liadi, a master of kabbalistic wisdom, explained this to mean that the Torah is more than just a glimmer of the Divine but "completely one with God Himself."[60] God has so invested Himself in the Torah that He is completely one with it. This is a difficult concept to grasp because God is an infinite Being, whereas the Torah is a finite text of laws and rituals.[61] However, the Kabbalah teaches that God compacted His will and wisdom into 613 commandments, investing the Torah itself with His very essence. Thus, by studying the Torah and observing its mitzvot, our souls become completely engulfed within the light of God.

By suffusing our physical selves with God's light, we reveal the light which lies within, namely our souls. Now bolstered by the Divine which has infused it, the soul bursts forth, "joining her beloved,"[62] finally manifest in the physical realm.

KABBALAH CORNER:
Mitzvot are like garments that allow our soul to manifest itself in this finite realm through their performance. Torah study is compared to *both* garments and food: Not only does the Torah we study envelop us like a garment – as does any mitzvah – but the Torah *itself* is God's wisdom, satiating our soul as bread satiates our physical body. (Rabbi Shneur Zalman of Liadi)

Now we can more deeply understand Rabbi Soloveitchik's interpretation of the talmudic passage about the angel teaching the child Torah. The Jew is born with an irrevocable, mystical connection to Torah. Through our immersion in Torah, the Jew reconnects with that lost part of his or her identity, stripping away the excess externalities and enabling us to discover the Godly within, which yearns for expression and recognition. The child, through the slap of the angel, may lose sight of this internal truth, but he somehow retains a connection to it and therefore continues to search and hopefully discover the deepest and most beautiful part of himself. With this, one achieves personal salvation, reaching the apex of human existence by rediscovering the most authentic element of himself. He or she who is immersed in Torah is redeemed.

> "The soul is a part of God above, the body its holy Temple." (Rabbi Shneur Zalman of Liadi)

THE KABBALAH OF CREATION

One of the most fundamental concepts found within Lurianic Kabbalah (the system of Jewish mysticism founded by Rabbi Isaac Luria, otherwise known as the Arizal) is called *tzimtzum* or contraction. Prior to creation of the physical world, all that existed was God and His Infinite Light. To allow for the creation of the physical world and for physicality itself, God contracted His essence to form a vacant space for the universe and humankind to exist. That space is where we and our material world live, sustained by God even as His presence and continued involvement appear hidden.

Tzimtzum, the kabbalists teach, also refers to God making Himself appear smaller or hidden so we can benefit from His Infinite Light. If God's presence were to remain too obvious, we simply would not be able to gain in any way from His existence. A famous metaphor illustrates this point. Imagine an electric bulb surrounded by a lampshade. The light emanating from the bulb is too bright to be enjoyed without a lampshade to block some of the brightness. Similarly, God makes Himself smaller, allowing Himself to appear hidden so we can benefit from His light and wisdom.

This metaphysical phenomenon of *tzimtzum* also allows us to maintain our free will. Think about it: If God's existence were too noticeable, if His light were too bright, we would have no choice but to follow His commands found in the Torah. It is only because God made Himself small, because He is hidden, that we can freely choose God and through our own volition become worthy of spiritual enlightenment. It is therefore no coincidence that the Hebrew word for the world, *olam,* shares the same etymological root *(ayin-lamed-mem)* with the Hebrew word *he'elem,* which means hidden. God purposely hides Himself for our benefit. "You are indeed a God who concealed Himself,"[63] declares Isaiah. Judaism teaches that our task is to reveal God amidst His concealment. God plays a cosmic game of hide-and-seek and enlists us to reveal His existence. We accomplish this by carrying out the various mitzvot of the Torah, each designed to reveal God and His Infinite Light in some way. Abraham, the first Jew, was the first to discover and teach the world about a supernatural God. His descendants, the Jewish people, are charged with ensuring God is not forgotten even as He remains hidden.

In reality, the kabbalists teach, we are sustained by God much as a child in utero is nurtured by its mother. God, however, created us to feel separate and independent of Him. For if we would feel God as our source, we would be completely nullified within Him and lose our distinct sense of identity. We would therefore be unable to carry out our mission to reveal God in the physical world.

PART 3: CAN YOU BE GOOD WITHOUT GOD?

One Yom Kippur, a young man approached me to give thanks for what he said was truly "an inspirational service." "Rabbi," he said, "this was my best High Holiday ever. You can count on me being here next year again." "Next year?" I asked. "What about next week on Shabbat? If the service was so good, why do I have to wait a whole year to see you again?" The young man gave me an honest answer. "Rabbi, I don't come every week because I'm not religious. And I'm not religious because I don't think you need to believe in God to be a good person."

Is this true? Does one have to be religious to be considered "good"? Can't one still be a decent person without believing in God? Can we not naturally intuit or, through our own logic and reasoning, determine for ourselves what is right and wrong, or must we follow laws ordained by a Supreme Being for our actions to be "good" and "moral"?

Let's start by defining morality. What exactly establishes something as moral? From a purely religious perspective, since God is defined as a benevolent and all-knowing Being, His will ultimately defines morality. As we will discuss in our chapter on the Torah, classical Judaism teaches that the Torah is the expression of that divine will and therefore represents an objective code of morality.

> "Morality without the light of Torah is merely cultural behavior without the depth of sanctity." (Rabbi Yitzchak Hutner)

On the other hand, if there is no God, humanity is left to define morality on its own. Some believe that through a careful analysis of human nature one can determine a system of right and wrong which holds true for all of humanity, while others argue that morality is relative to one's culture and society. Either way, since it is a humanly constructed system, it is susceptible to all the limitations of humanity – our personal and cultural biases as well as our inability to ascertain absolute truth. Besides this, there are two additional problems with a Godless morality:

- Shifting Sands – It is not sustainable since it changes as society changes.

- Conflicting Values – It fails to provide a guide for the moral triage that life requires.

SHIFTING SANDS

We all know people who, though they may not believe in God, live moral and ethical lives. This would appear to contradict the religious approach to morality, which is rooted in the divine will. This question was addressed by one of my revered teachers, Rabbi Dr. Norman Lamm, of blessed memory, in a sermon he delivered in 1965 where he acknowledged that we have all met moral people who do not believe in God. Still, he contends, "such goodness cannot last forever. The moral instincts that prevail today are but the residue of a religious reservoir which is rapidly drying up. We are living off the ethical interest from the quickly dwindling religious capital of two generations ago.... For ethical living is the branch of a tree of life, of which the roots are religion. When you cut off the root, the branch does not wither immediately, but eventually it must die."[64] This is inevitable because the moral foundations upon which Western society was originally founded – Judeo-Christian values – are based on God, not people's opinions. If belief in God fades, eventually those values will be replaced by humanly created ones, and we will be left to determine the most important life-and-death questions based on the opinions, and sometimes whims, of a particular generation.

> "Without belief in a higher will, human morality is bound to fail when it confronts self-interest." (Rabbi Meir Simcha of Dvinsk)

A "Godless goodness" is therefore unreliable.[65] It is constantly changing. We see this idea expressed in the Bible when Abraham and Sarah are forced to leave Israel because of a famine, and they go down to Egypt to find some food. They know Egypt is a place bereft of morality, so Abraham is afraid that when the Egyptians see how beautiful Sarah is, they will kill him and take her into Pharaoh's harem. To avoid this, Abraham tells the Egyptians he is Sarah's brother. The identical episode is repeated shortly afterward in the Bible, this time involving another ruler named Avimelech, king of Gerar. In that story, Abraham again tells the people of Gerar that Sarah is his sister. Upon discovering this deception, Avimelech asks Abraham why he felt the need to lie: "What did you see that caused you do this thing?"[66] To which Abraham answers: "Because I said there is no fear of God in this place."[67]

Two great nineteenth-century rabbinic figures, the Malbim[68] and the Netziv,[69] explain that Avimelech was saying to Abraham: "I understand why you felt the need to trick the Egyptians; they are, after all, immoral. But why did you feel it necessary to deceive us, the people of Gerar? We are ethical and just!" Abraham responds: "It is true you are good and moral, but if there is no fear of God, how can I trust that your morality will remain, that you will *always* be decent? You may be decent now, but if there is no religion, no faith in something beyond yourself, what is to stop you from making up your own laws to justify whatever behavior fits the situation?"

When there is no fear of God, what was considered morally wrong yesterday can become commonplace tomorrow.

The Brisker Rav, Rabbi Yitzchak Zev Soloveitchik,[70] notes the glaring hypocrisy Abraham confronted. He was afraid the Egyptians and Gerarites would murder him but was unafraid that they would commit adultery by abducting Sarah as a married woman. Abraham understood they would not leave him alive and take Sarah because they had a sense of morality when it came to adultery, but they had no ethical problem with murder. That, suggests Rabbi Lamm, is precisely what Abraham meant when he said, "There is no fear of God in this place": When goodness is divorced from God, the resulting morality is "spotty and inconsistent"[71] and can produce a society in which one may kill a man to take his wife, but will never take his wife as long as the husband is alive. There is respect for marriage but not for human life. That was the case in ancient times. Today, though, I would suggest that the situation has been reversed. In Western society today, murder is thankfully viewed as immoral, but adultery has become more acceptable as the entire institution of marriage has been called into question. Morality without God can mean one thing in one time and something else in another. The only way both murder and adultery are *always* wrong is if a higher authority like God says so.

> "Place your full trust in God with all your heart.... In all your decisions acknowledge Him, and He will guide you on the right path." (Proverbs 3:5–6)

CONFLICTING VALUES

This is arguably one of the most pressing philosophical issues of our day: Is there an *objective* morality or is everything subjective and humanly constructed? Most people, whether they believe in God or not, view murder as immoral and helping the old lady cross the street as moral. But life is not black and white, and so these are not the moral dilemmas we generally face. The more common and challenging moral questions we confront are not whether to steal or give charity. We all know one is right and the other is wrong. The question we are more likely to confront is whether it is moral to support a struggling family if the only way to do so is by fudging your taxes. We all condemn slander and admire those who speak the truth. But what if a colleague is about to seal a business deal with your less-than-honest friend, and he asks you about your friend's integrity? Or if a good friend is getting married while another has lost a parent – do we attend the wedding or the funeral? We can't be in two places at once, so we need a moral system to prioritize our values when they come into conflict.

During the COVID-19 pandemic, when ventilators were scarce, how should the medical professionals in the hospitals have prioritized patient care? Should it be illegal to sell or purchase an organ, even at the cost of losing a life? Can we allow people with terminal diseases and who are suffering to end their own lives? The controversial Dr. Jack Kevorkian invented a way for end-stage patients to take their own lives and assisted in the euthanizing of over 130 patients. Was this compassion or murder?

Life is complex, our time and resources are limited, and therefore our moral decisions are more about conflicting values than whether something is moral at all. Any real moral system must contain more than platitudes as to what is moral and what is not; it must also provide specific guidelines for establishing a hierarchy of values. What is more or less important and under what circumstances? When should we sacrifice one value for another?

Judaism prides itself on providing answers to these specific moral questions. And herein lies the infinite value of a God-given system. As we will explore in the next chapter, through every phrase, word, and even letter of the Bible, God reveals to us a moral code. Through its analysis, we arrive at a hierarchy of values to navigate our complex lives. The 2,711 pages of the Talmud are filled with textual analysis of

Young women learning Torah at Manhattan Jewish Experience (MJE)

countless words of the Torah so we can know what values take precedence and under what circumstances. This is precisely why Jewish students spend years studying in yeshivah (school for Torah study), and why in the Jewish prayers we refer to Torah study as "our lives and the length of our days." As Jews, we spend our lives learning the vast system of halachah (Jewish law), designed to cover virtually every moral issue and dilemma.

Recognizing our human imperfections, can we *really* rely on intuition and even logical analysis to definitively answer life-and-death questions, especially when they get so specific? When making decisions which can establish you as a hero or a criminal, an objective divine moral arbiter is imperative.

> "The Torah is light, its precepts the path to a life of righteousness." (Proverbs 6:23)

GOOD - BUT NOT GOOD ENOUGH

The Jewish people have lived in so many different cultures and societies: Egypt, Greece, Persia, Rome, each with their own value systems. Societies change but God does not. I believe we have remained a people for as long as we have because we have adhered to a code of ethics that goes beyond any civilization in which we have dwelt. We should learn from and participate in the culture in which we reside. Indeed, the Jewish people have contributed marvelously to many cultures and countries throughout the millennia. But to allow the unique Jewish code of ethics, which is thousands of years older – and, more importantly, rooted in divine wisdom – to be replaced by the values of whatever country in which we happen to live would be a tragic mistake.

Judaism's unique values inform every activity and moment of our lives – from the way we speak and dress to the manner in which we engage in our professional lives and our most intimate relationships. The way we approach these activities is not merely cultural but a reflection of Judaism's moral system, based on objective values rooted in an eternal and unchanging God. Other value systems may carry merit and even varying degrees of morality. At times, they may be good. But if a system is Godless, it will never be fully reliable, and it will never be detailed enough to provide us with the guidelines that are the prerequisite to living truly moral lives. It may be good – but not good enough.[72]

TRANSCENDING OURSELVES

A God-based morality enables us to take one step further. When we act based on our own intuition, we may be expressing ourselves, but no more. As contemporary author Rabbi Akiva Tatz writes: "If I am the source of my own command, I express only myself.... But when the source of my command is outside myself, I express that source when I act; a connection is forged between that point of origin and myself.... The individual who acts in accord with the Divine commandment has locked into the infinite and reveals in the world what the infinite source intends to reveal."[73]

KINDNESS AND CONVICTION

The relationship between belief in God and the way we relate to our fellow human being runs deeper than the issue of objective morality. Judaism believes that it is specifically through one's relationship with God that one can achieve the highest levels of *chesed,* the Hebrew word for kindness. This is taught most directly through the well-known biblical phrase "Love your neighbor as yourself, I am God."[74] Although this saying is probably quoted more than any other in the Bible, it is hard to understand it literally. Is it really possible for us to love another person as much as or more than ourselves? Maybe a spouse or child, but our "neighbor"?

Some suggest that the answer to this question is found in the verse's last phrase: "I am God." When the Torah commands us to love others as we love ourselves, what aspect of ourselves does the Torah wish us to love? Our physical appearance? How successful we have become? Rather, it is the aspect of God within us – our soul – which we are commanded to love.[75] If we can nurture a love for that part of who we are, presumably we can love other people since we are all created in God's image. It is ultimately our souls which unite us. The country in which we are born or reside, the language we speak, and our different cultures create distinctions and separations between different people, but what all human beings have in common is the soul. The soul or divine image, in which we are all created, is also what makes all people, irrespective of race and ethnicity, worthy of fair and just treatment. It is the basis for the Jewish imperative to extend kindness to all humanity.

STOP AND REFLECT:
Practically speaking, how would we act differently if we truly treated each other as having been created in the image of God?

ABRAHAM AND HUMAN RIGHTS

This is why Abraham, the founder of Judaism, is depicted in Hebrew Scripture as not only the first person to discover and spread the belief in God, but also the great promoter of *chesed,* acts of loving-kindness.[76]

KABBALAH CORNER:
Abraham revealed the oneness of God to the world through the trait of *chesed,* kindness. By inviting guests and spreading the word of God with care and compassion, he touched the hearts and minds of others. In Kabbalah, Abraham is considered the "chariot" or archetype of the *Sefirah* (divine emanation) of *Chesed,* embodying divine kindness. It was through his acts of *chesed* that God's kindness and unity were revealed to the world. (Zohar)

There are plenty of characters in the Bible. Surely there could have been one biblical personality who discovers God and another who champions acts of kindness. However, Judaism's founding patriarch is known for both, to teach us that the ultimate expression of one's belief in God is the way one treats their fellow human being. Abraham's hospitality and kindness to family and strangers alike was not incidental or coincidental but a direct manifestation of his belief in God. For if one believes in a God who creates all humanity in His divine image, it becomes incumbent to treat others in a respectful manner. The divine image in which we are all fashioned – the basis for the modern concept of human rights – demands that we show greater levels of consideration for all people.

EVEN HIGHER

Extending kindness to others is therefore not simply a nice thing to do but an act of religious devotion. The story is told of a chasidic master – known to be a very holy and beloved Rebbe to his many students – who had the reputation of coming late to synagogue for morning prayers. His devoted disciples would always defend him, explaining that their Rebbe's tardiness was due to his dealings in the heavenly spheres, communing with the Almighty before morning prayers. One skeptic did not buy the explanation and decided to spy on the Rebbe to see for himself why he always came late to synagogue. One morning the skeptic awoke at dawn and headed to the Rebbe's home. He saw the chasidic master emerge from his home dressed like a lumberjack with an axe in hand. The Rebbe started on his way, heading toward the forest, the skeptic following from a distance. The Rebbe stopped to chop some wood, gathered the lumber, and continued deeper into the forest. The skeptic saw that he had a bag in his other hand and continued to follow him to an isolated log cabin in the woods. The Rebbe knocked on the door, went inside, and began to speak to an elderly woman who was shivering from the cold. He built a fire for the woman from the wood he had chopped, set out some milk and eggs from the other bag, and left. After the Rebbe's long trek back home, he got dressed for synagogue and, sure enough, he arrived late for services.

At the synagogue, the skeptic saw the group of Chasidim who were defending their teacher. He approached the group and remarked: "You say your Rebbe ascends to the heavens every morning, and that is the reason he is late to synagogue. You are mistaken. He ascends even higher."

Our relationship with God is best expressed in the way we treat other people. Belief in God is not just an abstract concept but something manifest in our everyday behavior – in the sensitivity and kindness we extend to others. As the prophet Micah famously declared: "He has told you, O man, what is good, and what God requires of you: only to do justice and to love kindness, and to walk modestly with your God."[77]

PUTTING FAITH INTO PRACTICE: THE SHEMA

The central mitzvah expressing the Jewish belief in God is the *Shema.* "More than just a prayer, the *Shema* is the Jewish creed."[78] It is the declaration of the Jewish belief in an omnipotent, omniscient, and one God who serves as the source for all reality. Believing in this God also means that life is not random but was deliberately designed for a greater purpose. If we know our purpose, we can live accordingly.

Believing in *one* God does not simply mean we believe in a single God as opposed to multiple Gods. It means that, of course, but so much more. By reciting the *Shema* once in the morning and once in the evening,[79] we affirm our belief that everything we see in the world is ultimately an expression of God, since according to Jewish tradition God is the source of all reality. Affirming a belief in *one* God is therefore to acknowledge the *one and only* cause for all existence. Some suggest that this is the idea behind the custom to cover one's eyes while saying the words "Hear O Israel, God is our God, God is One."[80] For as long as our eyes are open, we see a world full of division and separateness. Closing our eyes helps us see the unity and interconnectedness behind all of reality.

The kabbalists take this idea further, explaining the last phrase in the *Shema,* "God is One," to mean that there is *only* God. This teaching is based on the biblical phrase *ein od milvado,* "There is nothing besides Him,"[81] which reflects the idea that only God exists. This does not mean that we and the world of physical reality in which we live are illusions. Judaism accepts the notion that the universe exists, but only because God is constantly engaged in recreating it. Jewish tradition emphasizes that God did not simply create the world but remains involved in it. The Kabbalah teaches that if God were to cease investing His creative energy into the world, even for a moment, all physical creation would revert to its original state of nothingness.[82] Thus, another idea upon which we meditate when saying the *Shema* is that only God's existence is completely independent and absolute, unlike the world and humankind, which are dependent on God for their survival.

STOP AND REFLECT: How would your life be different if you believed that God is directly involved in your everyday life?

The words of the *Shema* have been the last uttered by Jewish martyrs,[83] and it is also the very first prayer Jewish children learn. During the Holocaust, tens of thousands of distraught Jewish parents, seeing the fateful writing on the wall, deposited their small children with Christian neighbors and even local churches in the hope that their children would survive the war. Tragically, most of these parents were murdered by the Nazis. In 1945, after the war was over, Rabbi Eliezer Silver of the United States and Dayan Isadore Grunfeld of the United Kingdom were dispatched as military chaplains to Europe to rescue these children. Rabbis Silver and Grunfeld approached the priests who ran a monastery in Alsace-Lorraine, France, asking for the Jewish orphans to be transferred to their next of kin. The priests insisted that documentation would be needed to identify the children. When the rabbis were able to identify children with Jewish surnames, the priests said that last names could not prove the children's Jewishness. The rabbis asked if they could return that night, and the priests reluctantly agreed. The two spiritual leaders arrived as the children were in their beds, about to go to sleep for the night. The rabbis walked through the room and began to sing the *Shema* – the declaration of faith Jewish children learn at a very young age. Immediately, the little children, began to cry out "Mommy, Mamushka, Maman..." The rabbis were able to identify the Jewish children and return them to their relatives.

Hearing the *Shema* brought these children back to their earliest memories with their mothers. Deep down, perhaps even subconsciously, these Jewish orphans, left only with fleeting memories of their beloved parents, understood who they were at their core. When they heard the call of *Shema,* their souls responded.

Reciting the *Shema* is thus not only a way to express our belief in God but also a way to feel connected to the entire Jewish people, who have recited this declaration under the most challenging circumstances. It is also a way, not only for those who *already* believe in God to express their faith, but, as I have shared with many of my students, a way to start developing that connection in the first place.[84] In short, the *Shema* helps us return to our divine essence, to our souls.

Shema Yisrael

Further Reading

The Practical Tanya: The Book for Inbetweeners
Rabbi Shneur Zalman of Liadi
adapted by Rabbi Chaim Miller

Endless Light
Rabbi David Aaron

The Way of God
Rabbi Moshe Chaim Luzzatto

Letters to a Buddhist Jew
Akiva Tatz and David Gottlieb

Handbook of Jewish Thought, Vol. 1
Aryeh Kaplan

To Be a Jew
Rabbi Hayim Halevy Donin

TAKEAWAYS

- We can find God by looking at external sources such as history and science, and by tapping into the soul, our inner spiritual core. Both are authentically Jewish pathways to discovering and cultivating a relationship with God.
- The survival of the Jewish people against all odds strongly suggests that there is a God.
- The vast complexity and intricate design of the universe point to the existence of a Creator.
- Judaism's mystical teachings tell us that our souls are a part of God, offering us an internal connection to the Divine.
- Only divine moral rules are strong enough to stand the test of time and provide an objective way to decide when ethical values come into conflict.
- The *Shema* is a central prayer expressing the Jewish belief in one God and connecting us to the entire Jewish people

Notes

1. See Rebbe Nachman of Breslov, *Sichot HaRan*, chapter 32.
2. Maimonides, *Mishneh Torah*, Laws of Foundations of the Torah 1:1, Positive Mitzvot 1. In his *Sefer HaMitzvot* (Maimonides's treatise on the 613 commandments), he writes that the first mitzvah is to believe in God. However, Rabbi Menachem Krakowski (in his commentary *Avodat HaMelech*) points out that our Hebrew version of the *Sefer HaMitzvot* is actually a translation from the original Arabic, and the word which was translated into "belief" is actually more similar to "knowledge."
3. This "stroll through Jewish history" is not meant to be academic or exhaustive. Rather, it is a general survey of Jewish history intended to demonstrate my main point, namely that the continued existence of the Jewish people against all odds is best explained by the existence of a supernatural creator.
4. Rony E. Gabbay, *A Political Study of the Arab Jewish Conflict* (1959), pp. 92–93.
5. Robert Hull, *Welcome to Planet Earth – 2050 – Population Zero* (AuthorHouse, 2011), p. xiii.
6. William Nitardy, *Understanding the Anatomy of Evil* (Outskirts Press, 2016), p. 210.
7. Mitchell G. Bard, *The Complete Idiot's Guide to Middle East Conflict* (Alpha, 2002), p. 197.
8. Radio broadcast, June 1, 1967, as quoted in Michael Scott-Bauman (1998), *Conflict in the Middle East: Israel and the Arabs*. In stark contrast to all this, Israeli Prime Minister Levi Eshkol said, "Israel wants to make it clear to the government of Egypt that it has no aggressive intentions whatsoever against any Arab state at all" (Michael Brecher, *Decisions in Israel's Foreign Policy* [Oxford University Press, 1974]).
9. Mitchell G. Bard, *Death to the Infidels: Radical Islam's War Against the Jews* (St. Martin's, 2014), pp. 57–58.
10. Ibid., p. 63.
11. Interview on CBS, October 5, 1956.
12. *The Complete Works of Mark Twain, American Artists Edition* (Harper and Brothers, 1899), p. 286.
13. https://www.jewishvirtuallibrary.org/jewish-nobel-prize-laureates

14. The three Jewish thinkers were Albert Einstein, Sigmund Freud, and Carl Marx. Many take issue with the theories of the fourth, Charles Darwin. Although this is just a joke, it reflects the disproportionate influence of the Jewish people.
15. Exodus 19:5–6.
16. Sforno on Exodus 19:6.
17. Jeremiah 30:11.
18. Jeremiah 31:36.
19. Malachi 3:6.
20. Ibid., Radak.
21. Deuteronomy 7:7.
22. Leo Tolstoy, "What Is the Jew?" quoted in *The Final Resolution* (Doubleday, 1962), p. 189, originally printed in *The Jewish World Periodical*, 1908.
23. Nikolai Berdyaev, *The Meaning of History* (1935).
24. This approach to God's existence was articulated in the eleventh century by the Spanish rationalist Rabbi Bachya ibn Pakuda and in the fourth-century rabbinic text Genesis Rabbah, which attributes Abraham's discovery of God to the teleological argument. The Midrash, Genesis Rabbah (39:1), comments: "Rabbi Yitzchak said: This may be compared to a man who was traveling from place to place when he saw a castle aglow. He said: 'Is it possible that this castle lacks a person to look after it?' The owner of the building looked at him and said to him: 'I am the master of the castle.' What happened with Abraham our father was similar. He said: 'Is it possible that this universe lacks a person to look after it?' The Holy One, blessed be He, looked at him and said to him: 'I am the Master of the Universe.'" Rabbi Enoch Zundel, the nineteenth-century Polish talmudist, in his commentary on this midrash (known as *Etz Yosef*), explains that "the matter of the parable is that whoever sees a beautiful and orderly building understands and acknowledges that there is a master and owner of this palace, and that a wise artisan built it."
25. DNA is millions of times more storage efficient than any hard drive and lasts staggeringly longer (https://www.economist.com/science-and-technology/2019/12/12/dna-could-be-used-to-embed-useful-information-into-everyday-objects). In fact, scientists are attempting to use DNA to replace hard drives in order to store information more effectively, demonstrating that this tiny molecule, within the body's every cell, is more powerful than the most advanced technology humankind has been able to artificially produce (George M. Church et al., "Next-Generation Digital Information Storage in DNA," *Science* 337, no. 6102 [2012]: p. 1628; doi:10.1126/science.1226355).
26. Michael Denton, *Evolution: A Theory in Crisis* (Adler and Adler, 1986), p. 334. Although Denton's research was published in 1986, its veracity was confirmed in a 2017 article in *Science*, which discusses storing vast amounts of data in DNA: "Capable of storing 215 petabytes (215 million gigabytes) in a single gram of DNA, the system could, in principle, store every bit of datum ever recorded by humans in a container about the size and weight of a couple of pickup trucks" (Robert Service, "DNA Could Store All the World's Data in One Room," *Science*, American Association for the Advancement of Science, 2 Mar. 2017, https://www.science.org/content/article/dna-could-store-all-worlds-data-one-room).

27. Lawrence Kelemen, *Permission to Believe* (Targum, 1990), p. 48.
28. Ibid., pp. 48–50.
29. *Beit Yosef, Orach Chayim* 6:1; *Aruch HaShulchan, Orach Chayim* 6:2.
30. Fred Hoyle and Chandra Wickramasinghe, *Evolution from Space* (Simon & Schuster, 1984), p. 148.
31. This parable is put forth by the eleventh-century rationalist Rabbi Bachya ibn Pakuda in his classic work *Chovot HaLevavot.*
32. *Dialogues* 2; emphasis added by author.
33. Since his theological writings became available to scholars in 1936, scholars have discovered that Newton's belief in God was an extremely important part of his thinking. Newton accepted the divine authorship of the Bible and wrote treatises on the rules for interpreting Scripture correctly and the dimensions of the Temple, which was based on a close reading of the book of Ezekiel. He studied Maimonides carefully and owned his own translated copy of part of at least one section of Maimonides's voluminous work on Jewish law, the *Mishneh Torah.* As Albert Einstein wrote in a 1940 letter, "The divine origin of the Bible is for Newton absolutely certain.... From this confidence stems the firm conviction that the seemingly obscure parts of the Bible must contain important revelations." See Mitchell First, https://jewishlink.news/isaac-newton-and-judaism/.
34. Quoted in Des MacHale, *Wisdom* (Prion Books, 2002).
35. Stephen Hawking, *A Brief History of Time* (Bantam Books, 1988), p. 123.
36. Scientists Herbert S. Wilf and Warren J. Ewen, who authored "There's Plenty of Time for Evolution," published in *Proceedings of the National Academy of Sciences* (PNAS), the official journal of the National Academy of Sciences (NAS), argue that with the joint effort of random mutations and natural selection, nature alone can probabilistically produce the complexity of a human being and our universe.
37. In an article entitled "Peer-Reviewed Science: There Isn't 'Plenty of Time for Evolution,'" Casey Luskin notes the flaws and inconsistencies of the aforementioned paper, quoting a later-written paper (Winston Ewert, William A. Dembski, Ann K. Gauger, Robert J. Marks II, "Time and Information in Evolution," in *BIO-Complexity*, 2012) to refute its conclusion. The authors contend that Wilf and Ewen's method "does not accurately reflect biological evolution" for multiple reasons. First, it assumes "a highly informed oracle that prophesies when a mutation is 'correct,' thus accelerating the search by the evolutionary process. Natural selection, in contrast, does not have access to information about future benefits of a particular mutation." Second, they "assume no epistasis between beneficial mutations, no linkage between loci, and an unrealistic population size and base mutation rate, thus increasing the pool of beneficial mutations to be searched." Finally, in their model, "they represent each genetic locus as a single letter. By doing so, they ignore the enormous sequence complexity of actual genetic loci (typically hundreds or thousands of nucleotides long), and vastly oversimplify the search for functional variants. In similar fashion, they assume that each evolutionary 'advance' requires a change to just one locus, despite the clear evidence that most biological functions are the product of multiple

gene products working together." The authors conclude that "ignoring these biological realities infuses considerable active information into their model and eases the model's evolutionary process," thereby shortening their estimation significantly.

38. Shroeder powerfully explains that "neglecting spaces between the words, the chance of getting the entire sonnet by chance is 26 multiplied by itself 500 times. That seems as if it may be a fairly big number. And it is. Surprisingly so. That number comes out to be a one with 700 zeroes after it. In conventional math terms, it is 10700 or 10 to the exponent power of 700. To give a sense of scale for reference, the known universe including all forms of matter and energy, weighs on the order of 1056 grams; the number of basic particles (protons, neutrons, electrons, muons) in the known universe is 1080; the age of the universe from our perspective of time, 1018 seconds. Convert all the universe into microcomputers weighing a billionth of a gram and run each of those computers billions of times a second nonstop from the beginning of time, and we still will need greater than 10500 universes, or that much more time for even a remote probability of getting a sonnet, any meaningful sonnet. Chance does not produce intelligible text and certainly not a sonnet, not in our universe."
39. Gerald Schroeder, *God According to God* (HarperOne, 2010), pp. 35–36.
40. Max Tegmark, "Parallel Universes," *Scientific American*, May 2003, p. 35.
41. George Ellis, "Opposing the Multiverse," *Astronomy & Geophysics* 49, no. 2 (April 2008): 2.33–2.35, https://doi.org/10.1111/j.1468-4004.2008.49229_1.x.
42. Indeed, as Easterbrook notes, not only is it not uncommon for scientists to be believers, but many see religion and science as complementary. For example, Charles Townes, winner of the Nobel Prize in 1964 for his work on inventing lasers, maintains that religion and science are not contradictory but complementary. As he puts it: "Science wants to know the mechanism of the universe, religion the meaning. The two cannot be separated." Rabbi Lord Jonathan Sacks made a compelling case for the same view of the relationship between science and religion in his 2011 book *The Great Partnership*.
43. https://drmsh.com/TheNakedBible/SCIENCE%20Aug151997%20Science%20and%20God%20-%20A%20Warming%20Trend.pdf.
44. https://times-journal.com/dekalb_living/article_d427b5da-aab2-11e7-9a28-2f44fa886da9.html.
45. Genesis 2:7.
46. For example, when creating light, the Bible says: "And God said, 'Let there be light,' and there was light" (Gen. 1:3).
47. "Feeling a breeze on a hot summer day is pleasant but it is very different than having someone you are close to breathe down on your neck; this bears a certain intimacy." Aryeh Kaplan, *Innerspace: Introduction to Kabbalah, Meditation and Prophecy* (Moznaim, 1991).
48. Talmud, Niddah 30b.
49. Joseph B. Soloveitchik, "Redemption, Prayer and Talmud Torah," *Tradition* 17, no. 2 (1978): 69.
50. Shneur Zalman of Liadi, *Lessons in Tanya*, vol. 1, trans. Yosef Wineberg et al. (Kehot, 1999), p. 47.

51. Yehuda Ashlag,. *Hakdamos L'Chochmas HaEmes – Sefer HaZohar* (Ohr Boruch Shalom, 2003).
52. https://m.youtube.com/watch?v=6EAnJegnpq4.
53. Maimonides, *Mishneh Torah,* Laws of Foundations of the Torah 1:9–12.
54. This idea is expressed by Rabbi Soloveitchik in his monumental work *Halakhic Man,* a term Rabbi Soloveitchik developed to describe someone who endeavors to infuse every aspect and moment of physical reality with the laws and precepts of the Torah: "When halakhic man pines for God, he does not venture to rise up to Him but rather strives to bring His divine presence into the midst of our concrete world.... When [halakhic man's] soul yearns for God, he immerses himself in reality, plunges, with his entire being, into the very midst of concrete existence, and petitions God to descend upon every mountain and to dwell within our reality, with all its laws and principles" (Joseph B. Soloveitchik, *Halakhic Man* (Jewish Publication Society, 1991), p. 45.
55. The laws pertaining to the times and quality of the sexual encounter between husband and wife.
56. Moshe Chaim Luzzatto and Chaim Friedlander, *Daas Tevunos* (Seferati, 1998), section 24.
57. Moshe Chaim Luzzatto, *The Way of God,* trans. Aryeh Kaplan, 6th ed. (Feldheim, 1998), pp. 254–55.
58. Zohar II, 82b.
59. Zohar I, 24a.
60. *The Practical Tanya, Part 1: The Book for Inbetweeners,* adapted by Chaim Miller (Kol Menachem, 2016), p. 68.
61. To explain the concept that "the Torah and God are totally one," Rabbi Liadi quotes Maimonides, who explains that unlike humans, God is simultaneously the "power to know," "the knower," and "the known" – meaning that one cannot separate between God and the knowledge He possesses. Thus, God and the Torah are one.
62. Abraham Isaac Kook, *Olat Re'iyah,* vol. 1, (Mossad HaRav Kook, 2015), p. 19. In the quotation, Rabbi Kook draws on Solomon's biblical work the Song of Songs 8:5.
63. Isaiah 45:15.
64. "Godless Goodness," available at https://archives.yu.edu/gsdl/collect/lammserm/index/assoc/HASHfae6.dir/doc.pdf.
65. Contemporary author Rabbi Akiva Tatz makes a similar argument: "If my sense of obligation derives from my own intuition and from no point of reference outside of myself, it cannot guarantee a constant standard. It is likely to wax or wane with the quality of my own conscience. With no point of fixity external to the self, no anchor locked to an immovable bedrock, the ship of my consciousness and conscience is adrift. Of course that does not mean that it will drift, but the fact that it may changes everything. If I am my own judge, if there is no standard outside of myself... we have pitifully shrunken the world of the immoral." Akiva Tatz and David Gottlieb, *Letters to a Buddhist Jew* (Targum, 2004), p. 27.
66. Genesis 20:10.
67. Ibid. 20:11.

68. Rabbi Meir Leibush, Ukraine, 1809–1879.
69. Rabbi Naftali Berlin, Poland, 1816–1893.
70. Belarus, Jerusalem, 1886–1959.
71. Rabbi Norman Lamm, *The Shema* (Jewish Publication Society, 2000).
72. Ibid.
73. Tatz and Gottlieb, *Letters to a Buddhist* Jew, p. 41.
74. Leviticus 19:18.
75. Heard from Rabbi Richard Mann.
76. The Bible portrays Abraham sitting at the entrance of his tent, waiting for strangers to pass by so he can extend hospitality. He prays and pleads on behalf of the evil residents of the cities of Sodom and Gomorrah and saves his nephew Lot when he is in danger. Abraham remains a paradigm of kindness for future generations: "We are obligated to be careful in the mitzvah of charity, to a greater extent than all other positive commandments, for charity is the mark of a righteous person, a descendant of Abraham our patriarch" (Maimonides, *Mishneh Torah,* Laws of Gifts to the Poor 10:1).
77. Micah 6:8.
78. Rabbi Ephraim Buchwald, *Crash Course in Basic Judaism* (NTC/Contemporary Publishing Company, 1999), p. 5.
79. The mitzvah to recite the *Shema* twice a day includes all three paragraphs, each of which is taken from a different section of the Bible.
80. The verse is taken from Deuteronomy 6:4.
81. Deuteronomy 4:35.
82. Rabbi Shneur Zalman of Liadi, *Shaar HaYichud veHaEmunah* 111.
83. This is based on the example of Rabbi Akiva, who uttered the *Shema* as he was executed by the Romans in the second century CE. See Talmud, Berachot 61b.
84. For more on the *Shema* see pages 127–132 of this book.

CHAPTER 2
Torah

CHAPTER 2

Torah

Reverberations from On High

About ten years ago, I was invited to sit on a panel at Manhattan's 92nd Street Y to discuss the Jewish concept of *chosenness* – the notion that the Jewish people are a "chosen" people. The panelists included a Reform, Conservative, and Reconstructionist rabbi, and I was asked to share the Orthodox viewpoint. In my presentation, I spoke of the long and glorious history the Jewish people have enjoyed with God, dating back to the patriarchs – Abraham, Isaac, and Jacob – and the matriarchs.

KABBALAH CORNER:

Kabbalah teaches that to understand the essence of something, one must meditate on the word that represents it. The Hebrew word Yisrael (ישראל, Israel, the name of the Jewish people, spelled *yod-sin-resh-alef-lamed*) is an acronym for all the patriarchs and matriarchs:

Yod (י) = Yaakov and Yitzchak

Sin (ש) = Sarah

Resh (ר) = Rivka and Rachel

Alef (א) = Avraham

Lamed (ל) = Leah

This powerful allusion reveals that the essence of Israel is to follow in the footsteps of our forefathers and foremothers. (Roke'ach; Rabbi Aryeh Kaplan)

I spoke of the ups and downs the Jews experienced with God in the wilderness and of the unique relationship Moses enjoyed with the Almighty. I argued that when it came time for God to choose a nation through whom to communicate His vision for humankind, it was only natural for God to choose the Jews, since they had already chosen God.

When I finished my presentation, one of my colleagues on the panel rose to respond. "Everything Mark said is very nice and sweet," he told the audience, "but none of it is true. You see," he went on, "the Bible is a mythical book of fiction, written by people who invented characters and stories to convey certain ideas and lessons. But none of those people existed. There was no Abraham, Sarah, Isaac, Rebecca, or Moses. All those Bible stories were made up by people to teach lessons for living the best life.

"And why," continued the rabbi, "do we need to believe the Torah is true anyway? Why must we believe the Bible was written by God about real people when the whole point is simply to learn the right values for life?"

I was given two minutes to respond. I had to think fast.

I turned to the packed audience and said: "I don't have enough time to explain why I believe the Torah was divinely authored and why I think the stories in the Bible are true. But I will say this. My colleague asserts that it does not matter. I believe it does matter," I explained, "and here's why. By a show of hands, how many of you would make a critical life decision based on the teachings of a book which may or may not be true? Would you, for example, decide the morality of taking a loved one off a respirator based on a teaching from a fictional Torah, written by a person or group of people? By a show of hands, how many of you would be willing to pull the plug on a close relative on life support if the source justifying that behavior was a humanly authored book filled with mythical figures?"

No one raised a hand.

"Let's take a less dramatic example," I continued. "If you lived in a neighborhood with a good public school, which of course is free, would you be willing to spend the approximately $30,000 annual tuition to send your son or daughter to a Jewish school so they can learn teachings invented by people and which are not based on any real events?"

Again, no one raised a hand.

I suspect no one responded because *who* wrote the Torah and whether it contains history really *does* matter. If the Torah was written by human beings, even great scholars, not by God, the simple fact is that most people would not take it as seriously – and for good reason. True, Jewish tradition reveres scholars of all disciplines. The Jewish Sages even prescribed a blessing upon meeting a great scholar in any field of study: *Blessed are You, God, sovereign of the world, who has given of His wisdom to human beings.*[1] But even the greatest sage is mortal, his wisdom finite and imperfect. The teachings of a great scholar or group of scholars should be taken seriously, but they will never carry the authority of an infinite and supernatural Creator. Only a divinely authored Bible gives us access to a higher truth, and, as we will see, an *objective* moral system.

At the same time, the notion that a supernatural Being transmitted a body of knowledge to a segment of humanity is difficult for many to grasp. Still, a God who is sophisticated enough to create a universe as complex as ours can certainly figure out a way to speak to humankind. And if, as many scholars and laypeople believe, humanity is the centerpiece of creation, it is more than reasonable to assume that such a Creator would at some point wish to communicate with His creations.

The Revelation at Sinai is considered by Judaism to be that dramatic moment in human history.

> "When God gave the Torah...the sea did not stir and no creature uttered a sound. The world was silent and still, and the voice went forth: 'I am the Lord your God.'" (Midrash Rabbah)

The Revelation also serves as a foundation for the traditional Jewish belief in the divine origin of the Bible,[2] a principle embraced by billions of people across different faiths and cultures for thousands of years. Is this belief simply a matter of blind faith or is there some rational basis for believing that God is behind the oldest and most influential book ever written?

Evidence from Without

We'll consider two kinds of evidence for the divine authorship of the Torah: logical arguments that stem from *outside* the Torah and internal arguments that emerge organically from *within* the Torah itself. Let's jump in with the first.

A Glaring Contradiction

Maimonides, the brilliant medieval philosopher and physician, points to a glaring contradiction between two sets of verses. The first reads: "The Israelites saw the great power that God had unleashed against Egypt, and the people were in awe of God. They believed in God and in His servant Moses."[3] These verses refer to the reaction of the Jewish people to one of the great miracles of all time: the Splitting of the Sea. After the Jewish people were freed from Egyptian slavery, Pharaoh sent his legions to pursue the Jews. In a dramatic scene described in the Bible, the Jews find themselves confronted on one side by the Reed Sea and on the other by Pharaoh's fast-closing forces. The sea miraculously splits, the Jews walk across safely, and the Egyptians attempt to follow suit. But God causes the waters to come crashing down on the

Splitting of the Reed Sea

Egyptians, drowning them in the sea. Immediately following this spectacular event, the Torah tells us: "They believed in God and in His servant Moses."[4] Witnessing the Splitting of the Sea inspired the Jewish people to believe in God and the authenticity of Moses as His true prophet.

But this seems to be contradicted by a second set of biblical verses which appear just a few chapters later. When God discloses to Moses His plan to reveal the Torah at Sinai, God tells the prophet: "I will come to you in a thick cloud, so that all the people will hear when I speak to you. They will then also believe in you forever."[5] These verses teach that the Jewish people will be inspired to believe *after* the Revelation at Sinai. But didn't the Torah previously inform us that the Jews *already* believed after witnessing the splitting of the sea?

Miracles Are Fleeting

Maimonides answers this contradiction by presenting his unique view on miracles. Moses did not cause the people to believe in God or in his prophecy based on the miracles he performed because "one who believes based on miracles possesses within his heart doubt [entertaining the notion that] it is possible that [the miracle] was performed through sorcery and witchcraft."[6] The reason Moses performed these miracles, suggests Maimonides,[7] was not to prove the validity of his prophecy but to serve a practical end: "It was necessary to drown the Egyptians; [therefore] He split the sea and sank them in it. We needed food, [so] He brought down for us the manna. They were thirsty, [so] He split for them the rock. The assembly of Korach rebelled, [so] the earth swallowed them up. And similarly [with] the rest of the signs."[8]

Miracles, then, were never intended to serve as the basis for the Jewish people's faith. Since miracles leave us with questions and doubts as to the cause of the event, they are unreliable sources of faith. We might see something that *looks* miraculous, but the observer may think it came about through witchcraft or sorcery. That, of course, was back in the time of Maimonides, when witchcraft and sorcery were practiced. Today, our minds are more likely to go to technology; we might wonder whether the supernatural event was generated by a computer or by some other device, not God.

> "Miracles can awaken belief, but only daily acts of faith sustain it." (Rabbi Moshe Feinstein)

Miracles are therefore *not* a good foundation for faith. So what is? According to Maimonides, the greatest source of faith is the Revelation at Sinai: "For our eyes saw and not a stranger's, and our own ears heard and not another's. There was the flame, the thunder and lightning, and he [Moses] drew near the thick cloud and the Voice spoke to him [Moses], and we heard: 'Moses, Moses, go and tell them such and such....' Thus, 'The Lord made not this covenant with our fathers but with us (Deut. 5:3)....'"[9] It is the direct and personal nature of the Sinai experience that made this event a superior basis for faith.

But why is the Revelation at Sinai a better basis for belief in God and His Torah than miracles, which Maimonides says are unreliable? Because, as I heard from one of my teachers, Rabbi Israel Chait,[10] a miracle is an *indirect* encounter with God, whereas the Revelation at Sinai was a *direct* encounter. Someone who experiences a supernatural event needs to decipher how the event took place and who or what caused it. After witnessing a miracle, the person is left with a question: Was this occurrence really caused by God, or is there some other explanation?

The Revelation at Sinai, however, sidestepped that issue altogether because the Revelation was a direct confrontation – not with a miracle, but with God Himself. At the Revelation, God appeared to the Jewish people and spoke to them directly, transmitting the Ten Commandments and leaving less room for questions and doubts. Maimonides adds that this is why after the Splitting of the Sea the Bible simply states that the Jews believed in God, whereas it says after Sinai that the Jews will believe in God "forever."[11] The miracle of the Splitting of the Sea may have inspired faith, but it was only temporary.

And that's just it. Miracles can have a powerful impact on us. They can even inspire belief. But they also leave us with questions, and so faith inspired by a miracle is short lived. Only an encounter with God Himself – what Jewish tradition teaches the people experienced at Sinai – could create a more permanent and everlasting faith in God.

Mass Revelation

Judaism lays claim to what is called "mass revelation" – the belief that every Jewish man, woman, and child stood at Sinai and received the Torah *directly* from God, in contrast to other faith systems, which maintain that only one or a few prophets experienced a revelation from God. Prophets of the other faiths attempt to prove the authenticity of their revelations using miracles since no one else was there to see it happen. But Moses didn't need to prove the Revelation at Sinai to the Jewish people because they experienced the same event he did. They saw what he saw. Maimonides describes how the Jews at Sinai served as witnesses to Revelation: "Our eyes saw and not a stranger... our ears heard and not another."[12] It was therefore unnecessary for Moses or anyone else to prove that the Revelation occurred because everyone saw it with their own eyes.

The Ten Commandments, 1907

The great Jewish sage Nachmanides similarly wrote that God elevated all the Jewish people present at Sinai to the status of prophets so that every Jewish person's belief could come from their *own* experience and not from another person's account.

Judaism remains the only monotheistic faith, and virtually the only religion, to lay claim to a mass revelation. Neither Christianity nor Islam makes this claim, and for good reason: It is almost impossible to invent such a public event if it did not take place. For the same reason, both Christianity and Islam accept that the Sinai Revelation occurred.

What About Me?

Many of you reading this are probably thinking: This all makes sense for those who witnessed the Revelation themselves, for those who were physically present 3,300 years ago at Sinai when the Torah was given. But what about me? I wasn't there! What basis is there for a modern person living in the twenty-first century to believe in Revelation?

To answer this question, we must ask ourselves how we know any historical event occurred which we ourselves never experienced. Generally, we believe in the occurrence of such events based on secondhand knowledge. We have little choice but to rely on secondhand information since there are many instances in which there are no remaining eyewitnesses or physical evidence. Take the Holocaust for example. What happens when there are no more survivors alive to give firsthand accounts of their experiences? True, you could still visit any of the many Holocaust museums filled with physical evidence of the concentration camps, or you can simply go to Auschwitz and see the crematoria. But what happens if somehow all that evidence is lost or destroyed? Will we stop believing that there was a Holocaust? What then becomes the basis for believing that six million Jews were killed at the hands of the Nazis? The only basis for believing remains secondhand knowledge.

SECONDHAND KNOWLEDGE

Rabbi Chait explained that there are two criteria which must be fulfilled when relying upon secondhand information. First, we need to know that the person or people who witnessed the event understood it correctly and could transmit the account to others. And second, we must be sure that they or subsequent generations did not fabricate that account.

What happens when we apply these criteria to the Revelation at Sinai? The first one is easy to satisfy. The Bible describes it as an experience that was simple enough to perceive so that ordinary people could understand what was happening and communicate it to the next generation.[13] But what about the second criterion? Couldn't one still argue that the entire event was simply invented? Maybe Moses or some later Jewish leader conspired with the people and just made the whole thing up! How can we rule out the possibility of fabrication?

We are more likely to accept information as true when *many* people claim they personally witnessed the event. Since we consider mass conspiracy absurd or at least highly unlikely, the more people who say that they themselves experienced a certain event, the more believable that event becomes. For example, imagine you and twenty other people are waiting at the subway station for the train to come. One of the twenty people approaches you and claims that the train is not coming – he saw it derail at an earlier station. He then leaves the station. Nineteen others remain on the tracks waiting for the train. Do you leave? Let's say a few moments later, five more people tell you that they too witnessed the train derail at the earlier station. They also walk away, leaving fourteen people remaining. Do you go now? What if those fourteen people tell you the same thing and they all leave too? Would you still wait for the train? Doubtful. Why? What changed from when the first person told you that the train derailed and the twentieth? The information was the same, but *the likelihood of twenty people conspiring to lie is much less than if it was one or two people*. This is precisely why lawyers employ the legal strategy of corroboration, meaning that they bring numerous people to testify to the same facts. The more people who attest to the same set of facts, the more believable their testimony becomes. Corroboration may not prove that the testimony is true, but each new witness who steps forward reduces the likelihood of fabrication.

IS THIS ALL MADE UP?

As a result, the Jewish claim that millions of people witnessed the Revelation – in contrast to other faiths' claim that only a handful of people witnessed their foundational religious event – reduces the chances that the Revelation event was invented.

> "The idea that millions of people would conspire to lie is implausible; human nature does not lend itself to such mass deception over generations." (Rabbi Eliyahu Dessler)

It is possible, of course, that the Jewish community living at the time of the Exodus, or some person or group from a later generation, conspired and lied, claiming that millions of Jews stood at Sinai when in fact there was no such event. But the Jewish claim that there were so many witnesses present makes that possibility highly unlikely. Rabbi Judah HaLevi, in his famous work the *Kuzari,* explains why: If one or more people were going to fabricate the Revelation at Sinai, that person or group would never make the claim that the entire nation was present at the event since that is a much harder "truth" to sell. Think about it. An event witnessed by millions of people would have been known by many others. There would be some memory of the incident. And so it would be much harder to convince people that the supposed event never transpired. Remember also that the person or group fabricating the Revelation story would need to convince *the Jewish people* that this event took place with their own ancestors. Is it really possible that they have no knowledge of their own history, of what happened to their own forebears? Therefore, it is argued in the *Kuzari,* if a person or group of people had invented the Revelation story, they would have never claimed that the entire nation witnessed the event. And since that is the Revelation story taught by parents and teachers to every generation of Jews, we are left with the only alternative: The Revelation story is believed by so many because it actually happened. And even if this argument does not rise to the level of evidence or proof, it is far more reasonable to believe that the Revelation at Sinai occurred than to claim that it was fabricated.

> "Has anything so great as this ever happened, or has anything like it ever been heard of? Has any other people heard the voice of God speaking out of fire, as you have, and lived?" (Deuteronomy 4:32–33)

THE CHARISMATIC LEADER

The most popular response to the argument from mass revelation is that it assumes Moses led the Jewish people out of slavery and brought them to Sinai to receive the Torah. Perhaps later in history, a charismatic person approached a group of people with an ancient scroll in hand, claiming that a thousand years earlier, God took an enslaved nation out of Egypt, brought them to Sinai, and gave them the Torah. The charismatic leader could have told the group that they were the descendants of the slaves God had saved, and the scroll he possessed was the Torah. God, the leader would proceed to claim, instructed him to tell the people to follow him and the Torah scroll he possessed.

Since there would be no way for the people hearing this story to falsify this claim, the people could have conceivably believed the charismatic leader's story. That could explain the account of Sinai which we have to this day: not a direct revelation from God to a mass of people who all claim to have experienced the same event, but a single person who later convinced the people that the Sinai event had taken place long before.

A DISTANT MEMORY

But this rebuttal is unconvincing. If a charismatic leader would try to convince a group of people of this story, the first question they would ask is: If we are the descendants of this group called the Jewish people, why don't we know who they are? Why are we not aware of their story, of the plagues and miracles and this whole revelation you claim took place? Wouldn't we have some tradition of these very public events? And if the Torah was given to our ancestors a thousand years ago, why are we not observing any of its commandments? Wouldn't we have some distant memory of at least some of those laws? And if the answer to that question is that we received the Torah but over time it was forgotten or lost, wouldn't that be our story too? Wouldn't parents and teachers be telling their children and students that we received the Torah at Sinai but then we lost it and forgot it, and thanks to some great person later in history we regained our lost tradition?

Presumably we would also know the name of that person if he was responsible for restoring our religion. The Jewish story, though, told again and again through the millennia, is that the Jewish people received the Torah at Sinai. There are no versions of the story which claim the Jewish people received the Torah, lost it, and someone later in history gifted it to them again.

Human Authors: The Documentary Hypothesis

Proponents of a theory known as the "Documentary Hypothesis" posit that the Torah was written by multiple human authors at different points in history and that what we refer to as the "Pentateuch" or the "Five Books of Moses" is a compilation of four independent documents which were combined at various points by a series of editors or "redactors." The response to this claim is similar to our response to the assertion that a charismatic leader later came on the scene and convinced the people that their ancestors had received the Torah but forgot it, namely: Why has that not been the story of our people? If the Torah had been written by multiple human authors in separate documents which were later combined, why haven't parents and teachers been recounting that narrative to their children and students? The Jewish story told again and again throughout history is that the Jewish people received the Torah at Sinai. There are no versions of the story which claim that different people wrote the Torah and then combined it at some later date to form the Torah we have today.

EVIDENCE FROM WITHIN

The ultimate indication of the divinity of the Torah, though, is the Torah itself.

> "God's Torah is perfect, restoring the soul; God's testimony is reliable, making the ignorant wise." (Psalms 19:8)

If the Bible was written by a person or a group of people, the following teachings in the Torah are very difficult to make sense of:

A Bit Too Honest

The Torah gives an incredibly critical account of the story of the Jewish people. From the Jews' repeated complaints in the wilderness to the sin of the Golden Calf, the Torah seems to have no qualms about sharing a less than flattering account of the children of Israel's trek through the desert. This is not to mention that the Torah, in an equally transparent manner, discloses the failings of Israel's greatest leaders, including that of its greatest prophet, Moses. The Gospels and Quran focus overwhelmingly on the positive qualities of Jesus and Mohammed, respectively. Kings and other leaders of antiquity generally only wrote of their victories, almost never their defeats. If the Torah were written by a Jewish king or someone who lived in antiquity, it is hard to believe the account would have been so critical.

> "The greatness of the biblical personalities lies in their ability to confront their own failures and imperfections, to repent, and to grow. The Bible portrays them as real human beings, not idealized figures." (Rabbi Joseph B. Soloveitchik)

The Pilgrimage

On the three Jewish festivals of Passover, Sukkot, and Shavuot, the Torah commands all able-bodied men to embark on a pilgrimage to the Temple Mount in Jerusalem to bring special offerings. The dates of all three holidays appear in the Torah. And before the advent of modern travel, this meant that people who lived far from Jerusalem were away from home for weeks at a time. This meant that the borders of Israel would be left unprotected on a predictable schedule for long stretches of time every single year. All the surrounding nations needed to do was read the Bible or just pay a bit of attention to their enemy's schedule. Why would any human leader enact a law that leaves the nation vulnerable to attack? Only a leader capable of protecting the people without an army – a dvine Being – would institute such an edict.

Shemittah: Free Food!

The Torah forbids the Jewish people from working the Land of Israel in the seventh year of the Sabbatical cycle – what is called the law of *Shemittah*. Jews are not the only ones to know that unless you let your land rest, it will be depleted of its nutrients and unable to grow crops – for centuries, farmers have rotated their crops. The Bible, however, requires the entire Land of Israel to lie fallow every seventh year. In a completely agrarian society, as Israel was for millennia, such a law would effectively starve the populace. What kind of ruler would create such a foolish law – unless it was one who could somehow feed an entire population?

KABBALAH CORNER:
The number seven in Kabbalah represents completion and renewal. Just as the world was created in six days and renewed on the seventh with Shabbat, so does *Shemittah* renew the land and the soul. Every seventh year, the land rests, mirroring the cycle of Shabbat and allowing the people to reconnect with the deeper, spiritual dimension of existence. (Rabbi Moshe Cordovero, based on the Zohar)

PROPHECIES COMING ALIVE

Many people are inspired by what seems to be the modern-day realization of certain biblical prophecies concerning the Land of Israel. For example, the prophet Amos prophesied at the end of his book: "And I will bring back the captivity of My people Israel and they will rebuild desolate cities. They will return and plant vineyards and drink their wine and they will make gardens and eat their fruit."[14] Modern Israel is the only country that entered the twenty-first century with a net gain in its number of trees, which is even more remarkable when we consider that this happened in an area considered mainly desert. In the Middle East, the average date tree is about 18–20 feet tall and yields about 38 pounds of dates a year. In Israel today, date trees yield 400 pounds of dates a year and are short enough to be harvested from the ground!

Working the Land of Israel

Amos's prophecy informs us that the Land of Israel will be rebuilt only when the Jewish people return to Israel from "captivity." Despite other nations ruling over the land for centuries, Israel remained desolate until the middle of the twentieth century, when Jews began returning in increasing numbers. When Mark Twain visited Israel in 1867, he described it as a "desolate country whose soil is rich enough, but is given over wholly to weeds – a silent mournful expanse.... A desolation is here that not even imagination can grace with the pomp of life and action.... We never saw a human being on the whole route.... There was hardly a tree or a shrub anywhere. Even the olive and the cactus, those fast friends of the worthless soil, had almost deserted the country."[15] True to the prophecy, only when waves of Jews poured into Israel in the late eighteenth to early nineteenth centuries did the land began to blossom.

Last summer I personally witnessed the realization of another biblical prophecy, this one from the book of Isaiah: "The dry place shall become a pool, and the thirsty place shall become springs of water; in the habitat of jackals, a resting place, a grassy place for reeds and rushes."[16] Knowing of this verse from the Bible, I brought a group of my students to a place in Israel called Arugot Farms. In the middle of the Judean Desert, in the thick of the Middle Eastern summer heat, lay these exquisite vineyards and farmlands with an ecological pool and a self-filtering pond which cleans itself through its own plant and fish life. When he spoke to the group, my friend Ari Abramowitz, a farm owner who helped build up the area, wondered aloud: "Was it our vineyards that the prophet saw?"

Even before these agricultural innovations, though, Isaiah's prophecies were already being fulfilled. In 1917, Lord Arthur Balfour, foreign secretary of the United Kingdom, issued the Balfour Declaration, a document proclaiming Israel the national homeland of the Jewish people. After thousands of years of dispersion in the Diaspora, the Jewish people returned to Israel just as Isaiah had prophesied: "For a brief moment [God] deserted you, and with great compassion [God] will gather you, and the scattered ones of Judah shall gather from the four corners of the earth."[17] After the Jewish people were expelled from Israel in 70 CE, the Romans, Byzantines, Muslims, Crusaders, Mameluks, Ottomans, and British all ruled over the Land of Israel. Nearly two thousand years later, the prophecy of Isaiah was fulfilled: The Jewish people were gathered back to Israel from the "four corners of the earth."[18]

Another prophecy, this one from the book of Ezekiel,

KABBALAH CORNER:
The symbolism of four corners runs deep: There are four major elements (fire, air, earth, water), four seasons, four cardinal directions, four oceans, four states of matter (solid, liquid, gas, plasma), four physical forces (strong, weak, gravitational, electromagnetic), and four levels of life: inanimate, plant, animal, and human. The number four is thus foundational to the structure of the physical world. (Rabbi Yitzchak Ginsburg)

has also been realized in our time: "And I will multiply men upon you, all the House of Israel, all of it; and the cities shall be inhabited, and the ruined places shall be rebuilt."[19] In 1948, when the State of Israel was created, there were approximately 700,000 Jewish people living in Israel. Today there are over seven million – ten times the size in seventy-five years! The prophecy of the Jewish people returning to Israel and making the land blossom has been realized in modern times.

> "Rabbi Abba said: There is no greater sign of the end of days than the blossoming of the Land of Israel." (Jerusalem Talmud)

A Moral Revolution

The Torah brought ethics and morality to the world. Before the Bible, might made right. From Greece and Sparta all the way down to Nietzsche, it was all about power. Ethical monotheism, the root of classical Judaism, introduced the concept of *chesed* or acts of kindness, which was transmitted through prophets such as Isaiah and Ezekiel. Before Sinai, no one preached compassion for the poor or the oppressed. There were laws such as the ancient Hammurabi Code, but none had ethical mores, only practical laws to maintain civil society. Up until a hundred years ago, war was glorified and viewed by countries and their leaders as a good thing. But back in the year 700 BCE, the Jewish prophet Isaiah was communicating God's word: "To beat their swords into plowshares and their spears into pruning hooks; nation shall not lift up sword against nation, neither shall they learn war anymore."[20] Such pronouncements are thankfully commonplace today. But set in context of the battles and bloodshed of the ancient world, it is difficult to conceive of any one person or group of people, on their own, calling for peace.

Thinking for Ourselves

Dr. Joshua Berman, a historian and professor of Bible at Bar-Ilan University, in his book *Created Equal: How the Bible Broke with*

Ancient Political Thought, argues that the culture of the Ancient Near East, where most of the biblical narrative is set, was dominated by a strict class system dividing powerful kings, gods, and rulers from the rest of the population, who served the ruling classes. In stark contrast, the Torah emphasizes the equality of all people created in the image of God. What person or group of people in those times, contends Dr. Berman, could have created such a system given that it was completely contrary to the prevailing culture? As he puts it: "Every great thinker is allowed one major innovation, but there are just too many innovations on this particular front, about taking power away from the powerful, and empowering the powerless.... Either it's from God or there is some guy in a cave, who we don't know about, who is the most brilliant political thinker of all time."[21]

There was also little mobility in the strict class system of the ancient world. Those on the bottom were simply not considered important. The Torah, in which God speaks to an entire people and not simply to the elders or leaders, pushes back against this. In other ancient civilizations, if the gods spoke, it was only to the king. In the Hebrew Bible, though, the Jewish king was also subject to laws – something unknown in antiquity. The Jewish Temple celebrated the connection between God and the people, while the Egyptian temples only celebrated the relationship between the deity and the king. In the Torah, people appoint judges. God commands that the Land of Israel be distributed to the tribes, to the people. Every family in Israel gets a portion of land, a means of economic sustenance. The idea that the land belongs to the people, not the ruler, has no precursors in history and did not come about until modernity with the Homestead Act in the 1860s. The Torah has an incredibly modern and enlightened view of power and the imperative of empowering the powerless.

"A Mighty Hand and an Outstretched Arm"

The Bible teaches that the enslaved Jews of Egypt were liberated by God, as described in the story of the Exodus. There is a biblical phrase, which many are familiar with from the

Earliest reference to Israel found, Merneptah Stele, Egyptian Museum, Cairo, Egypt

Passover Seder, that God took the Jewish people out of Egypt with a "mighty hand and an outstretched arm." This phrase is not very common in the Bible; it appears only in relation to the Exodus. Interestingly, in the inscriptions of the ancient Pharaohs of the Egyptian kingdom (who ruled in the period of Jewish enslavement by traditional dating, roughly 1500–1200 BCE), the Pharaohs are routinely described as having "mighty hands and outstretched arms." Dr. Berman suggests that the Torah is engaging in what he calls "cultural appropriation" – using a phrase familiar to people who lived at that time, typically used to express Pharaoh's might, to describe God's power. By using a term normally used in Egyptian propaganda, the Bible is not only making the text more relatable for the people of that generation, but "out-Pharaoing the Pharaohs." This too suggests that the Torah was written at the same time as the Exodus – not later, as some who do not accept the divinity of the Torah claim.

Stealing the Egyptian Thunder

The cultural appropriation motif also applies to the biblical claim that the Jews were pursued by Pharaoh's chariots and army, who drowned in the sea, after which the Jews offered praise to God. There is a fascinating parallel between that story, as recorded in the Hebrew Bible, and the composition of the Kadesh inscriptions of Pharaoh Ramses II regarding his battle in Kadesh against the Hittite empire. The Egyptians and Hittites vied for control over a certain area in the region, and the Egyptians ultimately forced the Hittite army to retreat. It became a victory of which Ramses II was most proud. This frames the Exodus in a way that the Israelites can see their God as greater than the most powerful Pharaoh at the moment of his greatest achievement – the battle of Kadesh. Again, by describing the Exodus in the same language used by the Egyptians, the Torah is, to borrow Professor Berman's phrase, "stealing their thunder." And, as he goes on to argue, this type of biblical description is only plausible if there were a significant number of Israelites in Egypt who had experienced something they construed as a liberating event in the time of Ramses II. While this is certainly not proof of the divine origin of the Torah, it does support the traditional view that the Bible was written after the Exodus from Egypt and not later in history, as the Bible critics claim. Just as important is the Torah's ethical message that might does not make right, and that true power lies with God – not with human kings or armies.

Beyond Beethoven

Beyond these telling examples, to me, the overall profundity and wisdom of the Bible bespeak a divine origin. There is just too much depth and insight into the human condition for such a document to have been created by a single human being or by a group of people, themselves a product of creation. We simply could not know ourselves that well. As extraordinary as the writings of Shakespeare, the philosophy of Plato and Kant, the music of Beethoven, and the science of Einstein might be, their brilliance is dwarfed by the wisdom of the Torah. The more we study it, the more insight into the human condition it reveals. The more we plumb its depths, the more it manifests its true Author, God.

STOP AND REFLECT: Is there any aspect of Judaism you have been uncomfortable taking on? Do you think you might feel differently if you just "took the plunge" and tried it out?

> "These words, which I command you today, shall be in your heart. Teach them diligently to your children and talk of them when you sit at home, when you walk on the road, when you lie down to sleep, and when you awaken." (Deuteronomy 6:6–7)

In addition, to see the divinity of the Torah requires more than study; it also requires practice. When the Jewish people were first presented the Torah, they famously responded: *Naaseh venishma,* "We will do it and we will hear."[22] Why did the Jewish people first say, "We will do it," and only afterward that they would "hear it"? Usually, we first listen to something and only after hearing what it is all about, determine whether to proceed or not. Why, when it came to accepting the Torah, did the Jewish people put "doing" before "hearing"? The great medieval scholar Rabbeinu Yonah suggests that the Jewish people understood that to experience the divinity inherent in the Torah, one must practice and live by its teachings. Observing the Torah, alongside appreciating its psychological depth, is key to finding God in the Torah.

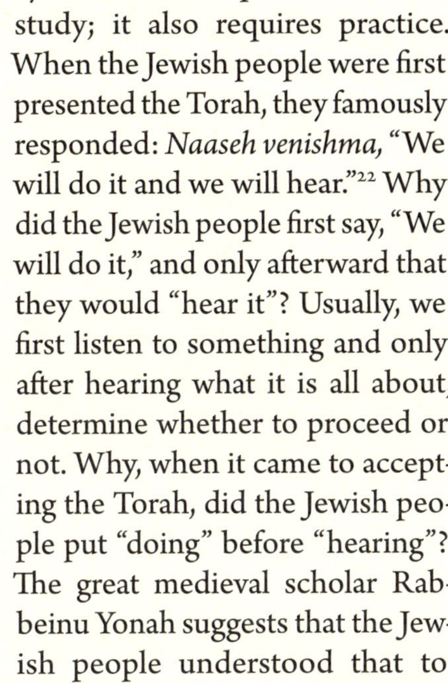

KABBALAH CORNER:
In Kabbalah, the first letter of both *naaseh* ("we will do") and *nishma* ("we will hear") is *nun,* which is the first letter in the Hebrew word *nofel,* meaning falls, representing the theme of humility. The key to experiencing God's word is to make oneself small, recognizing that we are mere vessels for God's light. When we humble ourselves, we make space to receive the wisdom of the Divine. (Rabbi Yitzchak Ginsburg, based on the Zohar)

THE WRITTEN TORAH

Our discussion thus far has largely focused on the Five Books of Moses, otherwise known as the *Chumash.*[23] This is comprised of the books of Genesis (*Bereshit*), Exodus (*Shemot*), Leviticus (*Vayikra*), Numbers (*Bemidbar*), and Deuteronomy (*Devarim*). These five books are also commonly referred to as "Torah." Traditionally, the five books of

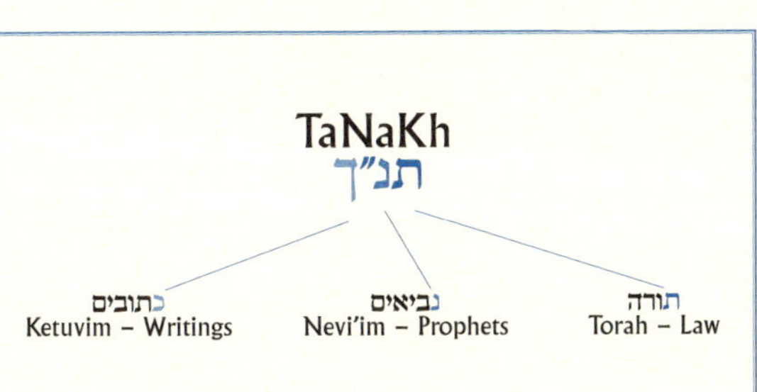

Moses are the parts of the Bible traditionally considered divine in origin, since Moses received them directly from God. After receiving the Five Books, Moses wrote them down on parchment in the form of a scroll. There are two more sections of the canonized Hebrew Bible: "The Prophets" (*Nevi'im*) and "The Writings" (*Ketuvim*). "The Prophets" was composed by the various prophets following Moses (Joshua, Samuel, Ezekiel, Jeremiah, Isaiah, and others) through the medium of prophecy, albeit a lower form than that with which Moses wrote the Five Books of the Torah. "The Writings," which include David's book of Psalms, Solomon's Proverbs, and other great works, was written by these prophets utilizing the medium of *ruach hakodesh* or divine inspiration.

A famous acronym helpful to remembering the three parts of the Bible or Written Torah is *Tanach,* which stands for *Torah* (the Five Books of Moses), *Nevi'im* (Prophets), and *Ketuvim* (Writings). Taken together, the three parts of Tanach consist of the following twenty-four books:

- **Five Books of Moses (*Torah*)**: Genesis, Exodus, Leviticus, Numbers, and Deuteronomy.
- **Eight Books of the Prophets (*Navi*)**: Joshua, Judges, Samuel, Kings, Isaiah, Jeremiah, Ezekiel, and the Twelve Minor Prophets.
- **Eleven Books of the Writings (*Ketuvim*)**: Psalms, Proverbs, Job, Song of Songs, Ruth, Lamentations, Ecclesiastes, Esther, Daniel, Ezra and Nehemiah, and Chronicles.

THE ORAL TORAH

Even if one accepts that God authored the Torah, so much of what observant Jews practice in their everyday religious lives is not explicitly mentioned anywhere in the Bible. Where did all these religious observances come from? Also, there are certain verses or phrases in the Torah, such as "an eye for an eye," which are not read literally. How do we know when to read a verse in the Bible literally and when not to? And since there are no vowels or punctuation in the Torah, how do we know how to pronounce words found in the Bible, or when one verse begins and another one ends? The answer is that along with the Written Torah[24] came an oral explanation of the Torah, which was also transmitted by God to Moses, to teach us how to define and understand terms and phrases found in the Written Torah. That explanation or guide is called the "Oral Torah."

> "The essence of the Oral Torah is its dialogue, the eternal conversation between teacher and student, past and present, God and Israel. This dialogue is where the truth of our tradition is continually reaffirmed and renewed." (Rabbi Joseph B. Soloveitchik)

Although the Oral Torah, as its name implies, was not originally written down, it is very clear that this body of information existed and was followed by generation after generation. The following examples unmistakably illustrate this:

- ***Shechitah***: The Written Torah speaks about the commandment of *shechitah* – that before a Jewish person may eat an animal which the Torah permits, the animal must be slaughtered in a particular type of way: "You may slaughter from your cattle and your flocks that God has given you as I have commanded you."[25] Nowhere in the biblical text does it explain what ritual slaughter is or how to perform it, but the phrase "as I have commanded you" implies that Jews were familiar with the method of slaughter.[26] In fact, when I was in rabbinical school, I spent months studying the many laws and details regarding *shechitah* – laws that continue to be practiced by kosher butchers today. Yet those specifics are not found anywhere in the Written Torah. Where did this information come from?

- **Tefillin:** The Written Torah speaks about the commandment to don tefillin: "And you shall bind it as sign on your arm and a *totafot* between your eyes."[27] What is this "sign" and what is a *totafot*? There is no definition for these terms found anywhere in the Written Torah, yet tefillin always consist of black-colored boxes containing the same parts of the biblical text. If there is nothing in the Written Torah about these details, why has there never been a red or round pair of tefillin?

Tefillin

- **Yom Kippur**: When it comes to the holiest day of the year, the Written Torah commands, "And you shall afflict your souls,"[28] yet it does not define what constitutes "affliction." I'm sure if I asked different people what activities fall under the term "affliction," I would get a wide variety of responses. Yet for thousands of years on Yom Kippur, Jews have always refrained from the same activities: eating, drinking, wearing leather shoes, washing, anointing oneself with oils, and engaging in sexual relations. How did these very specific restrictions originate if they are not mentioned in the Bible?

The fact that the Torah leaves these words such as *affliction* or *totafot* undefined, or that it states "as I have commanded" but it is not written anywhere, shows that the Torah is assuming a complementary interpretative body of information to fill in the gaps. What is that body of information?

The answer is the Oral Torah.

Following the Revelation at Sinai, God revealed to Moses not only the Written Torah (which he wrote down on parchment in the form of a scroll), but also the particulars of various mitzvot and how to define the myriad phrases and terms found in the Written Torah. This is how the Jewish people learned all the detailed laws and traditions concerning the abovementioned examples of *shechitah,* tefillin, and Yom Kippur, and so many other areas of Judaism.[29] These laws were then passed from generation to generation, all the way down to us, in a process of transmission known as *mesorah.*

> "The Oral Torah is the bridge between the finite words of the Written Torah and the infinite wisdom of God." (Rabbi Adin Steinsaltz)

The Jewish Supreme Court

Jewish tradition also teaches that Moses received certain rules or legal principles for deriving laws from the Written Torah. The Sanhedrin, the Jewish High Court consisting of seventy-one of the greatest scholars of each generation, was authorized to use those legal or hermeneutical principles to interpret the biblical text in order to arrive at halachah, or Jewish law.[30] Just as the Supreme Court of the United States serves as the legal body charged with interpreting the Constitution, the Sanhedrin was similarly authorized to interpret the biblical text. Whether a law was received directly by Moses from God, or it was derived through one of these rules by the Sanhedrin, the law would have the same status as any command mentioned explicitly in the Written Torah since it was ultimately derived from the biblical text.[31] In addition, the Sanhedrin[32] also acted like Congress in that it was also authorized to enact *new* laws to ensure that the laws of the Torah were safeguarded. Those laws are called "Rabbinic Law,"[33] and they too became part of the Oral Torah.

According to Maimonides, when it comes to the laws transmitted to Moses directly, you will never find debates. This is why, for example, no one in the Jewish tradition disputes that the color of tefillin should be black, since that was a law given to Moses directly. However, when it comes to some of the laws derived by the Sages, there were differences of opinion which were resolved through majority rule.

To Write or Not to Write: The Mishnah and Talmud

The Oral Torah was passed down from generation to generation – teacher to student and parent to child. It was kept oral for many centuries, and for good reason: Its oral transmission

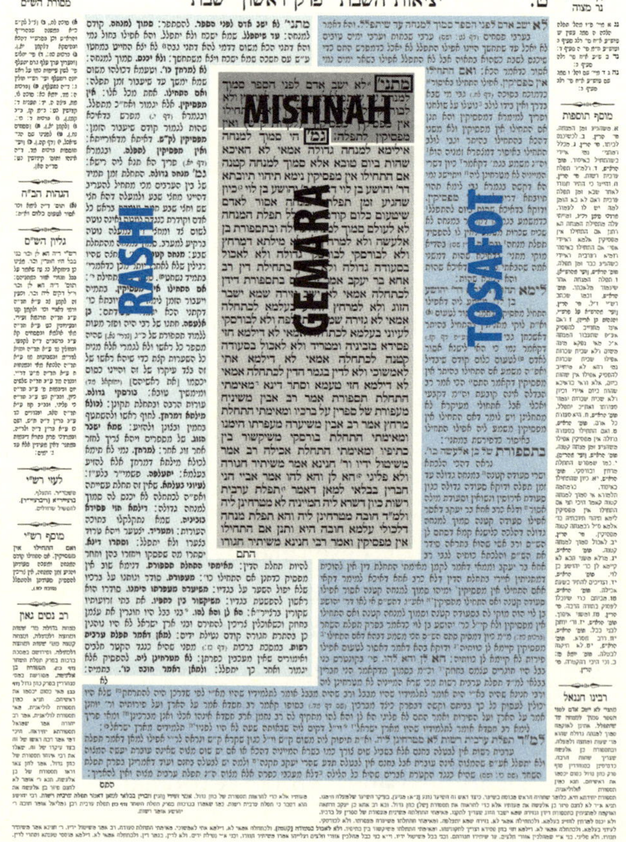

Understanding the Talmud; Gemara and Mishnah

required parents and teachers to study with their children and students or else it would be forgotten. Its oral nature guaranteed a high level of engagement with the wisdom of the Torah, as it does to this day. However, by the second century CE, the Jewish Sages became concerned that due to the Jewish expulsion from Jerusalem by Rome, the Oral Torah would be forgotten. The rabbis of that generation were faced with a conundrum: risk losing the priceless wisdom of the Oral Torah or violate the strong Jewish tradition to maintain the unwritten nature of the Oral Torah. In roughly 200 CE, the generation's leading rabbinic scholar, Rabbi Judah the Prince, relied on a verse from the Torah permitting the suspension of a Torah prohibition for a national emergency[34] and published what is known as the *Mishnah* – a written work containing the laws of the Oral Torah. The Mishnah was ratified by the leading rabbis of the generation, and it became the basis for the Talmud, which was composed over the next few centuries. The main purpose of the Talmud was to clarify the laws of the Mishnah, establish which opinions were binding, and provide derivations and applications for the laws. The Talmud also contains stories and discussions on philosophy and ethics and, to this day, serves as the most important source for Jewish law, ethics, and philosophy.

Virtually all Jewish observances and practices come from the Oral Torah, now found in the Talmud and legal works of codification which followed.[35]

> "Turn it [Torah] over and over again, for everything is in it. Reflect on it and grow old and gray with it, and do not stir from it, for you have no better portion than this." (Mishnah, "Ethics of the Fathers")

The Oral Torah includes everything from lighting Shabbat candles, to the mitzvah of paying one's employees on time, to celebrating the Jewish festivals; all the details of how to perform the many mitzvot – how a *mohel* performs a circumcision, a cantor leads a prayer service, or a rabbi conducts a wedding ceremony.

How should we pray? How much charity are we responsible to give? Is it ever acceptable to disobey our parents? What responsibility do we have to our siblings if the relationship causes us pain? How do we deal with the death of a loved one? The Oral Torah covers virtually every aspect of human existence. Even modern phenomena such as in vitro fertilization, euthanasia, cloning, artificial insemination, and stem cell research can be found in the Oral Torah. Although these technologies did not exist at the time of the Revelation, the principles of how to approach these breakthroughs are spelled out in the Oral Torah. This is possible because the Oral Torah is an expression of God's wisdom and will and is therefore not subject to the human limitations of time and space. And so, although there was no electricity when the Torah was given at Sinai, the Oral Torah contains the principles necessary to analyze questions such as whether using electricity violates the prohibition of "work" on Shabbat. It is ultimately left to us to apply the principles of the Oral Torah to these modern-day questions. In doing so, we are given the opportunity to live every aspect of our lives based on God's ideals and to imbue the physical world with spirituality.

The Oral Torah is also the main source for Jewish thought. The unique Jewish outlook on values and ethics, the spiritual impact of mitzvah observance, what happens after we die, free will, the Messiah, why bad things happen to good people, and so many other pressing theological issues appear in the Oral Torah, which today can be found in the Talmud.

The Talmud, though, is much more than just a book of rules and ideas. It is a window into the deliberations and debates of some of the greatest scholars struggling to define the scope and application of virtually every Jewish law, biblical and rabbinic alike. Studying these debates today allows us to get to the very heart of Jewish law and philosophy, providing us with the tools necessary to answer modern-day ethical and legal questions. Although Talmud study used to be limited to scholars and students of the yeshivah (an academy for advanced Torah study), since its translation into English and other languages,[36] it is now studied by scholar and layman alike.

The modern publications of the Koren and Artscroll editions of the Talmud offer the opportunity for anyone, scholar and layperson alike, to study and understand the Talmud and its commentaries. Hundreds of thousands of people are now enrolled in the *Daf Yomi* (a-page-a-day) program, in which participants study the two sides of a page of Talmud each day, allowing for the completion of the 2,771 folios of the Talmud in seven and a half years. There are also excellent online video and audio classes available to study the Talmud.

THE KABBALAH

The Oral Torah contains both a revealed and concealed part.

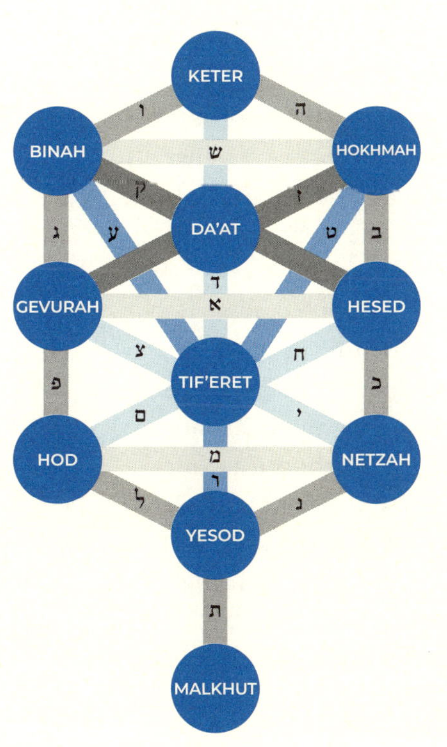

The *revealed* part of the Oral Torah consists of all the details of the 613 mitzvot as well as the great ideas and philosophy of classical Judaism – all found today in the Talmud. The *concealed* part of the Oral Torah refers to the esoteric and metaphysical explanations of the mitzvot and our relationship with God – what is commonly referred to as the Kabbalah. The word Kabbalah means "to receive," and it refers to an entire system of thought received by the Jewish prophets to explain the Torah on a deeper metaphysical level. Kabbalah is not a foreign system to Judaism. It is a critical part of the Oral Torah transmitted by God to Moses designed to give us a more penetrating understanding of the human soul, why God created the universe, and how our actions impact not only our physical world but also the spiritual realms.

> "Kabbalah is the tradition of inner knowledge, the spiritual path that leads to enlightenment and union with God." (Rabbi Aryeh Kaplan)

The Kabbalah deals with spiritually sensitive topics and can be easily misunderstood. As such, its study and transmission were restricted to a small circle of prophets and students. It was never taught publicly. The Kabbalah's communication from teacher to student also remained entirely oral until the Bar Kochba revolt in 132–135 CE, when the Romans became intent on uprooting the Torah from the Jewish people. As a result, according to tradition, Jewish scholars of that time, including the great Sage Rabbi Akiva ben Yosef and his student Rabbi Shimon bar Yochai, began to commit some of this body of wisdom to writing in book form. These books included the *Sefer Yetzirah* (Book of Formation); the *Sefer Habahir* (Book of Illumination); and the Zohar (Book of Splendor), considered one of the great sources of Kabbalah. To this day, these profound works are generally studied only by advanced students of Kabbalah. But generations later, certain masters of the Kabbalah wrote works intended to be read by the general Jewish public.[37] A contemporary scholar, Rabbi Aryeh Kaplan (1934–1983), published outstanding books on Jewish mysticism[38] for the layman. Writing in an exceptionally user-friendly manner, Rabbi Kaplan realized the appeal of Kabbalah and the need for such works to be made available to spiritual seekers. It is imperative, though, to choose authors of such works who are masters of both the revealed and concealed parts of the Oral Torah since both parts of the Torah work in tandem. Rabbi Kaplan was such a scholar, and I highly recommend his books. Other more classic works with which to begin a study of the Kabbalah are *The Way of God,* by Rabbi Moshe Chaim Luzzatto (1707–1746), and the *Tanya,* by Rabbi Shneur Zalman of Liadi (1745–1812).[39] Although both books are translated into English, they should ideally be studied with someone more knowledgeable. However, my teacher and friend Rabbi David Aaron has written several wonderful works based on kabbalistic teachings that can be read alone.

Making the Oral Torah Yours

The Talmud recounts a fascinating story involving Rabbi Akiva, a great rabbinic figure of the talmudic era:

"When Moses ascended on High, he found the Holy One, Blessed be He, sitting and tying crowns on the letters of the Torah. Moses said before God: 'Master of the Universe, who is preventing You from giving the Torah [without these additions]?' God said to him: 'There is a man who is destined to be born after many generations, and Akiva ben Yosef is his name. He is destined to derive from each and every tip of these crowns mounds upon mounds of halakhot.' [Moses] replied: 'Master of the Universe, show him to me.' God said to him: 'Return, behind you.' Moses went and sat at the end of the eighth row [in Rabbi Akiva's classroom] and did not understand what they were saying. Moses's strength waned, until [Rabbi Akiva] arrived at the discussion of one matter, and his students said to him: 'My teacher, from where do you derive this?' [Rabbi Akiva] said to them: 'It is a halachah transmitted to Moses from Sinai.' When Moses heard this, his mind was put at ease" (Menachot 29b).

According to this passage, after Moses ascended Mount Sinai to receive the Torah, he found God working on the finishing touches of the manuscript. In the traditional calligraphy of a Torah scroll, seven letters of the Hebrew alphabet have special ornamentations called "crowns." It seems from this talmudic passage that God was waiting until this calligraphic work was finished before handing over the Torah, which confused Moses. Why would God delay giving the Torah because of these crowns? God explained that in the future a man named Akiva will use these little crowns to interpret "heaps and heaps" of laws. Moses is intrigued. He wants to meet this man. So God transports Moses into the future, where he is able to sit in on a class taught by the great Sage Akiva. But in the classroom Moses becomes perturbed. He understands *nothing* that is being said. How is that possible? Isn't Moses the one who brought the Torah to the people? And why is it that Moses feels better – that "his mind was put at ease" – after Akiva cites Moses's authority? What is this story trying to teach us?

Apparently, the Oral Torah had developed so much since the time of Moses that he was not able to follow the classroom discussion. In the centuries between the days of Moses and Akiva, scholars and students of each generation had studied and applied the Oral Torah's teachings to their own unique circumstances, so the discussion was unfamiliar to Moses. The intervening generations of Jews had not changed the Torah but had developed it through their own learning and application to their daily lives. The Oral Torah was therefore more complex and sophisticated, having been applied to many new circumstances, even as it was still based on the same principles God had revealed to Moses and the Jewish people. That is why Moses was comforted when he heard Rabbi Akiva answer his student: "It is a halachah transmitted to Moses from Sinai." When Moses saw that the classroom discussion was rooted in the same laws and traditions he had received at Sinai, he was reassured that Rabbi Akiva and his students were continuing the transmission of the Oral Torah, ensuring a Jewish future.

Each of us is presented with the same opportunity today: to develop the Oral Torah by becoming students and even scholars of Torah. By studying and applying the teachings of the Torah to our lives, we further develop the Oral Torah and bring its values and laws into the twenty-first century. This task is not meant to be restricted to the great rabbis or scholars of each generation; it is a privilege in which all Jews are invited to participate. Jewish tradition teaches that there are three "crowns" a Jew can wear: the crown of priesthood, the crown of kingship, and the crown of Torah. Maimonides wrote that whereas the crown of priesthood is only open to *kohanim* (Jewish priests) and the crown of kingship is only accessible to descendants of King David, the crown of Torah is open to all: "It is standing and ready for all Israel; anyone who wants it can come and take it."[40] Perhaps that explains why it was Rabbi Akiva's classroom to which Moses was transported. For Rabbi Akiva had been an illiterate shepherd who knew little of his Jewish heritage until the age of forty, when he first began to study.

> "Until age forty, Rabbi Akiva was ignorant. One day, while standing near a well in Lydda, he pondered aloud, "Who hollowed out this stone?" He was told, "Akiva, have you not read that water wears away stone (Job 14:19)? It is the constant drip of water, day after day." Rabbi Akiva asked himself: Is my mind harder than this stone? I will go and study a portion of Torah." (*Avot DeRabbi Natan*)

He also did not have much of a Jewish lineage to speak of, having descended from converts. Nonetheless, Rabbi Akiva immersed himself in Jewish learning and eventually became one of the greatest Torah scholars of all time, teaching us that you do not need to be born into an illustrious rabbinic dynasty to become a scholar or leader in the Jewish community. You just need the will and determination to study Torah and a desire to live by its teachings. In doing so, we not only enrich our own lives but ensure the continuity of the Oral Torah's teachings.

A LETTER IN THE SCROLL

KABBALAH CORNER:

For a Torah scroll to be kosher, there must be enough space around each black letter so that no two letters are touching. Our Sages teach that each of our souls corresponds to one of the 600,000 letters of which a Torah scroll is comprised. However, if one actually counts all the letters, they total just over 300,000! There are those of us who are "black letters," who are deeply connected and have found our place in Judaism. Yet, there are also those of us who are "empty space," who are still exploring our Judaism and developing our personal connection to our heritage. Yet for a Torah scroll to be kosher, both the black letters and the empty spaces must be included. (Rabbi Shneur Zalman of Liadi)

The great mystical commentator Rabbi Chaim ibn Attar (1696–1743), in his commentary on the Torah,[41] wrote that whereas every human being is comprised of two elements, a body and soul, every Jewish person possess a third element: a part of the Torah which is "betrothed to every Jew."[42] Each Jewish person's soul is metaphysically connected to a different part of the Torah.

Since it is unique to him or her alone, it is imperative for each person to find their own special portion in the Torah. Some are attracted to the more rational parts of Torah and others to the more spiritual or mystical. Some are drawn to the laws governing interpersonal relationships such as the Torah laws regarding torts, damages, contracts, or property law, and some gravitate toward the parts that connect us directly with God, such as lighting Shabbat candles or donning tefillin. This is not to say we should *only* pay attention to the parts of Jewish tradition that speak to us personally, but different aspects of the Torah will resonate with some more than others, since every Jewish person has their own unique portion.

STOP AND REFLECT: Is there a Jewish teaching or mitzvah to which you feel deeply attached? What do you think makes you feel so connected to it?

Another great mystical thinker, Rabbi Abraham Isaac Kook, taught that when one feels drawn to a certain part of the Torah, whether from the Written or Oral Torah, they should take that interest seriously and deepen their understanding of that part of Judaism. Rabbi Kook believed that each Jewish person's soul is rooted in a different part of the Torah, and that when a Jew learns that portion of Torah, he or she builds a greater awareness of their own self and personality. Learning those parts of Torah grants us access to our own inner world. Failure to learn about the parts of Torah that resonate will result in a lack of self-understanding.[43] The Kabbalah teaches that each Jewish person possesses a special letter of the Torah[44] which is uniquely theirs. Studying those parts of Torah is necessary to reach our true essence.

Rabbi Abraham Isaac Kook, 1924

> "Each of us has significance precisely insofar as we are part of a story, an extraordinary and exemplary story of a people dedicated to certain ideas. We are not free-floating atoms in infinite space. We are letters in the scroll." (Rabbi Jonathan Sacks)

Devekut: Spiritual Intimacy

Studying *any* part of the Torah, though, even the parts *not* unique to who we are individually, can also have a great impact upon us. Besides the opportunity to acquire spiritual and moral wisdom, something even deeper takes place when we learn Torah. The great chasidic master, Rabbi Shneur Zalman of Liadi, otherwise known as the Baal HaTanya,[45] quoted from the primary source of Kabbalah, the Zohar, which says: "God and the Torah are one." The Torah is not merely an expression of God's wisdom but a manifestation of God Himself. The letters and words of the Torah are the means through which God originally created the world and through which He continues to interact with the physical world. And so learning Torah leads to what the kabbalists call *devekut* – an attachment with God Himself. Studying Torah is not just an intellectual or academic exercise. It provides us with the information necessary to follow the uniquely Jewish spiritual path and enables us to become one with God.

A Word of Encouragement

Some people are put off or intimidated by Torah study since it requires a Jewish educational background, which many lack. However, with today's plethora of excellent English translations and commentaries, one really does not need a background to engage in Torah study. The great Maimonides penned a letter to a simple Jew in Baghdad named Joseph ibn Gabir expressing a similar sentiment. Joseph, not knowing any Hebrew, was unable to read the *Mishneh Torah*, Maimonides's major work on Jewish law. Ibn Gabir therefore asked Maimonides to respond in his own hand and offer him some encouragement.

In response, Maimonides wrote: "First of all, I must tell you, may the Lord keep and increase your welfare, that you are not justified in regarding yourself as ignorant. You are our beloved pupil; so is everyone who is desirous of studying even one verse or a single law. It also makes no difference whether you study in the holy language, or in Arabic, or in Aramaic; it matters only whether it is done with understanding.... But of the man who neglects the development of his spirit it is said, 'He has despised the word of the Lord' (Num. 15:31); this applies also to a man who fails to continue his studies even if he has become a great scholar, for the advancement of learning is the highest command. I say, therefore, in general, that you must not belittle yourself nor give up the intention of improving. There are great scholars who did not begin their studies until an advanced age, and who became scholars of distinction in spite of this."[46]

Judaism is supposed to be attainable. Although at times we might be intimidated by the complexity of the Torah's many laws and its philosophical intricacies, it is supposed to be within our reach. As the Torah itself declares: "It is not in heaven, that you should say, 'Who will ascend into heaven for us and bring it to us, that we may hear it and do it?' Nor is it beyond the sea, that you should say, 'Who will go over the sea for us and bring it to us, that we may hear it and do it?' Rather the matter is very near you, in your mouth and in your heart, that you may do it."[47]

Judaism is not in the heavens. It may feel like Torah is a world away or on the other side of the planet. But as Torah itself tells us: "It is very near you, in your mouth and in your heart."[48]

Further Study

Studying Torah is my favorite mitzvah. Learning Jewish texts, whether from the written or oral parts of the Torah, fills me in a way nothing else does. And it never gets boring.

> "The soul craves Torah, the spiritual sustenance that provides it with true satisfaction and delight." (Rabbi Chaim of Volozhin)

The more I study, the more I grow intellectually and spiritually, and the more convinced I become of the Torah's divine nature.

But even if one becomes convinced of the divine origin of the Torah and of its profound impact on our lives, there are other issues some have with the Bible that I could not address in this section: seeming contradictions between the Bible and the scientific approach to the age of the universe, the existence of dinosaur fossils when the Bible makes no reference to them, or the lack of direct archaeological evidence of Egyptian slavery or the Exodus (although there are references in Egyptian sources to the Jews as slaves, the plagues, and the Exodus); certain laws and commands in the Bible that, on the surface, seem xenophobic, sexist, homophobic, and even racist; and an entire section of the Bible – the book of Leviticus – which focuses on animal sacrifice, a practice most modern Westerners find difficult to accept. These and other issues are real questions – some with which I personally struggle – that deserve answers. The important thing to know is that there *are* real answers and approaches to these questions, some of which I have taught and incorporated into my classes over the years, but which are beyond the scope of this work. If any of these questions bother you, I would urge you to do further reading on these issues.

Further Reading

Is the Good Book Bad? A Traditional Jewish Response to the Moral Indictments of the Bible
Michoel Stern

The Written and Oral Torah: A Comprehensive Introduction
Nathan Lopes Cardozo

In Good Faith: Questioning Religion and Atheism
Scott A. Shay

Genesis and the Big Bang: The Discovery of Harmony Between Modern Science and the Bible
Gerald L. Schroeder, PhD

The Great Partnership: Science, Religion, and the Search for Meaning
Rabbi Jonathan Sacks

Ani Maamin: Biblical Criticism, Historical Truth, and the Thirteen Principles of Faith
Dr. Joshua Berman

Permission to Receive
Lawrence Kelemen

Handbook of Jewish Thought 2
Aryeh Kaplan

TAKEAWAYS

- Judaism is the only major faith that claims a mass revelation. Since a mass conspiracy is highly improbable, the Revelation at Mount Sinai is exceedingly unlikely to be a fabrication.
- The Torah's honest account of the shortcomings of the Jewish people and their leaders points toward a divine origin, as authors of antiquity routinely painted their ancestors far more favorably.
- The fulfillment of biblical prophecies such as the return of the Jewish people to Israel and the land's stunning rebirth indicates that the Torah's origin is divine.
- The Written Torah comprises the Five Books of Moses, the Prophets, and the Writings. The Oral Torah provides the laws and explanations passed down orally from Moses that are necessary to unlock the code of the Written Torah.
- Jewish mysticism or the Kabbalah offers profound metaphysical insights into the spiritual dimension of the Torah and our relationship with God.
- Studying Torah is a great mitzvah. According to a renowned master of Kabbalah, every Jewish soul is metaphysically connected to another part of the Torah. Since it is unique to him or her alone, each person can find their own special portion in the Torah.

Notes

1. *Koren Shalem Siddur*, p. 1002.
2. The traditional Jewish belief in the divinity of the Bible or the Torah refers to the Five Books of Moses (also called the Pentateuch). The other canonized books of the Bible, such as the book of Joshua, Isaiah, or the Book of Esther, are believed to have been authored by prophets or others endowed with divine inspiration.
3. Exodus 14:31.
4. Ibid.
5. Ibid. 19:9.
6. Maimonides, *Mishneh Torah*, Laws of the Foundation of the Torah 8:1.
7. Ibid.
8. Ibid.
9. Ibid.
10. Rabbi Israel Chait, *Philosophy of Torah: A Collection of Articles*, 2nd ed. (Targum, 2010), p. 16.
11. Exodus 19:9.
12. Deuteronomy 5:4.
13. Referring to the Revelation, Moses tells the people: "You are the ones who have been shown, so that you will know that God is the Supreme Being and there is no one besides Him. From the heavens, He let you hear His voice admonishing you, and on earth He showed you His great fire, so that you heard His words from the fire" (Deut. 4:35–36).
14. Amos 9:14.
15. Mark Twain, *The Innocents Abroad* (1881).
16. Isaiah 35:7.
17. Ibid. 54:7.
18. Ibid.
19. Ezekiel 36:10.
20. Isaiah 2:4.
21. The WildesCast: An MJE Podcast, February 8, 2023, "Is the Torah Authentically Divine?"

22. Exodus 24:7.
23. From the Hebrew word *chamesh*, or "five."
24. When I use the term "Written Torah" I am referring specifically to the Five Books of Moses (Genesis, Exodus, Leviticus, Numbers, and Deuteronomy), which are written upon scrolls and kept in the synagogue in the Holy Ark.
25. Deuteronomy 12:21.
26. Rashi, the great biblical commentator, writes on this phrase: "This teaches us that there was already a commandment regarding the slaughtering of animals – as to how one should slaughter; it is not written in the Torah, but it comprises the traditional regulations regarding the slaughter of animals that were given orally to Moses on Mount Sinai" (*Sifrei*, Deuteronomy 75:7; Chullin 28a; Rashi, Deut. 12:21). The Talmud also interprets the phrase "as I have commanded you" to teach "that Moses was previously commanded about the halachot of slaughter, even though they are not written explicitly in the Torah. He was commanded about cutting the gullet and about cutting the windpipe, and about the requirement to cut the majority of one *siman* for a bird, and the majority of two *simanim* for an animal" (Chullin 28a).
27. Deuteronomy 6:8.
28. Numbers 29:7.
29. Another famous example regarding the Sabbath is the biblical term *melachah*, which is loosely translated as "work." The Oral Tradition, however, teaches that this term refers to the thirty-nine activities that went into the building and maintenance of the Tabernacle.
30. This power of the Sanhedrin was derived from the biblical verse "According to the teaching that they will teach you and according to the judgment that they will say to you, shall you do; you shall not deviate from the word that they will tell you, right or wrong" (Deut. 17:11).
31. A well-known example is the way Jews have gotten married for thousands of years. The Torah says, *"Ki yikach ish ishah"* (Deut. 24:1), meaning that a man takes a woman in marriage, but it never specifies how. Today it is common practice for a man to marry a woman by giving her a coin or other object of value, especially a ring. But how do we know that this is a valid form of Jewish marriage? This is derived from a *gezeirah shavah*, one of the thirteen hermeneutical methods with which the Rabbis interpreted the Torah. The same phrase *ki yikach* appears in regard to Abraham's purchase of a burial plot for his beloved wife Sarah. The Rabbis explain that just as Abraham bought the field by handing its previous owner an object of value (money), so too, when the Torah says *ki yikach* regarding marriage, it refers to giving a woman an item of value. Even though this law is only known through rabbinic derivation, it remains a biblical law because the Rabbis are not legislating marriage but using certain principles to interpret the Bible.
32. The Sanhedrin existed for thousands of years, from the time of Moses until roughly 358 CE, when the Roman Empire put down a Jewish revolt. See Rabbi Aryeh Kaplan, *Handbook of Jewish Thought* (Moznaim, 1992), p. 209.

33. For example, the Rabbis created the category of *muktzeh,* which means that certain items may not be moved on Shabbat. While this prohibition serves to protect the sanctity of Shabbat, it remains a rabbinic enactment, not a biblical prohibition.
34. The Torah prohibits setting down the Oral Law in written form. But the Sages accepted Rabbi Judah the Prince's application of the verse "It is time to act for the sake of God; they have overturned Your Torah" (Ps. 199:126) as the basis to save the Oral Torah. Rabbi Judah applied the verse to mean that in order "to act for God," meaning to preserve the Oral Tradition, it was necessary to overturn the Torah and negate the restriction against committing the Oral Torah to writing.
35. Examples include the *Mishneh Torah* by Maimonides, the *Tur* by Rabbi Jacob ben Asher, and *The Code of Jewish Law* by Rabbi Joseph Karo.
36. The Talmud was written in Aramaic.
37. *The Way of God* by Rabbi Moshe Chaim Luzzatto (known as the Ramchal) and Rabbi Shneur Zalman Liadi's *Tanya* are two noteworthy examples, both of which are translated into English with excellent commentaries.
38. Some examples of Rabbi Kaplan's books include *Infinite Space: Introduction to Kabbalah, Meditation, and Prophecy; Meditation and Kabbalah;* and *Jewish Meditation: A Practical Guide.*
39. My personal favorite English translation of the *Tanya* is *The Practical Tanya, Part 1: The Book for Inbetweeners.*
40. Maimonides, *Mishneh Torah,* Laws of Torah Study 3:1.
41. *Or HaChayim* on Deuteronomy 22:3.
42. Ibid.
43. In *Orot HaTorah,* chapter 9, section 1, Rav Kook writes that when one studies and involves oneself in the parts of Torah in which their soul is rooted, it "enhances their spirit." Contemporary scholar Rabbi Shlomo Aviner (*Commentary to Orot HaTorah* [Mesorah, 2005], p. 150) explains this to mean that studying those parts of Torah builds one's personality, spiritually elevates their soul, and adds joy and God-consciousness to one's life.
44. This kabbalistic idea is discussed by the Baal Shem Tov and by Rabbi Kook, in *Orot HaTorah* 11:2.
45. The Baal HaTanya (1745–812), also known as the Alter Rebbe, was the founder and first Rebbe of Chabad. He is best known for his authoring of the *Tanya* – a foundational work on Jewish mysticism which underlies the philosophy of chasidic thought.
46. Isadore Twersky, *A Maimonides Reader* (Behrman House, 1972), p. 478.
47. Deuteronomy 30:12–14.
48. Ibid.

CHAPTER 3
Prayer

CHAPTER 3

Prayer

Mindfulness for Anxious Times

I have prayed three times a day since my early teens, but it never came naturally to me. As a child, I remember seeing my mother, of blessed memory, totally focused and plugged in to her praying. There was always a book of Psalms next to her bed. Sometimes she even cried. When I would see her tears welling up as she prayed, I remember wondering what she was thinking about – and feeling badly that I couldn't manage to muster that kind of emotion myself. My personal relationship with God was forged primarily through Torah study. It was always more natural for me to connect spiritually through my mind. But Judaism wants our connection to God to be more than just cerebral. Judaism's primary goal is to imbue our lives with God and His eternal values, and for that we need to develop more than an intellectual connection. It must penetrate deeper; it needs to be emotional. And for that, prayer is indispensable. *Tefillah,* the Hebrew word for prayer, is defined in the Talmud as *avodah shebalev* – service of the heart.[1] Prayer is a deeply emotional experience.

STOP AND REFLECT: Have you ever had a powerful prayer experience? What made it so meaningful?

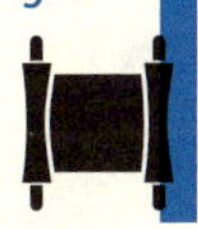

THE PHILOSOPHY OF PRAYER: FOUR APPROACHES

How does prayer connect us emotionally, and why does Judaism view prayer as such a powerful vehicle for developing ourselves spiritually?[2] Here are four main answers that I found have spoken to me and my students throughout the years:

#1: Prayer transforms us into better people.
#2: Prayer helps us create a deeper bond with God.
#3: Prayer cultivates mindfulness.
#4: Prayer serves as a conduit for God's blessings in this world.

1. PRAYER TRANSFORMS US

Embedded in the Hebrew language are some of Judaism's deepest messages. The Hebrew word "to pray" – *lehitpallel* – is an excellent example. The three-letter root of this word, *peh-lamed-lamed,* means to judge or evaluate. What do judging and praying have to do with one another? *Lehitpallel* is the reflexive form of the word, meaning to judge or evaluate oneself. Prayer is a means to evaluate whether we are living our lives in accordance with our ultimate goals.

How does prayer enable us to self-evaluate?

The Jewish prayers express the most fundamental beliefs, principles, and values of the Jewish faith. As one of my teachers once remarked, virtually all of Jewish philosophy can be found in the pages of the siddur (the Jewish prayer book). When we articulate the ideas and ideals of Judaism found in the siddur and then reflect

on our *own* lives in relation to those ideals, we judge or evaluate ourselves. We recite a phrase from the prayer book, reflect on that idea as it is played out in our own personal lives, and ask ourselves: Are we living up to these ideals and aspirations?

Gazing into the Mirror

The siddur in this sense is like a mirror, allowing us to see ourselves and reflect on how we are faring in relation to our own values. That is why it is important to *hear* the words as we pray, a tradition dating back all the way to the prophetess Chanah, who taught us to pray with our lips – not just our minds. Psychologically speaking, hearing ourselves say things out loud makes a greater impact on us than reading the same words on paper. It can take months, even years of therapy, for us to say certain things out loud. But once we hear ourselves say the words, we can begin the process of change. *Hearing* the words of the prayer book forces us to take an honest look at our lives, assess where we are, and make the changes we need to better live up to our own ideals.

As humans we easily get distracted, especially when it comes to the very purpose of our existence. This is another reason Jews pray daily. Consistent prayer creates space for a daily check-in to ensure our actions remain consistent with our life goals.

STOP AND REFLECT: Identify one area where your actions and your ideals are not aligned. What can you do to try to bring them closer together?

Although we are taught not to judge other people, it is imperative for our own growth to "judge" ourselves. We should be a fair judge, understanding our own fears and challenges, but not refrain from being introspective while using the prayer book as our guide. As the Greek philosopher Socrates famously declared: "The unexamined life is not worth living."[3]

The Chutzpah to Pray

It takes a lot of chutzpah to pray. Think about it: We come before God and ask Him to help us get that promotion at work or the big bonus at the end of the year. Judaism classically defines God as an all-knowing and benevolent Being, so how do we have the nerve to ask the Almighty to change reality? If God knows everything and has our best interests in mind, then, by definition, the way things are is the way God meant them to be! How dare we ask God to change that reality, just so it can be more in line with our own desires and needs? What's more, prayer seems nonsensical. If God is perfect and therefore unchanging, we cannot change His mind anyway. So why bother praying at all?

The medieval Jewish philosopher Rabbi Joseph Albo submits[4] that *prayer is not intended to change God; prayer is meant to change us*. God is perfect and we cannot change His mind. But through the prayer experience, as we articulate Judaism's values and ideals and reflect on our own lives in relation to those ideals, we transform ourselves into better people – really into *different* people. Every time we improve ourselves through prayer, we create ourselves anew. God's prior decree or judgment no longer applies to "us" because we are no longer that same person. The prior decree was for the *old you*. The new and improved "you" warrants a new divine evaluation because prayer has helped you become a different person.

Prayer also changes us because the experience of communicating with God often inspires us to take on something new. The prime example of this is the prayer of the prophetess Chanah. Chanah struggled with being childless, so in her prayers she vowed to dedicate her future son to God if He would only bless her with one. In a similar way, when we pray, we may be moved to take on a new mitzvah or commit to do better at one we are already observing.

Whether it is the experience of praying itself or the potential to become inspired and take on something new, prayer has the power to transform us into different people than we were the day before.

2. PRAYER CONNECTS US TO GOD

The Rabbis do something that seems very odd: They learn a basic principle of prayer from a failed prayer – Moses's request to enter the Land of Israel, which is denied. Moses begins as follows: "My Lord, God, You have begun to show Your servant Your greatness and Your strong hand, for what power is there in the heavens or on earth that can perform according to Your deeds and according to Your mighty acts?"[5] Only afterward does Moses ask: "Let me now cross and see the good land on the other side."[6] From here the Talmud derives that before we ask something of God, we must first recite words of praise.[7]

Why do the Jewish Sages use the example of Moses to illustrate this principle of praising before requesting? Why would the Sages choose an unsuccessful prayer to demonstrate their point? Why not instead cite a prayer that is accepted?

By referencing a prayer that was denied, the Sages teach us that prayer – even when it seems unsuccessful – is a valuable practice in and of itself. The very experience of standing before God and engaging one's Creator in dialogue is a worthwhile experience – even if we don't get what we ask for. Rabbi Joseph B. Soloveitchik put it best: "In praying we do not seek a response to a particular request as much as we desire fellowship with God. Prayer is not a means of wheedling some benefit from God. Despite our prayer 'Accept our prayer in mercy and favor,' it is our persistent hope that this may be fulfilled but it is not our primary motivation."[8] Petitioning or beseeching God for our needs is an important part of the prayer experience,[9] but it's not *why* we pray. We pray to connect. We pray to develop a more intimate relationship with our Creator. We pray to express our hopes, desires, and values, and thereby to create a closer bond. So even if He does not grant us a particular request, we are still connecting with God.

> "Where is God found? Wherever we let him in." (Rabbi Menachem Mendel of Kotzk)

Is Anyone Listening?

Of course, it is a huge letdown when God does not grant us our wishes. When that happens, we may conclude that God is simply not listening. But Jewish tradition teaches that God *always* listens. Rabbi Soloveitchik taught that God is a *shome'a tefillah* – He hears our prayers – but He is not always a *mekabel tefillah,* One who always accepts our prayers favorably. As with Moses's entreaty to enter the Land of Israel, God sometimes denies our requests. It is difficult to understand why, especially when those requests are critical to us and seem so legitimate. But it does not mean God is not listening.

I remember when my children were younger, and, on occasion, I would muster the strength to deny them one of their many requests. (I was the pushover and my wife the disciplinarian.) My children invariably responded: "Daddy, you're not listening!" And my answer was always the same: "I *am* listening. I just don't think a sixteenth candy bar is a good idea right now!" I do not mean to make light of an experience that can be painful, but God, like any human parent, is aware of all the issues at play and therefore has a broader perspective on reality. A negative response to our prayers is not a reflection of a deaf or uncaring God, but of an all-knowing Being who is privy to infinite issues of which we are unaware.

Prayer as a Dialogue

Prayer is therefore more about our relationship *with* God than what we can get *from* God. That is why if one is unable to pray in a synagogue, it is still a mitzvah to pray at home – because prayer is ultimately a personal encounter. For this reason, the most important part of any prayer service is called the *Amidah*, which literally means "standing." Standing or appearing before our Creator, communicating our thoughts, hopes, and values – with the Jewish prayer book's guidance – is key to developing an emotional connection with God.

A final question remains. Communication usually implies a dialogue, an exchange between two parties. But when it comes to prayer, it is just us talking to God! Where is the dialogue? Although we no longer live in an age of prophecy when God spoke to specific individuals, we still have the Torah, through which God communicates His will to humankind. In this sense, prayer can still be seen as a dialogue: God speaks to us through His Torah, and we respond through our prayers.

> "God is close to all who call out to Him in truth." (Psalms 145:18)

3. PRAYER CULTIVATES MINDFULNESS

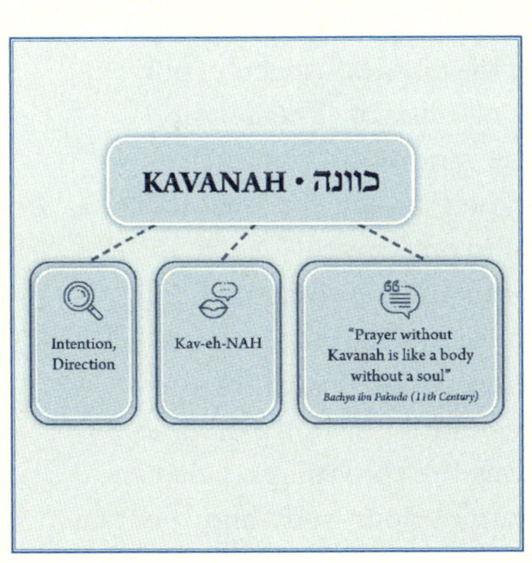

What is the first thing you do in the morning? Eighty percent of people check their phones. The average person checks their phone forty to fifty times a day, two to three times an hour.[10] In 2010, 50 percent of American teens received at least 50 text messages a day;[11] by 2023 that number had increased nearly fivefold to 237.[12] Studies suggest that smart devices are contributing to a global mental health crisis for our children.[13] Our addiction to stimulation has made our generation exceptionally distracted – not to mention anxiety ridden – making it harder than ever for us to be "in the moment."

In the search for coping mechanisms, many have turned to the modern-day mindfulness movement with its Zen Buddhist roots. But as Jews, we need not turn elsewhere. Few are aware that Judaism's ancient system of daily prayers and blessings is also a path to mindfulness – though with a different goal and methodology. The Eastern approach to mindfulness, which conjures the image of a monk meditating on a mountain far from civilization, is aimed at removing oneself from the physical world – in a word, transcendentalism.[14] The goal of Jewish mindfulness is not to remove oneself from the world but to engage the physical world through the mitzvot, all of which require some physical activity. Whether it is eating matzah on Passover, kindling a flame to light the Sabbath candles, or wrapping tefillin on one's arm, all mitzvot involve some physical activity. *Imbuing our daily physical activities with spirituality helps bring about Judaism's main objective, which is not transcendentalism but holiness.* In Judaism, we attain holiness not by breaking free of the physical world but, as the Kabbalah teaches, by elevating the physical aspects of our existence through the observance of mitzvot. The physical activities involved in carrying out the various mitzvot, such as moving one's lips to recite a prayer, help us achieve what the kabbalists call *devekut* or attachment to our Creator.

> **STOP AND REFLECT:** How do you think Judaism can help us deal with today's technology-driven mental health challenges?

Rabbi Shneur Zalman of Liadi,[15] the founding rabbi of the Chabad Lubavitch movement and a mystical scholar, wrote that performing the physical actions associated with the various mitzvot engages and spiritually elevates the body and the "animal soul." Praying, which involves the throat, lips, palate, tongue, and teeth, elevates these parts of our body and the part of our soul most connected to the body, the "animal soul." To impact the higher part of our soul, the "Godly soul" – the part of us taken directly from God[16] – one requires *kavanah* or mindful focus. *Kavanah,* within the context of prayer, means being aware that we are addressing God and understanding the words we are saying.[17] Our ability to maintain that kind of mindfulness while we pray elevates the highest part of who we are. However, as Rabbi Shneur Zalman pointed out, even if one fails to achieve that level of *kavanah*, prayer still elevates the body and the lower part of the soul.

APPRECIATING OUR BLESSINGS WHILE WE STILL HAVE THEM

On a much simpler level, though, prayer brings about mindfulness by causing us to become more aware of the reality of our own existence and of God Himself.

KABBALAH CORNER:
Each of the three daily prayers focuses on a specific spiritual energy. The morning prayer empowers us to concentrate on renewal and innovation. In the afternoon, we carve out a few moments to find calm in the midst of our daily chaos. Finally, as evening arrives we find peace in the stillness of night. (Rabbi Tzadok HaKohen of Lublin)

Reciting words or praises about God makes us more God-conscious, which is critical for making the right choices and decisions throughout our day.

Reciting certain words and phrases regularly – almost like a mantra – also enables us to remain mindful of our mission and the basic gifts of life, such as the ability to see or walk. These are all necessary to becoming a grateful person. Whether it is simply thanking God for being alive or that our bodies are functioning properly (see below for the *Modeh Ani* and *Asher Yatzar* blessings), Jewish prayer reminds us of our blessings. Instead of making our happiness depend on acquiring what we do not possess, prayer enables us to take joy in what we already have.

STOP AND REFLECT:
What is one thing in your life you are deeply grateful for, and how can you use the morning blessings to deepen your sense of gratitude?

Having greater God and soul awareness can, over time and with regular practice, change our natures. We are, after all, where our mind and are thoughts are.[18] Remaining mindful of our true purpose and mission, as well the gifts we have been given to carry out our mission, will direct our thoughts upward toward the spiritual realm. Eventually our nature and disposition will follow suit. It will not happen overnight, but over time, prayer has the power to make us more spiritually sensitive, ethically refined, and ultimately holier people.

4. PRAYER IS A CONDUIT FOR GOD'S BLESSINGS

The masters of Jewish mysticism provide a comprehensive framework that helps us understand the deeper meaning of the prayer experience. According to the teachings of the Kabbalah and Chasidism, prayer is a profound co-creative process between humanity and the Divine. Man, who is created in the image of God, participates in the mission of creation itself. Just as God continuously sustains the world, we too play an active role in shaping reality through our prayers.

According to this model, which is rooted in the thought of Rabbi Moshe Chaim Luzzatto, known as the Ramchal, through prayer we build spiritual vessels or pipelines known as *partzufim*.[19] The words of our prayers form these pipelines, and God in turn uses them to interact with and sustain the world. In this way, prayer is a partnership with God, where we create channels through which He pours His abundance into the world.

This idea of co-creation is rooted in the very beginning of the Torah. In Genesis we read that "the shrubs and grasses of the field had not yet sprouted because God had not caused it to rain, and there was no man to work the land."[20] Rashi, the famed medieval French Bible commentator, explains that God withheld the rain until creating Adam so humankind would recognize the need for rain. This lack would inspire the first man to pray. Only once he prayed would God cause the rain to fall, allowing the plants to grow. In other words, God orchestrated a world that was incomplete, leaving space for humanity to pray and thereby partner with God in bringing reality to fruition.

This concept of spiritual pipelines suggests that prayer also serves to purify the world. Thus, the Ramchal explains elsewhere[21] that prayer removes obstacles that block this flow of divine blessing, allowing us to draw down the spiritual energy necessary to elevate the world. The kabbalists similarly teach that every day, we elevate spiritual sparks that have fallen into the lower worlds. Through prayer, these sparks are refined and raised back to their source in the highest heavenly realm of *Atzilut,* where they are rectified and returned to their purest state.[22]

THE CREATIVE POWER OF WORDS

The Baal Shem Tov, founder of the chasidic movement, also emphasizes that prayer is a creative experience. Through the process of *devekut* – clinging to God – one transcends intellect and body, connecting with the Divine through the letters of prayer. The letters themselves possess mystical power, representing sparks that have fallen from their original source. When we pray with intention, merging love and awe of God, we elevate these letters back to their divine origin.[23]

The words of our prayers are thus compared to stones that build worlds.[24] As Rabbi Nachman of Breslov taught, when we pray with the proper intention, our words ascend to higher spiritual realms and effect changes in the physical and spiritual worlds. Each letter we utter serves as a vessel, receiving divine light and directing it into creation.

THE ROLE OF LOVE AND AWE

The emotions of love and awe are central to the creative capacity of prayer. Awe, or *yirah,* is a recognition of our smallness in comparison to the infinite vastness of the Creator, causing us to step back from His overwhelming presence. Yet awe also leads naturally to love, or *ahavah,* the desire to draw close to God and be absorbed in His light. This love is the force that pulls us closer, inspiring *devekut*, in which we seek to be unified with the Divine.[25]

As the Baal Shem Tov taught, prayer is not simply about reciting words. It is about elevating those words, returning them to their source with love, awe, and deep connection to God. In this way, we become partners in creation, sending our prayers upward, trusting that God will use them to shape and sustain the world.

By framing prayer as a partnership with God, chasidic and kabbalistic teachings show us that we are not mere passive recipients of divine blessings. We are active participants, co-creators with God, building vessels through which the world is sustained and transformed.

The Synagogue and the Japanese Koi

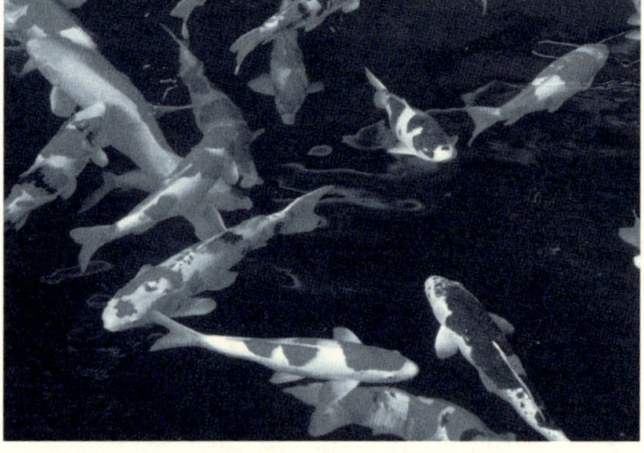

Koi Fish, Japan, 2020

Many Jewish people are turned off to prayer. There are many reasons for this, chief among them the close association between prayer and the synagogue. Although some have had a positive experience in synagogue and attend services regularly, the vast majority of American Jews only attend synagogue on the High Holidays. But while the ideal place to pray is the synagogue, a synagogue is *not* fundamentally necessary for Jewish prayer.[26] Indeed, during the COVID-19 pandemic, when synagogues throughout the world were forced to shut down, people did not stop praying. Prayer, as we have seen, goes well beyond the synagogue to the very essence of how we connect emotionally with God. It is a profoundly personal experience that fulfills a critical spiritual purpose: to connect with something greater and become attached to "our deeper selves, to our purpose, to our community, to the world around us, and ultimately to God."[27]

Still, Judaism places great value on communal prayer for two reasons. First, we are deeply impacted by our surroundings – a Jewish principle powerfully illustrated by the Japanese koi fish. If you put the koi fish into a small tank, it grows to about three inches. If you place the koi into a larger tank, it can grow to six or seven inches. And if you move it to a pond, the koi fish can grow to a foot and half. Put the koi into a huge lake where it can really stretch out, and it will grow up to three feet long! Human beings are just the same – we also grow when we are in the right environment and when we surround ourselves with the right people.

There is a story told of a little boy who would run into the forest when it was time to pray. After the father saw his son do this a few times, he asked: "Son, why do feel the need to run into the forest every time you pray? Don't you know God is the same everywhere?" "Yes, I know," the boy answered. "But *I'm* not." We are not the same everywhere. Our surroundings affect us. That is one reason Jewish tradition mandates praying with a community, in a public setting called a synagogue.

> "Wherever the Israelites are exiled, the Divine Presence is with them. And wherever they build a synagogue, the Divine Presence is found." (Talmud, Megillah 29a)

Another reason Jews value praying in a community with a *minyan*[28] is that when we pray *with* others, we are more likely to pray *on behalf of* others – a critical Jewish ethic. Virtually all Jewish prayers are written in the plural. On Yom Kippur, when we ask God for forgiveness for sins committed throughout the year, we run through an extensive list of transgressions[29] – not because any one of us alone committed all those sins but because we are praying on behalf of the entire community. Indeed, the Talmud teaches that one who prays for others is more likely to have his or her own prayers favorably answered. This is another reason we should get used to praying for other people. One way of doing that, besides praying in a synagogue, is taking a moment to say a prayer when you hear an ambulance whiz by with its siren blazing – a suggestion I once heard from the popular author Rabbi Joseph Telushkin.

There is a story about praying for others that I find very moving. A Jewish woman from Beverly Hills, California, traveled to Israel with her family and rented a suite with a beautiful ocean view in a hotel in Herzliya. When they arrived, the dining room had already closed for the night, so they decided to order room service. A young Israeli waiter entered the hotel room, set down the food, and said to the family: "My name is Barak. If you need anything else, please do not hesitate to call." The woman's husband called him back. "Your name is Barak?" "Yes," the waiter answered. "By chance, is your mother's name Orna?" "Yes," the waiter answered again. "Did you fight in the Gaza War last summer?" "Yes. How did you know?" "Because I got a call to pray for a Barak ben Orna," explained the husband. "We had your name on our refrigerator door in California. Our family prayed for your safety every day. Every morning we prayed for Barak ben Orna – may he have a *refuah sheleimah,* a complete recovery. And every day I would ask myself: 'Is he wounded? Did he survive the war? Is Barak ben Orna still alive?'"

The waiter broke down in tears, deeply moved that someone six thousand miles away was praying for him to survive and be well – to come home safely to his family. The husband hugged the waiter and the two parted.

Prayer has the power to unite and help us feel connected – wherever we live.

A shul (Yiddish for synagogue) is valuable for another reason. It is not only a place Jews gather to pray, but it is also a place to take care of communal needs such as raising money to feed the poor or to support community institutions. It is not uncommon to see the rabbi taking time from the synagogue service to make an appeal for a worthy cause or on behalf of those in the community who need financial assistance. While praying is fundamentally a personal, introspective experience, praying in a synagogue environment helps us move beyond ourselves, making sure we pray for and help others.

Is the Prayer Book Too Structured?

Another challenge many of us struggle with is that Jewish tradition mandates that we pray at certain set times, using words written by other people in a language that is foreign to most. How frustrating! Why not just pray from the heart whenever we feel like it and in whatever language we prefer?

In fact, ideally prayer should be spontaneous. After all, as we mentioned, Jewish prayer is defined as "service of the heart." In keeping with the essence of prayer, we should only pray when our hearts motivate us – when we feel like it, using our own words in whatever language we are most comfortable.

STOP AND REFLECT:
Do you find it more meaningful to pray at home or in synagogue? What would you need to do differently – such as arrive earlier, go to a new synagogue, or learn more about the prayers – to enhance your synagogue experience?

But the Sages were concerned about spontaneous prayer. First, they were worried prayer would become a selfish enterprise, with people only praying when they need something or have something particular for which to be thankful. Praying at a set time, even when we don't feel emotionally compelled to pray for our own needs, offers us the opportunity to think about what others might need.

Second, as we know from our lives in general, when something is not structured, it rarely lasts. And so after the First Temple in Jerusalem was destroyed in 586 BCE and prayer began to take on a more prominent role in Jewish religious life,[30] the Sages formalized prayer. They did this not to create something mechanical but to ensure that this vehicle that is so necessary for divine emotional connection would endure, inspiring us to pray on behalf of ourselves and others for millennia.[31]

Abracadabra: The Magic of Hebrew

According to Jewish tradition, Hebrew is the language God used to create the universe, and it is the language of prophecy. The kabbalists teach that before anything else, God created the twenty-two letters of the Hebrew alphabet, which He then used to create the universe.[32] God combined the letters of the Hebrew alphabet into different words and phrases, investing each letter with a certain spiritual and creative energy.

For this reason, while other languages allow us to articulate our thoughts and ideas – to *express* reality – Hebrew gives us the power to *create* reality. This idea is conveyed by the well-known word "Abracadabra" (commonly used by magicians and stage performers), an Aramaic phrase which means "I will create as I speak." Using the Hebrew language enables us to create and lift the world as we know it. No translation can ever capture the power of Hebrew. For this reason, although one may pray in any language he or she chooses, Hebrew is preferred.

In addition, the Men of the Great Assembly – who composed the prayers in the siddur – were outstanding Sages, kabbalists, and prophets who wrote the Hebrew prayers in such a way as to enable us, thousands of years later, to use their words to pierce the heavenly spheres. It is comparable to a person who hires a lawyer to sue someone in court. Although the complainant knows all the facts, he or she still hires an attorney who is well versed in the court's language and can articulate the client's thoughts and feelings in way that will resonate with the judge or jury. The Hebrew prayers in the siddur similarly serve as a vehicle to ensure that our deepest thoughts, emotions, and desires will be most favorably received on High.

Having said this, since a lot of Jewish people are not well acquainted with Hebrew, many prefer to pray in English (or whatever is their first language) so they can better understand the meaning of the prayers. That too is an important value, which is why I advise my students whose Hebrew understanding is lacking to strike a balance between praying in Hebrew and English. On one hand, we do not want to forfeit the spiritual potency that only Hebrew and the words of our Sages can provide. On the other hand, it is important to understand what we are saying when we pray. While the ideal is to know Hebrew well enough to understand the meaning of the prayers, until that time comes it is perfectly acceptable to recite some prayers in Hebrew and others in English.

A SHORT HISTORY OF THE PRAYER BOOK

While prayer has existed since the beginning of human existence, the standardized Jewish liturgy we recite today first emerged with the destruction of the First Temple in 586 BCE and the Jewish exile to Babylonia. As the Temple sacrifices no longer occupied center stage in Jewish life, the institution of the synagogue began to emerge, and alongside it the development of more structured daily prayer services.

> "The synagogue is not just a building; it is a sanctuary in time, a place where heaven and earth meet." (Rabbi Abraham Joshua Heschel)

Around that time, according to tradition, a group of 120 leading rabbis known as the Men of the Great Assembly authored the *Amidah* prayer and began to establish a regimen of daily services. The prayers included the *Shema* and *Shemoneh Esrei*, and they developed over time. The unique services for weekdays, Shabbat, and holidays also began to emerge at this time.

As Jewish communities spread throughout the exile, different practices arose among various Jewish ethnic groups, most famously between Ashkenazic and Sephardic communities. These differences are captured in a number of medieval siddurim (prayer books), which ultimately became the basis for the modern siddur.

Today, one can purchase countless variations of the siddur. While some are written only in Hebrew, many popular prayer books come with translations into English and other languages. Siddurim following different community traditions continue to be available. One can also purchase a special siddur for the High Holidays and festivals known as a *machzor*. Of course, while it is certainly worth purchasing your own copy of the siddur, synagogues also have prayer books available for use as you enter the sanctuary.

STOP AND REFLECT:
Are you from a Sephardic or Ashkenazic background? Who in your family could help you learn more about your roots?

THE "HOW-TOS" OF PRAYER

The Men of the Great Assembly created three daily prayer services: Shacharit (Morning Prayers), Minchah (Afternoon Prayers), and Maariv (Evening Prayers). The Talmud[33] explains that the Sages drew on two sources in establishing this three-part structure. First, the Sages derived from various biblical verses that each of the patriarchs established one of these services: Abraham prayed in the morning, Isaac in the afternoon, and Jacob in the evening. The second source for the three daily prayers was the Temple service. There was a daily sacrifice brought in the Temple each morning and afternoon, which became Shacharit and Minchah. The burning of the fats and limbs in the evening formed the basis for Maariv.

The common denominator of all Jewish prayer services is the *Shemoneh Esrei,* literally translated as "The Eighteen Blessings."[34] This central prayer is also referred to as the *Amidah,* or "Standing."

KABBALAH CORNER:
Because of our spiritual closeness to God when reciting the *Shemoneh Esrei,* we recite this prayer in a whisper. Our near silence reflects the profound intimacy of this moment, when the soul is almost "one" with God. (Arizal)

As we will explore later in this chapter, it is considered the heart[35] and destination of each prayer service. The prayers that lead up to the *Amidah* are significant in their own right, each containing its own meaning and purpose, but they also serve as a way of preparing the worshipper for the *Amidah* – the experience of "standing" before God. The Shacharit service has more prayers leading up to the *Amidah* than Minchah and Maariv, which are shorter services. Shacharit is also the service I have always recommended people begin with when starting to pray.[36]

Praying at the Western Wall

Below is an overview of Shacharit and a brief explanation of some of the main prayers found in each section of the service. My hope is that you find this content helpful in learning how to pray and that it deepens your understanding of some prayers you may already be saying. The prayers I will discuss below are recited during the week as well as on Shabbat, the festivals (Passover, Sukkot, and Shavuot), and the High Holidays (Rosh HaShanah and Yom Kippur).

Shacharit: The Morning Prayer Service

The Morning Prayer Service consists of four main parts: The Morning Blessings, Psalms of Praise, the *Shema* and its surrounding blessings, and the *Amidah*.

This section, which begins our daily prayers, provides us with the opportunity to express gratitude for the simple blessings of life. The Sages felt it important to begin our day by recognizing the gifts we so often take for granted.

BIRCHOT HASHACHAR: THE MORNING BLESSINGS

Modeh Ani: Believing in Ourselves

The first such prayer is called the *Modeh Ani*, a short prayer to be said immediately upon rising:

מוֹדֶה אֲנִי לְפָנֶיךָ מֶלֶךְ חַי וְקַיָּם שֶׁהֶחֱזַרְתָּ בִּי נִשְׁמָתִי בְּחֶמְלָה רַבָּה אֱמוּנָתֶךָ.

Modeh ani lefanecha, Melech chai vekayam, shehechezarta bi nishmati bechemlah, rabbah emunatecha.

I thank You, living and eternal King, for giving me back my soul in mercy. Great is Your faith.

This prayer allows us to thank God for restoring life by acknowledging the return of our soul. "For giving me back my soul" is a reference to the Jewish belief that part of the soul leaves the body during the night and is restored upon awakening in the morning. We are recreated each day.

"*Modeh Ani* is a powerful practice that grounds us in humility and gratitude from the moment we open our eyes." (Rebbetzin Tziporah Heller Gottlieb)

The Sages purposely omit God's name so this prayer can be recited immediately upon awakening, even before we leave our beds to wash our hands. It was important to the Sages that our first words each day be words of gratitude and renewal, emphasizing that with each new day, God returns our souls to our bodies, enabling us to live another day. Reciting this short

KABBALAH CORNER: According to some kabbalists, our prayers mirror Jewish history. We start with the preliminary *Birchot HaShachar*, just as the patriarchs built a relationship with God before establishing a formal religion. We then move into the lengthy Psalms of Praise, in which we prepare to thank God for the Exodus, symbolizing our extended slavery in Egypt and preparation for freedom. The *Shema* speaks of the actual redemption from Egypt, while the silent *Shemoneh Esrei* represents the intimacy with God at the Reed Sea. Our wandering in the desert parallels life's challenges, which correspond to the afternoon prayers. Finally, in Maariv, recited in the dark, we ask God to end our exile and bring the Final Redemption. (Rabbi Yitzchak Ginsburg) prayer allows us to be mindful that we are entering a new day that presents new opportunities, not the same old grind. We are not the same people as the day before – not spiritually and not even physically. The cells in our bodies keep changing. Scientists believe that 98 percent of the cells and one-seventh of the atoms in our bodies are replaced every year. Reciting the *Modeh Ani* prayer connects us to this theme of newness and renewal.

> "Our goal should be to live life in radical amazement… get up in the morning and look at the world in a way that takes nothing for granted. Everything is phenomenal; everything is incredible; never treat life casually. To be spiritual is to be amazed." (Rabbi Abraham Joshua Heschel)

Another layer of insight is expressed in the last words of the *Modeh Ani* prayer: "Great is Your faith." This phraseology is curious. Usually when we speak about faith, we refer to the faith that we have in God. Here, instead of the prayer using the language of "*our* faith" in God, it says "*Your* faith," referring to God's faith in us! What does this mean?

Judaism is premised on the belief that life is not random, that we all exist for a reason. And so if we wake up in the morning, it is only because God believes we have the capacity to fulfill that purpose for our existence. Why else give us another day to live? We therefore begin each day by acknowledging *God's belief in us, which provides daily encouragement that our Creator thinks us worthy of life.* For a generation struggling with self-esteem, starting our day by being mindful of our self-worth is invaluable.

Asher Yatzar and Elokai Neshamah: The Gift of Life

The next two blessings in the Morning Blessings similarly express gratitude for the basic gift of life, both physical and spiritual:

Asher Yatzar

> Blessed are You, Lord our God, King of the Universe, who formed man in wisdom and created in him many orifices and cavities. It is revealed and known before the throne of Your glory that were one of them to be ruptured or blocked, it would be impossible to survive and stand before You. Blessed are You, Lord, Healer of all flesh who does wondrous deeds.

In *Asher Yatzar,* we thank God for the proper physical functioning of our bodies. For this reason, we recite this blessing not only upon arising, but also immediately after each time we use the restroom. It may seem odd to recite a blessing after discharging waste, but that is precisely the purpose of this blessing – to remain mindful of the intricacies of the human body and how grateful we must be for its proper functioning.

Elokai Neshamah

> My God, the soul You placed within me is pure. You created it, You formed it, You breathed it into me, and You guard it while it is within me. One day You will take it from me, and restore it to me in the time to come. As long as the soul is within me, I will thank You, Lord my God and God of my ancestors, Master of all works, Lord of all souls. Blessed are You, Lord, who restores souls to lifeless bodies.

Elokai Neshamah elaborates on *Modeh Ani*'s theme of the restoration of the soul. It refers to the soul as "pure," an important acknowledgment of Judaism's belief in the inherent goodness of humankind. This too provides us with an important boost of self-esteem: We are fundamentally good people. Sin is merely an aberration that may make it more difficult for our goodness to shine forth, but it can never corrupt the soul's inherent purity.

The Fifteen Blessings: Down to the Details

After expressing our appreciation for the gift of life in general, we get more specific in our gratitude by reciting a series of fifteen short blessings (*Koren Shalem Siddur,* p. 26), in which we thank God for the gifts of sight, clothing, and our ability to sit up, stretch, and walk – activities we might not otherwise think about at all. The morning blessings remind us to acknowledge the many blessings we possess but which we rarely notice and often take for granted. Starting our day by recognizing these gifts helps us become more grateful and ultimately happier people.

> "*Birchot Hashachar* are the morning symphony of gratitude, tuning our hearts to the blessings of a new day." (Rabbi Jonathan Sacks)

The Blessings over Torah Study: Keeping It Sweet

The Morning Blessings section also contains the *Birchot HaTorah,* the Blessings of the Torah recited in the morning each day (*Koren Shalem Siddur,* p. 8). These blessings are said as a way of preparing us for any Torah study in which we will be involved over the course of the day, whether it is attending a Torah class, studying a Jewish text, or reading a Jewish book. In this prayer, we ask God to make our Torah study "sweet in our mouths." Torah study is not a mere intellectual exercise but a joyful exploration of God's wisdom and His blueprint for humanity and the world.

Scholars[37] raise the following difficulty: When a person recites a blessing and later wants to perform the associated mitzvah again, as a general rule, he or she must recite a new blessing. So for example, on Sukkot, someone who recites the blessing over sitting in the sukkah, eats breakfast, and returns to the sukkah a few hours later for lunch, needs to recite a new blessing. So why do we not say a new blessing over the Torah each time we sit down to study? The Tosafists[38] answer that because the book of Joshua[39] commands that we study Torah day and night, there is no need for a new blessing each time we learn Torah. But is this really true? How many of us really study Torah day and night?

To answer this question, Rabbi Soloveitchik distinguishes between what he calls "latent awareness" and "acute awareness." Using the metaphor of a mother and her child: When a mother is in the middle of caring for her child, she is acutely aware of the child. But when she takes a break and steps out to read a magazine in the next room, she may not have an "acute awareness" of the child, but she still possesses a "latent awareness." No matter where she goes or what she may do, she always has the child in the back of her mind. The same is true of the Jew and Torah study. When we are engaged in Torah study, we have an "acute awareness" of Torah. But even when we are involved in other activities, whether it be working or just listening to some music, we still have a latent awareness of the Torah, just as the mother has a latent awareness of her child. For this reason, explains Rabbi Soloveitchik, there is no interruption between the blessings over the Torah in the morning and our involvement in Torah throughout the day: even when we are not actively studying, the Jew has a profound innate connection to Torah that never fades away.

PESUKEI DEZIMRAH: THE PSALMS OF PRAISE

It would be foolish to think one can attain the kind of focus and concentration prayer requires without preparation. In fact, the Talmud[40] tells us that the early pious Sages would meditate for an entire hour just to prepare for prayer! The Sages therefore created this section, the *Pesukei DeZimrah* or "Psalms of Praise," consisting mostly of sections from the biblical psalms, to be said each morning. In this way, by the time one reaches the *Amidah* (the Silent Devotion), one has attained what the Sages call *kavanah* – a certain focus or spiritual frame of mind. Meditating upon these psalms helps shift our awareness and remove distracting thoughts so we can leave behind the minutiae of our daily activities and achieve a prayerful state of being.

> "When I am present, all of me is here; when I am not present, none of me is here." (Based on Talmud, Sukkah 53a)

This section opens with the *Baruch She'amar* blessing (*Koren Shalem Siddur,* p. 62) and closes with another blessing called *Yishtabach* (*Koren Shalem Siddur,* p. 84). Sandwiched in between are the various psalms, over which we meditate and which we use to block out any distractions. If you are just beginning to pray, start with *Baruch She'amar* and *Yishtabach,* and recite Psalm 145, the *Ashrei* prayer, in between.

Ashrei

Happy are those who dwell in Your House; they
shall continue to praise You, Selah!

Happy are the people for whom this is so;
happy are the people whose God is the Lord.

A song of praise by David.

א I will exalt You, my God, the King, and bless
Your name for ever and all time.

ב Every day I will bless You, and praise Your
name for ever and all time.

ג Great is the Lord and greatly to be praised;
His greatness is unfathomable.

ד One generation will praise Your works to the
next, and tell of Your mighty deeds.

ה On the glorious splendor of Your majesty I
will meditate, and on the acts of Your wonders.

ו They shall talk of the power of Your awesome
deeds, and I will tell of Your greatness.

ז They shall recite the record of Your great goodness, and sing with joy of Your righteousness.

ח The Lord is gracious and compassionate, slow
to anger and great in loving-kindness.

ט The Lord is good to all, and His compassion extends to all His works.

י All Your works shall thank You, Lord, and Your devoted ones shall bless You.

כ They shall talk of the glory of Your kingship, and speak of Your might.

ל To make known to mankind His mighty deeds and the glorious majesty of His kingship.

מ Your kingdom is an everlasting kingdom, and Your reign is for all generations.

ס The Lord supports all who fall, and raises all who are bowed down.

ע All raise their eyes to You in hope, and You give them their food in due season.

פ You open Your hand, and satisfy every living thing with favor.

צ The Lord is righteous in all His ways, and kind in all He does.

ק The Lord is close to all who call on Him, to all who call on Him in truth.

ר He fulfills the will of those who revere Him; He hears their cry and saves them.

ש The Lord guards all who love Him, but all the wicked He will destroy.

ת My mouth shall speak the praise of the Lord, and all creatures shall bless His holy name for ever and all time.

We will bless the Lord now and for ever. Halleluyah!

The *Ashrei* is considered a centerpiece psalm because its verses begin with all twenty-two letters of the Hebrew alphabet (except for the letter *nun*), and because it expresses God's giving nature as stated in the verse "You open Your hand and satisfy the desire of all living beings."[41] These two reasons affirm Judaism's belief in a God who both creates and watches over the universe. The Jewish mystical tradition teaches that the letters of the Hebrew alphabet were used to create the world, and the phrase "You open Your hand and satisfy the desire of all living beings" confirms our belief in divine providence – that God didn't simply create the world but cares enough to sustain and govern it.

THE SHEMA AND ITS BLESSINGS

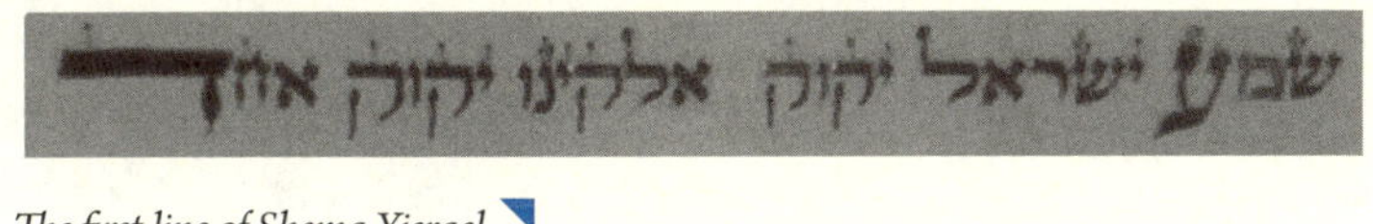

The first line of Shema Yisrael

שְׁמַע יִשְׂרָאֵל ה׳ אֱ-לֹהֵינוּ ה׳ אֶחָד

Shema Yisrael, Ado-nai Elo-heinu, Ado-nai Echad.

Listen, Israel: The Lord is our God, the Lord is One.

In this statement of faith, we express our conviction that everything in the physical world is ultimately an expression of God, the one and only Source of all existence. The spiritual purpose of the *Shema* is to achieve what the Jewish Sages call *kabbalat ol malchut shamayim* – the acceptance of God's sovereignty throughout the world and His authority over our lives. It's one thing to believe in God – and the *Shema* is certainly an affirmation of that belief – but another to accept what that means for our daily lives: the privilege to live by God's commands, the mitzvot. The *Shema* is therefore not only an expression of our faith in the one and only Creator and Sustainer of the universe, but also a personal pledge to live according to God's laws and values as expressed in the Torah.

The *Shema* is thus designed to bring about a deep sense of mindfulness of God's existence and the ongoing role of the Jew in bringing this message to the world. This idea is expressed in an interesting Jewish tradition practiced by Jewish scribes. When writing the words of the *Shema* in a Torah scroll, a scribe must enlarge two of the letters in the prayer: the *ayin*, the last letter in the first word, *shema* (which means "hear"), and the *dalet*, the last letter of the last word, *echad* (which means "One"). One explanation for this tradition is that the letters *ayin* and *dalet* spell the Hebrew word *ed*, or witness, for by reciting the *Shema* we serve as witnesses, testifying to the existence of God.

KABBALAH CORNER:
Our Sages teach that when we say the final word of the *Shema, echad,* we should prolong the final letter, *dalet,* which has the Hebrew numerical value of four. This is because God's unity exists in all four corners of the world, regardless of how distant He may sometimes appear. Our task is to discover that holiness and reveal it to those around us.
(Rabbi Yosef Yitzchak of Lubavitch)

Leaving Our Doubts Behind

Another explanation of this tradition is that the letter *ayin* is enlarged so it does not resemble the Hebrew letter *alef,* which would spell *shema,* meaning "maybe" or "perhaps." That would make the *Shema* declaration sound something like "Perhaps God is One." The Hebrew letter *dalet* is enlarged so it does not look like a letter with a similar appearance, the *resh,* which would spell the Hebrew word *acher* or "another" (instead of *echad* or "one"), implying the existence of another God. The *ayin* and *dalet* caution us that while questions have an important place in Judaism, we should set aside our doubts and hesitations for another time and place. The *Shema* is our moment, each day, to envelop ourselves in a belief in something beyond the physical world, in God Himself. As my teacher, Rabbi Dr. Norman Lamm, of blessed memory, wrote in his book on the *Shema*: "Our tradition makes room for the honest doubter, for without such doubt questions would never be asked, prejudices never challenged, and science would come to a halt. But when we are seriously engaged in prayer, endeavoring to experience the presence of God, it is not the time to entertain intellectual doubts. In prayer, taught R. Nahman of Bratzlav, we must cast aside all our "wisdom" and stand before our Maker as children; to be child-like in prayer is as appropriate as to be skeptical in thought. When seeking to wrest transcendent meaning out of existence and to pull ourselves out of the void, we should not cast ourselves into that very void. Rather, at that sacred moment, we can put our doubts aside and, in all integrity, proclaim the unity of God whole-heartedly."[42]

Light Through a Prism

The *Shema* is also meant to reflect upon God's oneness. What does that mean exactly, and why is it so important to be mindful of God's oneness?

Life often seems random. One day we wake up and everything is going well: Work is good, our social life progressing. The next day something changes: We lose our job, our girlfriend breaks up with us. Is it possible that the same God who allows for such goodness one day, permits so much to go wrong the next? And that is just in one person's life! Multiply that sense of randomness by the billions of events that take place every day, good and bad, all of which seem to have no rhyme or reason.

Of course, this is only how things appear from our own perspective. Judaism teaches that in reality, everything is somehow part of a greater plan. Things may seem random, but ultimately everything emanates from one place and happens for some greater good. That is one meaning of the words "The Lord is One": *There is a single source for everything we experience in the world.*

One way of understanding this is to imagine a light shining through a prism. Even though we see many colors of the spectrum, they all emanate from one light. This is one of the reasons for the custom to cover our eyes when saying the *Shema*.[43] When we look out at the world, things appear fragmented and disconnected. We cover our eyes to block out what seems random, so that for at least a few moments we can be mindful of the one, unifying source for all reality: God.

Is There a Plan?

It was the Jewish people who brought the concept of monotheism – the belief in one God – to the rest of the world. It remains the Jewish people's mission to demonstrate that nothing is accidental or haphazard; it is but an expression of a thought-out plan by the one true Reality. God willed us into existence for a reason and, as such, everything that happens is a necessary part of a greater design. Saying the *Shema* every day keeps us mindful of this and allows us to bear testimony to Judaism's core belief: Life has purpose and meaning.

The Three Paragraphs of the Shema

The *Shema* contains three paragraphs, all of which appear in the Torah.[44]

The first paragraph[45] starts with the declaration of faith. It goes on to speak about how to *live* that faith: by loving God "with all your heart, with all your soul," teaching these ideas to our children, reciting them when you "lie down and when you rise," binding these principles on our body (referring to the mitzvah of wearing tefillin), and attaching them upon our doorposts (referring to the mitzvah of affixing a mezuzah). This paragraph has become famous since it is often recited by parents with their children before they go to sleep at night.[46]

> KABBALAH CORNER:
> There are 248 words in the *Shema*, in which we declare our faith in God – the same numerical value as the name *Avraham*. Just as Abraham was the archetype of kindness, we too connect to our fellow human beings – and ultimately to God – through acts of kindness. (Rabbi Aryeh Kaplan, based on the Zohar)

> Love the Lord your God with all your heart,
> with all your soul, and with all your might.
> These words which I command you today shall
> be on your heart. Teach them repeatedly to
> your children, speaking of them when you sit
> at home and when you travel on the way, when
> you lie down and when you rise up. Bind them
> as a sign on your hand, and they shall be an
> emblem between your eyes. Write them on the
> doorposts of your house and gates.

The second paragraph,[47] which starts with the words "If you indeed heed" (*Koren Shalem Siddur*, p. 98) speaks of the blessings that will come as a result of fulfilling God's commands: rain in its proper season, grain, wine, and oil, grass in the fields, and abundant food. Failure to comply will result in the withholding of these blessings. This section affirms the principle of reward and punishment. Ultimately, while we cannot always discern God's master plan, by observing the mitzvot we will be rewarded in this world and the next.

The final and third section,[48] beginning with the words "The Lord spoke to Moses, saying" (*Koren Shalem Siddur*, p. 100), speaks of the mitzvah of tzitzit, the ritual fringes which serve as a reminder of God's presence and our mission to carry out God's will as expressed in the Torah. The verses mention a special dye with the color *techelet*, widely assumed to be a deep blue that comes from the murex trunculus snail found off the coast of the Mediterranean Sea.[49] The symbolism of this dye is particularly meaningful. In ancient times, it was generally only used for garments worn by royalty. For this reason, it was sewn into Jewish priests' clothing and used for the fabric of the Tabernacle that accompanied the Jews when they traveled in the desert. The *techelet* therefore serves as a sign that just as the Torah says that the Jewish people are so beloved that they are seen as God's metaphorical children,[50] by extension all Jews are considered part of the divine royal family.

The *Shema* is an integral part of the prayer service, but it is also an independent biblical mitzvah. Therefore, if for whatever reason one did not pray on a given day or in general does not pray, one should still endeavor to recite the *Shema*.[51]

The Blessings Surrounding the Shema: Creation, Revelation, Redemption

In Shacharit, the *Shema* is enveloped by three blessings.[52] Two are recited before the *Shema* and focus on the themes of creation and revelation; the third follows the *Shema* and speaks of redemption. As we will see, the two blessings preceding the *Shema* – the blessing of creation, referred to as "God as Creator," and the blessing of revelation or "The Great Love" – serve as "spiritual stepping stones to the *Shema*'s proclamation of faith."[53]

The Blessing of Creation

The first blessing (*Koren Shalem Siddur*, p. 88) emphasizes the Jewish belief in God as a *perpetual* Creator. God did not simply create the world, set it on an automatic timer, and take off. Instead, Jewish tradition teaches that God remains involved, continually renewing creation each day. This constant intervention creates a daily sense of newness and engenders a feeling of gratitude for the new opportunities we are granted each and every day.

KABBALAH CORNER:
In Kabbalah, the concept of *ratzo vashov* (run and return) represents the continuous process by which God recreates the world. Without God's ongoing involvement, the world would cease to exist. Yet at the same time, if His presence were fully revealed, it would overwhelm the physical realm. The back-and-forth rhythm of God's energy flowing into and withdrawing from creation allows it to subsist. (Rav Moshe Cordovero, based on the Zohar)

The Blessing of Revelation

The second blessing preceding the *Shema* (*Koren Shalem Siddur*, p. 96) has the character of a Torah blessing[54] and conveys the idea that God gave the Jewish people the Torah as an expression of love. This theme of revelation follows the preceding theme of creation since, as Rabbi Dr. Elie Munk points out, while God's existence may be perceived in the marvels of the universe, "nature remains silent on the question of man's position within the cosmos, how he is supposed to act in this world."[55] By studying science and observing the wonders of nature we can arrive at a belief in God,[56] but nature and science do not teach us how to live or behave – what kind of values or ethical system we should follow. For that we need the Torah.[57] The Torah provides a guide, a moral map to find the kind of meaning and purpose so many people are seeking today.

That is why the Blessing of Creation is followed by the Blessing of Revelation. Recognizing God as the One who both *creates* the world and *reveals* how to live in that world are essential stages to prepare for the *Shema,* when we accept God and His mitzvot into our lives.

The Blessing of Redemption

This blessing (*Koren Shalem Siddur,* p. 102), which immediately follows the *Shema,* celebrates God's deliverance of our ancestors from Egyptian slavery. The Sages teach[58] that this blessing must be directly linked to the *Amidah* (the Silent Devotion) to connect our past redemption from Egypt to our future redemption in the Messianic Age, which is reflected in the opening blessing of the *Amidah.*[59] Even though we make many individual requests in the *Amidah,* what has kept the Jews reciting these prayers for thousands of years is our belief that just as God redeemed the Jewish people in the past, so will He redeem us in the future.

The *Amidah*: The Heart of Jewish Prayer

This part of the prayer service represents the very essence of Jewish prayer. The *Amidah,* or "Standing," is the spiritual destination of all the preceding prayers, and it is through this prayer that we fulfill the Jewish imperative to pray. The name *Amidah* refers not only to the standing position in which we remain throughout this prayer, but also to the mindset we endeavor to maintain: an awareness that we are standing before God and addressing our Creator. Maintaining this mindfulness is considered by some[60] to be even more fundamental than understanding the words of the prayers. The *Amidah* is also referred to as the *Shemoneh Esrei* or "The Eighteen Blessings"[61] because the original version consisted of eighteen blessings composed by the 120 Men of the Great Assembly. This group consisted of outstanding scholars and prophets[62] who led the Jewish community at the beginning of the Second Temple era (516 BCE–68 CE). To this day, when we recite "The Eighteen Blessings," we tap into the wisdom and spirituality these great prophets possessed. This enables us to achieve a greater spiritual connection than by simply using our own words.

To stand implies to be present, to be mindful of the Being before whom one is standing. Standing is also the position in which testimony is given: A witness is required to stand when testifying in a Jewish court of law. Similarly, when we stand in prayer, we bear testimony to the existence of God, His great power, and His concern for our needs.

Every *Amidah*, whether it is recited on a weekday, Shabbat, or festival,[63] is divided into three parts: blessings of praise, the body, and concluding blessings. The opening blessings of praise and the concluding blessings always remain the same, but the body varies depending on the service. During the week, the body of the *Amidah* consists of thirteen personal and national requests, whereas on Shabbat and the festivals the body consists of one blessing which speaks to the unique sanctity of the day.[64]

What follows is an explanation of the main themes of the blessings of the weekday *Amidah*. It is my hope that these ideas will help you achieve the spiritual intimacy the *Amidah* is designed to engender, as it has for so many of my students over the last thirty years. Since these commentaries are by no means exhaustive, I will recommend other books and articles for further exploration at the end of the chapter.

Opening Blessings of Praise

> "O Lord, open my lips, so that my mouth may declare Your praise." (Psalms 51:15, opening words of the *Amidah*)

Blessed are You, Lord our God and God of our fathers,
God of Abraham, God of Isaac, and God of Jacob;
the great, mighty, and awesome God, God Most High,
who bestows acts of loving-kindness and creates all,
who remembers the loving-kindness of the
fathers and will bring
a redeemer to their children's children
for the sake of His name, in love.
King, Helper, Savior, Shield:
Blessed are You, Lord, Shield of Abraham.

We begin the *Amidah* by addressing God as "the God of Abraham, God of Isaac, and God of Jacob." In so doing, we present ourselves as descendants of the patriarchs,[65] the founders of Judaism with whom God enjoyed a special relationship. We do not stand before our Creator as strangers but as descendants of His beloved prophets. But even as we begin the *Amidah* by recognizing our common ancestry, we also acknowledge the unique relationship we forge individually with God. Some suggest that this is why God's name is repeated before each of the patriarchs, namely "the God of Abraham, God of Isaac, and God of Jacob," in the opening blessing. Why not simply say "God of Abraham, Isaac, and Jacob"? Adding "the God of" next to each name reminds us that the relationship Abraham developed with God was different from that of Isaac or Jacob. We may all come from the same place, but the relationship we cultivate with our Creator is different from everyone else's.

* * *

You are eternally mighty, Lord.
You give life to the dead and have great power to save.
(In fall and winter: He makes the wind
blow and the rain fall.)
(In Israel, in spring and summer: He
causes the dew to fall.)
He sustains the living with loving-kindness,
and with great compassion revives the dead.
He supports the fallen, heals the sick, sets captives free,
and keeps His faith with those who sleep in the dust.
Who is like You, Master of might,
and who can compare to You,
O King who brings death and gives life,
and makes salvation grow?
Faithful are You to revive the dead.
Blessed are You, Lord, who revives the dead.

The blessing of praise speaks of God's might and power. The Sages express God's power by describing His ability to create – more specifically, God's capacity to resurrect the dead: "You are eternally mighty, Lord; You give life to the dead."[66] The resurrection is mentioned three times in this one blessing! Although resurrection is usually associated with a cosmic event that will take place in messianic times, Jewish tradition teaches that we also experience the resurrection of the dead on a personal level every morning.[67] The Sages consider there to be an element of death in sleep since part of the soul departs the body each night. When our souls are returned upon awakening, a kind of resurrection of the dead has taken place. We come back to life, which is the reason we recite the *Modeh Ani* prayer upon arising to acknowledge God for restoring our souls. This is why it is particularly appropriate to thank God for the resurrection in the second blessing of the *Amidah* each morning.

> "Every morning, we thank God for returning our souls with compassion. For each new day is a sign of His faith in us." (Rabbi Yaakov Emden)

Another expression of God's creative capacity that appears in this blessing is God's power to bring rain: "He makes the wind blow and the rain fall."[68] This phrase is recited during the winter months when rain is needed in Israel and omitted in the summer when rain could damage the crops.[69] Since rain gives new life to the earth, this phrase fits nicely with all the references to resurrection.

* * *

You are holy and Your name is holy,
and holy ones praise You daily, Selah!
Blessed are You, Lord,
the holy God.

This final blessing in this section, the Blessing of Sanctification, references the concept of holiness three times. This mirrors the threefold mention of the word "holy" in the prophet Isaiah's declaration, which forms the centerpiece of the *Kedushah,* the communal prayer we recite during the repetition of the *Amidah.* Whereas the two opening blessings of the *Amidah* speak of God's power in the physical world, such as His ability to bring rain and heal the sick, this prayer conveys the idea that despite His concern for the earthly world, God is completely elevated and removed from all that is material.[70] As we will explore in our chapters on sexuality and *kashrut,* the idea of holiness as separateness is a divine value we aim to emulate through these and many other observances.

The Body: Petitions

The weekday *Amidah* contains thirteen requests: six personal appeals, six communal requests, and a final petition for God to "hear our voices."

Personal Requests

Each of these requests is meant to be personalized, and so, as I always encourage my students, try to relate each petition to something personal in your own life. I have made some of my own suggestions below.

1. **Knowledge**

You grace humanity with knowledge
and teach mortals understanding.
Grace us with the knowledge, understanding
and discernment that come from You.
Blessed are You, Lord, who graciously grants knowledge.

We begin with this request since we can only know what is truly worthy of asking of God if we first acquire knowledge.[71] In the

Jewish tradition, knowledge of God and the world around us are also prerequisites for religious devotion. As Maimonides writes: "In accordance with one's knowledge will be the love [for God] – if much [knowledge] then much [love], and if little [knowledge] then little [love]."[72] For these reasons, asking God for help acquiring knowledge is vital.

"True knowledge leads a person to humility, for the more we know, the more we realize how much we do not know." (Rabbi Eliyahu Dessler)

You may personalize this petition by asking God for wisdom and insight for an exam, interview, or whatever in your day ahead requires "knowledge, understanding, and discernment."

2. **Repentance**

Bring us back, our Father, to Your Torah.
Draw us near, our King, to Your service.
Lead us back to You in perfect repentance.
Blessed are You, Lord, who desires repentance.

Human beings are imperfect and inevitably sin. Since sins distance us from our Creator, Judaism urges us to repair our relationship with Him. The word describing this spiritual act, *teshuvah,* or return, implies that our natural state is to be close to our Creator. Sin and other negative forces keep us from enjoying that intimacy with God. Jewish tradition mandates *teshuvah* as the road back to where we began. In this blessing, reflect on what you are doing – or not doing – that may be keeping you from being in a greater state of spiritual connection. Ask God for help to bridge the gap and bring you back "in perfect repentance."

STOP AND REFLECT: What is one area in your relationship with God and your fellow human beings that you'd like to work on?

3. **Forgiveness**

Forgive us, our Father, for we have sinned.
Pardon us, our King, for we have transgressed;
for You pardon and forgive.
Blessed are You, Lord,
the gracious One who repeatedly forgives.

It is well established in Jewish tradition that God is looking to forgive since He desires a close connection with His creations. In this blessing, we seek God's forgiveness by acknowledging our wrongdoings. We might have assumed that this kind of request – along with the previous petition for repentance – is reserved for the High Holidays. But as with any human relationship, we have our good days and our bad days. We therefore ask God every day to help us stay close to Him through the observance of the Torah's mitzvot. We cannot wait until Yom Kippur to repair whatever needs fixing in our relationship, so repentance and forgiveness are necessary every single day. It is also interesting to note that both these blessings refer to God as "our Father" – invoking the parental connection we have with God. Like any parent, God wants to forgive us so He can remain close to His children.

4. **Redemption**

Look on our affliction, plead our cause,
and redeem us soon for Your name's sake,
for You are a powerful Redeemer.
Blessed are You, Lord, the Redeemer of Israel.

STOP AND REFLECT: What in your life is causing you anxiety right now? Consider sharing that with God the next time you pray.

In this blessing, we do not ask for redemption from exile but that God deliver us from our everyday troubles.[73] It presents us with an opportunity to share whatever issue in our life is currently "afflicting" us, be it physical, emotional, or spiritual. God is fully aware of what is causing stress or anxiety. But having the chance to bring that into our spiritual relationship is an important part of the healing process. Rabbi Samson Raphael Hirsch teaches that the first phrase of this blessing, "Look on our affliction," refers to suffering we may be experiencing due to our own issues, while the next phrase, "Plead our cause," refers to protection from those who seek our harm.

5. **Healing**

Heal us, Lord, and we shall be healed.
Save us and we shall be saved,
for You are our praise.
Bring complete recovery for all our ailments,
for You, God, King, are a faithful and compassionate Healer.
Blessed are You, Lord, Healer of the sick of His people Israel.

As Hayim Halevy Donin remarks in his wonderful work *To Pray as a Jew*, "While it is the doctor who treats the patient, it is God who cures him."[74] In this blessing, we pray on behalf of relatives, friends, and loved ones (including ourselves if necessary) who are ill. After the words "bring complete recovery for all of our ailments," there is an opportunity to insert the names of specific individuals in need of healing. The custom is to identify the person by their own Hebrew name and their mother's Hebrew name.[75] If the mother's Hebrew name is not known, one can use their father's name. If the ill person's Hebrew name is not known at all, one may simply insert their English name or any other name by which they are known.

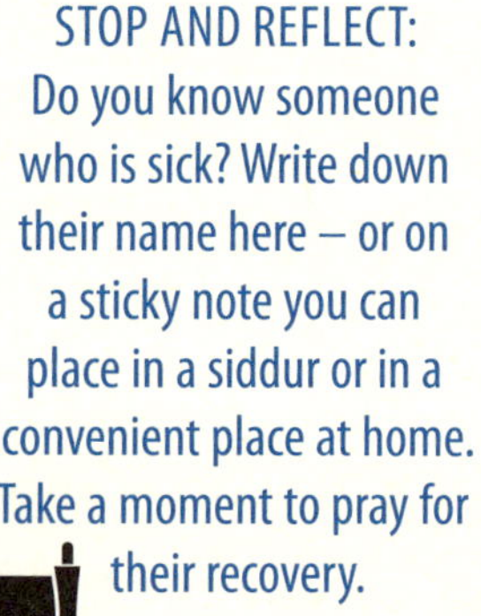

STOP AND REFLECT:
Do you know someone who is sick? Write down their name here – or on a sticky note you can place in a siddur or in a convenient place at home. Take a moment to pray for their recovery.

The language of "healing of both soul and body" in this blessing demonstrates the connection Judaism sees between our souls and our bodies. We ask God to treat not only the physical symptoms of sickness afflicting the body but also the underlying issue ailing the soul.

6. **Livelihood**

Bless this year for us, Lord our God,
and all its types of produce for good.
(In winter: Grant dew and rain as a blessing)
(In other seasons: Grant blessing)
on the face of the earth,
and from its goodness satisfy us,
blessing our year as the best of years.
Blessed are You, Lord, who blesses the years.

Earning a decent living so we can pay our bills – and not be stressed by money issues – is key for healthy living. Although this blessing is couched mainly in agricultural terms, we petition God "to bless our year as the best of years" – to achieve success at whatever we do professionally. To personalize this request, ask God to help you successfully negotiate that big deal coming up, or whatever else you need help with in earning a living. While Judaism certainly believes in working hard to achieve our professional goals, we also need God's blessing to achieve financial success.

Where Is the Blessing for Happiness?

STOP AND REFLECT: How does your Judaism make you happier?

A common question I often receive when it comes to these personal requests is, why is there no blessing for happiness? Considering that the Torah urges us to be in a state of joy when serving God[76] and how deeply we all desire happiness, it is curious that the Sages never added this request. Some answer that whereas God can bless us with all the necessities and even luxuries of life, being happy is ultimately up to us.[77] Jewish tradition teaches that it is only when we are content with our blessings that we can ultimately find happiness. As the Sages insightfully remark: "Who is a wealthy person? One who is satisfied with his lot."[78] Happiness is not a blessing to pray for, but a choice we make ourselves.

Communal Requests

7. **Ingathering of the Exiles**

Sound the great shofar for our freedom,
raise high the banner to gather our exiles,
and gather us together from the four quarters of the earth.
Blessed are You, Lord,
who gathers the dispersed of His people Israel.

In this blessing, the first of the national requests, we ask God to bring about the first phase of the messianic redemption: the return of Jews from all over the world to the Land of Israel. The physical return of the Jewish people to Israel creates the political and societal infrastructure necessary for a spiritual return.[79] This is why many contemporary rabbis see today's modern "ingathering" to Israel and the creation of a sovereign state in the land of our forefathers as step one in the messianic process.

According to Rabbi Joseph B. Soloveitchik, the last words of the blessing, "who gathers the dispersed of His people Israel," do not refer to the physically dispersed but to those who have become spiritually alienated from their Jewish traditions. According to this reading, this blessing is also a prayer for God to help Jews return to their lost Jewish heritage.

8. **Justice**

Restore our judges as at first,
and our counselors as at the beginning,

and remove from us sorrow and sighing.
May You alone, Lord,
reign over us with loving-kindness and compassion,
and vindicate us in justice.
Blessed are You, Lord,
the King who loves righteousness and justice.

Scales of justice

After the Jewish people are restored to Israel, the prophets envision the Jewish people following the Torah's unique judicial system of laws and values as the next step toward full redemption. Although many of today's Western legal systems have roots in the Judeo-Christian tradition inspired by the Bible, they are nonetheless human systems devised to maintain order and civility. The ideal situation is for the Jewish people to follow the Torah's laws, which are designed to promote not only law and order but also ethics and morality. "Restore our judges" is our request to begin that process.

9. Against Informers

For the slanderers let there be no hope,
and may all wickedness perish in an instant.
May all Your people's enemies swiftly be cut down.
May You swiftly uproot, crush, cast down,
and humble the arrogant swiftly in our days.
Blessed are You, Lord,
who destroys enemies and humbles the arrogant.

This blessing was originally composed by the Sages during the second century CE to petition God for help in confronting Jewish sects that were informing on their fellow Jews to the Roman authorities. When those groups ceased to be a threat, this blessing remained for us to use for praying for God's assistance in confronting anti-Semitism in all its forms. Some suggest that this request is specifically made after we ask God to help us return to Israel and create a just society in order to secure God's protection against those who would destroy or "sabotage our national redemption."[80] Its author, Shmuel Hakatan, famous for emphasizing the biblical verse "When your enemy falls do not take joy,"[81] possessed the necessary sensitivity to compose a blessing asking for God's help in confronting our enemies.

10. **For the Righteous**

To the righteous, the pious,
the elders of Your people the House of Israel,
the remnant of their scholars, the righteous converts, and to us,
may Your compassion be aroused, Lord our God.
Grant a good reward to all who sincerely trust in Your name.
Set our lot with them,
so that we may never be ashamed, for in You we trust.
Blessed are You, Lord,
who is the support and trust of the righteous.

STOP AND REFLECT:
Have you ever met a person you would describe as righteous? What makes that individual special, and how can you apply some of their characteristics to your own life?

The previous requests for the ingathering of the exiles, justice, and protection from enemies are all necessary to establish the physical aspects of what will be needed for the messianic redemption. This blessing for the righteous addresses what is needed on the spiritual level, namely to empower those "who can generate our nation's spiritual growth – the holy ones (*tzaddikim*) and the devout (*chasidim*)."[82] As great rabbinic figures have always done, the righteous leaders of Israel today remind and inspire us about the deeper purpose for our nation's existence – to illuminate the world by reflecting the spiritual and ethical teachings of our Torah.

11. Rebuilding Jerusalem

To Jerusalem, Your city, may You return in compassion,
and may You dwell in it as You promised.
May You rebuild it rapidly in our days as an everlasting structure,
and install within it soon the throne of David.
Blessed are You, Lord, who builds Jerusalem.

STOP AND REFLECT: Have you ever been to Israel? Do you live there? If so, try to recall an amazing experience you had there.

The city of Jerusalem receives its own blessing because it is considered the spiritual epicenter of the world. In 1967, the Jewish people experienced a *physical* return to Jerusalem with the liberation of the holy city during the Six-Day War. This prayer, however, refers to the rebuilding of Jerusalem in a spiritual sense, namely that God Himself return to Jerusalem: "And may You dwell in it as You promised." According to tradition, God's return to His holy city will accompany the messianic redemption.

12. Restoring the Davidic Kingdom

May the offshoot of Your servant David soon flower,
and may his pride be raised high by Your salvation,
for we wait for Your salvation all day.
Blessed are You, Lord, who makes the glory of salvation flourish.

In this blessing, we petition God for the final leg of the messianic redemption: the restoration of the Davidic dynasty. Unlike the kings of Europe, the powers of the Jewish king are subject to a higher authority – the laws of the Torah. The Jewish king's main function, in fact, was to ensure that the people live by the laws of the Torah, as the king himself was required to do. This ancient system of checks and balances was demonstrated by the command that the Jewish king possess not one Torah (as every Jewish person is technically required to have) but a second Torah scroll, which the king took with him wherever he went.

The language in this prayer – "for we wait for Your salvation all day" – expresses the longing that the Jewish people are meant to cultivate for a better tomorrow. This desire to elevate the physical world in which we now live is communicated in one of the six questions that the Talmud teaches every Jew will be asked by God after we pass on: "Did you anticipate the salvation?"[83] Anticipating the redemption is not merely expressing faith or hope in the advent of the Messiah, but actively working to bring the messianic redemption through the observance of the Torah's mitzvot.

> "We do not wait for salvation to descend from the heavens; we bring it about through our actions on earth." (Rabbi Yitzchak Hutner)

The mitzvot transform the physical world into a spiritually suitable place for God's presence to dwell, culminating in the messianic redemption.

> "Every individual has the potential to bring salvation through their deeds. A single act of righteousness can tip the scales of the world toward redemption." (Maimonides, Laws of Repentance)

"Hear Our Prayer"

Listen to our voice, Lord our God.
Spare us and have compassion on us,
and in compassion and favor accept our prayer,
for You, God, listen to prayers and pleas.
Do not turn us away, O our King,
empty-handed from Your presence,
for You listen with compassion
to the prayer of Your people Israel.
Blessed are You, Lord, who listens to prayer.

After all our personal and communal requests, we turn to God and ask that "in compassion" He "accept our prayer." We plead with God that He not turn us away empty-handed. In this blessing of the *Amidah*, we are granted the opportunity to insert any personal requests we did not include in the previous petitions. These requests can be made in any language and can relate to any need we may have for ourselves, friends, family, and loved ones.

Some suggest that this prayer follows the national request for the Messiah in order to convey the idea that even after the Messiah arrives, prayer will remain a critical way for us relate to God. The prophet Isaiah, in fact, refers to the Temple as a place of prayer for all the nations in messianic times.[84]

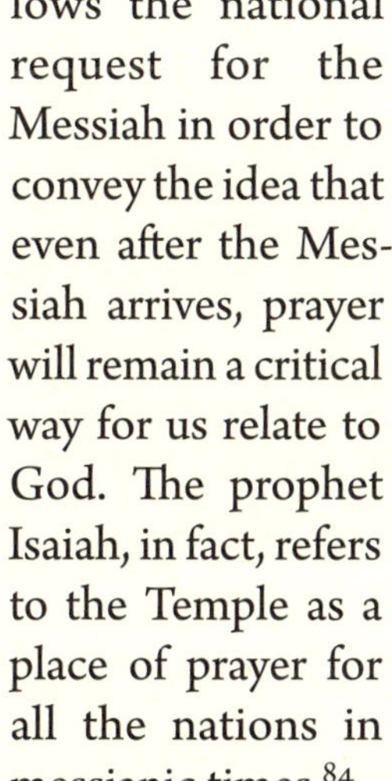

KABBALAH CORNER:

The balance of masculine and feminine energies is fundamental to kabbalistic thought. While God transcends such human categories, these energies help us understand divine actions. The masculine is linked to giving and the feminine to receiving. In the *Modim* prayer, the language shifts to the feminine: *Modim anachnu lach* ("We thank You"), because when we offer thanks, God, as it were, takes on the feminine aspect, receiving our gratitude. This reflects the balance of energies that kabbalists emphasize – the interaction between giving and receiving, both human and divine. Through *Modim*, we engage in this sacred exchange, acknowledging God's receptivity to our prayers. (Rabbi Joel David Bakst)

The Concluding Blessings

The first of the three concluding blessings, called *Retzeh,* speaks of how prayer today substitutes for the sacrifices (*Koren Shalem Siddur,* p. 126). Just as the Temple sacrifices were meant to draw our ancestors closer to God, so are our prayers meant to do the same for us today. At the same time, in this prayer we petition God "to restore the Temple service" since without the Temple service, prayer is lacking.

The prayer called *Yaaleh Veyavo* – said only on Rosh Chodesh (the New Month) and on the festivals (Passover, Shavuot, and Sukkot) – is inserted toward the end of the blessing of *Retzeh,* since reciting *Yaaleh Veyavo* is how we fulfill the Talmud's edict to declare the uniqueness of the day in the *Amidah* on those special days of the year.[85] We fulfill that mandate in the very blessing which calls for the Temple to be restored "because the day's uniqueness is manifest in the different sacrifices offered in the Temple."[86]

The second concluding blessing, *Modim* or "Thank You," expresses our gratitude to God for all of our blessings (*Koren Shalem Siddur,* p. 128).

Expressing gratitude is fundamental to being Jewish. To this day, one of the reasons we are called Jews is that the matriarch Leah named her fourth son Yehudah or Judah, from the Hebrew word *hodaah* or "thanks." The Sages explain that Leah understood that her husband Jacob was destined to have twelve sons. Since Jacob had four wives, Leah thought she was entitled to have only three sons. So when she gave birth to a fourth, she was moved to give thanks. We too are moved to express gratitude when we are gifted something we didn't expect or don't think we deserve. Judaism views everything we are given as a gift and therefore worthy of giving thanks. As you recite this prayer, think about specific things for which you are grateful, expressing your personal gratitude for those blessings in your life.

In this blessing of *Modim,* we also insert the special *Al HaNisim* or "For the Miracles" prayer, which is recited on the holidays of Hanukkah and Purim *(Koren Shalem Siddur,* p.

130). Since *Al HaNisim* is used to express gratitude to God for the miracles God performed for the Jewish people during the Persian and Greek periods, it is inserted in this prayer of thanksgiving.

Each morning in synagogue, following the silent *Amidah*, the leader recites the *Amidah* aloud as a form of communal prayer. During that repetition, instead of the congregation simply answering Amen to the leader's blessing (as is done for all the other blessings during the repetition), we recite the *Modim* of the Rabbis – a thanksgiving prayer for everyone in the congregation to say alongside the *chazan*'s repetition of that blessing (*Koren Shalem Siddur*, p. 128). The fourteenth-century commentator on the siddur, the Abudraham, explains that while it is permissible to petition God through an emissary, one cannot give thanks by delegating that responsibility to someone else. We must express gratitude ourselves.

We conclude the final set of blessings with the blessing *Sim Shalom* or "Grant Peace" (*Koren Shalem Siddur*, p. 132), because none of the blessings which we ask for in the *Amidah* can be realized without peace. As the Rabbis teach: "Great is peace for no vessel can retain blessing as effectively as peace.... The blessings in themselves are of no avail unless peace goes with them."[87] This is true not only on the national level but also individually. One can possess many blessings – intelligence, good health, and a respectable livelihood – but not have the inner peace to enjoy those blessings.

> "All the blessings are worthless unless there is peace." (Midrash Rabbah)

The *Amidah* closes with a personal meditation starting with the words "My God," which denotes the increased level of spiritual intimacy with God that we have achieved by this point.

My God,
guard my tongue from evil and my lips from
deceitful speech.

To those who curse me, let my soul be silent;
may my soul be to all like the dust.
Open my heart to Your Torah and let my soul
pursue Your commandments.
As for all who plan evil against me,
swiftly thwart their counsel and frustrate their plans.
Act for the sake of Your name; act for the
sake of Your right hand;
act for the sake of Your holiness; act for the
sake of Your Torah.
That Your beloved ones may be delivered,
save with Your right hand and answer me.
May the words of my mouth and the meditation
of my heart
find favor before You, Lord, my Rock and Redeemer.

In this meditation, which is really added to the text of the *Amidah*, we ask God to help us curb any ill speech we may say about or to other people, and we also ask God for protection against those who "plan evil" against us. The request "Open my heart to Your Torah and let my soul pursue Your commandments" is another way of saying: "Through Torah and mitzvot we want to be close to You, God, but we can use some help."

We formally conclude the *Amidah* with the phrase "May the words of my mouth and the meditation of my heart find favor before You, O Lord." This phrase parallels the introductory line of the *Amidah*: "O Lord, open my lips, so that my mouth may declare Your praise." We start the *Amidah* by asking God for help expressing ourselves sincerely, and we conclude by asking that God find those prayers acceptable.

"To be sincere is to stand before God with honesty, offering not perfection but the truth of who we are." (Rabbi Shlomo Riskin)

May He who makes peace in His high places,
make peace for us and all Israel – and say: Amen.

The final words of the *Amidah* are accompanied by some choreography: The phrase "May He who makes peace in His high places" is said as one bows to the left, "make peace for us" while bowing right, "and all Israel" while bowing straight ahead. We conclude with the words "and say: Amen." Just as we begin the *Amidah* by taking three steps forward, concretizing the sense that we are entering the realm of the Divine, we conclude by taking leave of that spiritual space. Some suggest that this is why we begin the three steps forward of the *Amidah* with the right foot and conclude the leaving with the left. Right demonstrates our eagerness to enter God's realm and left represents our reticence in leaving. A short prayer for the restoration of the Temple then follows.

THE KABBALAH OF PRAYER

The great kabbalist the Arizal taught that each of the four parts of the Morning Prayer Service we have discussed – the Morning Blessings, Psalms of Praise, the *Shema,* and the *Amidah* – transport us to another one of the four worlds of reality that exist according to Kabbalah: the World of Emanation, the World of Creation, the World of Formation, and the World of Action. These four worlds relate to the concept of *tzimtzum* or contraction we discussed in our chapter on God – the process by which God makes Himself smaller or hidden. You may recall the metaphor I mentioned of the electric bulb surrounded by a lampshade: The light emanating from the bulb is too

bright to be enjoyed without a lampshade to block some of the brightness. Similarly, God makes Himself smaller, allowing Himself to appear hidden so we can benefit from His light and wisdom. God's light is most obscured in the lowest world, the World of Action – the world in which we humans live. An increasing amount of spiritual light is revealed in the higher worlds, the Worlds of Formation and Creation, and the greatest revelation of God's light in the World of Emanation. The Arizal taught that by reciting each of the four parts of the prayer service, we ascend from one world to another, enabling ourselves to experience more and more of God's Infinite Light.

When we begin the prayer service with the Morning Blessings, we are, as it were, in the World of Action – the physical world in which we live. As mentioned, in the Morning Blessings section we express our gratitude for physical gifts such as eyesight, clothing, and strength. This section of prayer is therefore rooted solely in the physical realm. Only once we become cognizant of how much the physical dominates our experiences and perception are we ready to move on to the next sphere, the World of Formation.

The Psalms of Praise, the next part of our morning prayers, relates to the World of Formation. This is the world in which we discover the inner formation of the physical world. Here, we are still attached to the physical but recognize that there exists something beyond our material existence – the spiritual or metaphysical. In the Psalms of Praise section, we recite verses from the Bible recognizing God's greatness and splendor in the physical world[88] – all of which emanate from a supernatural source. Realizing the spiritual source of physical reality allows us to break through the physical barriers which prevent us from being spiritually connected. We are now ready to move to the next domain: the World of Creation.

We enter the World of Creation by reciting the *Shema* and its surrounding blessings – the next section of our daily prayers. Here, we see the existence of a completely separate realm of reality. In the *Shema,* we surrender to God as we recognize the Almighty's supremacy and His control over every aspect of existence. We also recognize that God is beyond our human comprehension and understanding.

> "God's essence lies far beyond human comprehension. The more we seek to understand Him, the more we realize how utterly unknowable He truly is." (Rabbi Nachman of Breslov)

Once we realize that God is the ultimate source of all existence and that He lies beyond our conception, we are ready to enter the fourth and final world: the World of Emanation.

We reach the World of Emanation as we begin the *Amidah* or Silent Devotion. As noted, the word *amidah* means to stand because it is at this point in the prayers when we are prepared to stand before God and address Him directly. Having broken through all physical barriers, we can now truly commune with God on a much more intimate level. The Hebrew word for Emanation is *atzilah,* which comes from the Hebrew root *etzel* or "to be near," since it is in this world that we are closest to God. In each of the three previous worlds, we prepared ourselves for this point, so that we can be elevated, come as near to God as possible, and attach ourselves to His holy presence.

A BROKEN HEART

> "There is nothing more whole than a broken heart." (Rabbi Menachem Mendel of Kotzk)

The sincerity we bring to the experience is just as important as the deep ideas underlying our prayers. When it comes to prayer, there is no substitute for being genuine and authentic.

There is a touching story I think about when reciting the moving High Holy Day prayer *Avinu Malkeinu,* "Our Father our King." There was once a man who owned a fine jewelry store in Israel. One day, a nine-year-old girl walked into the store to buy a bracelet. The little girl looked through the glass display case and pointed to an expensive piece of jewelry that cost about sixteen thousand shekels, which equals approximately four thousand dollars.

The owner of the store asked the girl: "Do you want to buy that?"

"Yes," replied the nine-year-old.

"Well, you have very good taste. Who is it for?"

"For my older sister."

"That's very nice, but why do you want to buy your sister such an expensive bracelet?" asked the storeowner.

"I don't have a father or a mother," the little girl responded. "My oldest sister takes care of all of us, so we collected all our money to buy her a present."

With that, the girl pulled a handful of coins from her pocket. The jeweler counted the change, which amounted to seven shekels and eighty *agurot* – about two dollars.

The storeowner, who was visibly moved by the little girl's story, excitedly told her: "You're in luck! That's exactly what this bracelet costs." He wrapped the gift and handed the bracelet to the little girl, who left the store with a big smile.

A few hours later, the little girl's older sister came into the store and apologized to the owner: "I'm terribly sorry, sir. My little sister shouldn't have taken this bracelet without paying."

The owner responded: "What are talking about? It's paid for in full."

"There is no way my sister could have afforded such a fine piece of jewelry," the older sister said.

"She paid in full," reiterated the storeowner. "Seven shekels, eighty *agurot,* and a broken heart." The storeowner continued: "My wife died a few years ago. People come into my store every day to buy expensive pieces of jewelry, and they can afford it. When your little sister walked in wanting to buy you something special, and then she showed me all the money she collected, it was the first time since my wife died that I remembered what it really means to love someone. So I gladly gave her the bracelet and wished her well."

When we pray, we make lots of requests from God. We ask for life, for good health, for a decent livelihood. And then we reach into our pockets to see what we have to pay for all these beautiful blessings. Maybe we have a few merits, but not nearly enough to pay for all the things we ask for. We manage to pull out a few shekels, a few dollars – a mitzvah here, a mitzvah there. A little Shabbat we observed, some charity we gave to the poor, a phone call to a lonely person, some Torah we learned, some support we lent to Israel. But we don't really have what it takes to pay God for all the blessings for which we ask on Yom Kippur and every day of our lives. That is why the *Avinu Malkeinu* prayer concludes with the stanza: "Our Father, our King, have mercy on us and answer us, though we don't have enough deeds." We've accumulated a few merits here and there, but not enough to justify our request.

But we *do* have one thing, something we must never underestimate: a broken heart. "The Lord is near to the broken-hearted, and He saves those of crushed spirit" (Ps. 34:19). If we come before God contrite and sincere, with a genuine interest in doing better in the year to come – to be kinder to our fellow human being, to give more charity, to speak less ill of one another, to study more Torah, to increase our Shabbat observance – that can go a long way. We conclude *Avinu Malkeinu* with the words "Treat us with charity and kindness and save us." We admit we do not have enough to pay for what we ask, but we turn to God and plead: "Please give us good health and a life of sweetness – in the merit of a broken heart."

STOP AND REFLECT: Have you ever turned to God with a broken heart?

IT'S NOT ALL OR NOTHING

We covered a good amount in our discussion on prayer. If much of this is new to you and you feel a bit overwhelmed, do not fret. As I've shared with my students over the years, Judaism is not an all-or-nothing enterprise, and this certainly applies to prayer too. If you are currently not in the practice of praying every day, start with the Morning Blessings – nothing better than beginning your day with some gratitude. After you become comfortable with the Morning Blessings, you can move to saying the *Shema* and after that the *Amidah*. Once you have that down to a routine, you can add in the Psalms of Praise and the blessings surrounding the *Shema*. One step at a time. Remember what the Sages of the Talmud said: "If you grab for too much, you will end up with nothing."[89] Judaism isn't a sprint, so take your time and enjoy the ride.

STOP AND REFLECT: If you were to choose to say one of the prayers we have discussed, what would it be and why?

Further Reading

To Pray as a Jew
Rabbi Hayim Halevy Donin

Soul-Powered Prayers
Rabbi David Aaron

The Rav on Tefillah: An Anthology of Teachings by Rabbi Joseph B. Soloveitchik on Jewish Prayer
Jay Goldmintz

Jewish Meditation
Aryeh Kaplan

A Guide to Jewish Prayer
Rabbi Adin Steinsaltz

Rav Schwab on Prayer
Rabbi Shimon Schwab

TAKEAWAYS

- Prayer allows us to reflect on our Jewish ideals as expressed in the siddur, the prayer book, and how well we live up to them.
- The purpose of prayer is to deepen our relationship with God, not just to get what we need.
- Prayer makes us mindful of and grateful for God's daily blessings, such as sight, clothing, and the ability to walk, which we so often take for granted.
- By reciting structured prayers at set times, we remain aware of our life's mission and ensure that we continue to pray, even when we don't feel inspired.
- Praying with others in a synagogue gives us the opportunity to stay mindful of the needs of others, tap into the power of the community, and recite special prayers that can only be recited with a *minyan*.
- While it is ideal to pray in Hebrew, since it is the language God used to create the world, one may nonetheless pray in any language.
- There are four main parts of Shacharit, the Morning Service: the Morning Blessings, Psalms of Praise, *Shema,* and the *Amidah,* all rungs in a spiritual ladder we climb every day in our relationship with God.
- When we pray with sincerity and heartfelt emotion, our prayers carry immense spiritual power.

Notes

1. In regard to the biblical verse "You shall serve God with all your heart" (Deut. 13:11), the Talmud states: "What is the service of the heart? That is prayer" (Talmud, Taanit 2a).
2. Observant Jews pray three times a day, and prayer is the primary means of securing atonement and forgiveness during the High Holidays.
3. *The Apology*, 38a, 5–6.
4. *Sefer HaIkkarim* 4:18.
5. Deuteronomy 3:23.
6. Ibid. 3:24.
7. Talmud, Berachot 32b.
8. Rabbi Joseph B. Soloveitchik, *Reflections of the Rav,* ed. Abraham Besdin, vol. 1 (Ktav, 1979), pp. 77–79.
9. The entire middle section of the weekday *Amidah,* recited three times a day, is devoted to specific requests we make of God.
10. Dr. Scott Barry Kaufman of the University of Pennsylvania. A brief summary of some of his findings appears at: https://www.wnycstudios.org/podcasts/notetoself/episodes/bored-and-brilliant-data-preview.
11. https://www.pewresearch.org/internet/2010/04/20/teens-and-mobile-phones/.
12. https://www.deseret.com/2023/9/27/23892484/how-many-texts-does-teen-get-day-study-cell-phone/.
13. https://www.latimes.com/opinion/story/2023-05-22/smartphones-and-social-media-hurt-teens-but-parents-face-a-hard-choice.
14. Technically speaking, transcendentalism refers to the nineteenth-century American-British movement that included figures such as Ralph Waldo Emerson. Since that movement was heavily influenced by Eastern ideas, and because the term captures the approach we are trying to convey, we are using the term loosely to refer to contemporary mindfulness.
15. 1745–1812, Liozna, Belarus.
16. See page 27 of chapter 1, "Finding God."

17. This is taken from the writings of Rabbi Chaim Soloveitchik, *Chiddushei Rav Chaim,* Laws of Prayer 4:1.
18. This is a teaching of the Baal Shem Tov, the founder of the chasidic movement.
19. *The Rules of Wisdom and Knowledge* (Mossad HaRav Kook, 2011), First Rule – Intention of Creation.
20. Genesis 2:5.
21. *Derech Hashem,* part 4.
22. Rabbi Benayahu Yisachar Shmueli, *Pathway of the River* (Sifrei Givat Shaul, 2007), p. 155.
23. Kamarna Rebbe, "Pillar of *Tefillah,*" in *Or Shivat Yamim,* (Mossad HaRav Kook, 2007), pp. 6–7.
24. Rabbi Shneur Zalman of Liadi, *Torah Or, Vayetzeh* 1.
25. Kamarna Rebbe, "Pillar of Tefillah," pp. 76–80.
26. Some prayers, as well as the Torah reading, can be recited only with a *minyan,* but the fundamental parts of prayer can be said alone.
27. Rabbi Dovber Pinson, *Inner Worlds of Jewish Prayer* (Iyyun, 2014), p. 23.
28. A quorum of ten men or more.
29. This prayer is called the *Al Chet,* which lists the various categories of sins.
30. Prayer, of course, has existed from the beginning of time. But while the Jewish Temple stood, sacrifices were a primary form of Jewish worship and prayer was less formalized.
31. Half of the requests found in the *Amidah* are personal and the other half communal. All are said in the plural.
32. This is a teaching by Rabbi Dov Ber, the Maggid of Mezeritch, who interpreted the opening verse of the Torah: "*Bereshit bara Elokim et*" or "In the beginning God created the" to mean, "In the beginning God created the letter *et,*" which is spelled *alef, tav,* the first and last letters of the Hebrew alphabet.
33. Talmud, Berachot 26b.
34. There are technically nineteen blessings in this prayer since an additional blessing was later added.
35. Rabbi Hayim Halevy Donin, *To Pray as a Jew* (Basic Books, 1972), p. 69.
36. There are a few reasons for this recommendation. As a general rule, tefillin are worn only at Shacharit. Minchah does not include the *Shema,* and Maariv is not considered to be on the same level of obligation as Shacharit and Minchah. Perhaps most important, Shacharit has the power to set a spiritual tone for the entire day. Many people report that when they begin their days with prayer, their entire day is transformed into one that feels more meaningful, peaceful, and connected to the Divine.
37. *Tosafot* (medieval Ashkenazic scholars) on Talmud, Berachot 11b.
38. Talmud, Berachot 11b.
39. Joshua 1:8.
40. Talmud, Berachot 32b.

41. Ibid. 4b.
42. Rabbi Dr. Norman Lamm, *The Shema*, p. 17.
43. The most well-known reason is to enable us to focus and concentrate.
44. The *Shema* is the only part of our daily prayers taken directly from and mandated by the Torah. The rest of the prayers were organized and composed by the Jewish Sages and prophets.
45. Deuteronomy 6:5–9.
46. Check out the powerful story I shared in chapter 1, p. 44, of the Jewish children discovered in a Christian orphanage because of the *Shema* their parents had sung with them at bedtime.
47. Deuteronomy 11:13–21.
48. Ibid. 15:37–41.
49. The precise identity of the dye was lost for thousands of years, and most scholars maintain that it has been recovered today.
50. Deuteronomy 14:1.
51. This is based on Deuteronomy 6:7: "Recite them ... when you lie down and when you rise up." The Sages derive from here that the *Shema* should be recited in the morning and evening. The *Shema* is therefore included in both Shacharit and Maariv services.
52. During Maariv, the Evening Service, the *Shema* is enveloped in four blessings, two before the *Shema* and two after.
53. Rabbi Hayim Halevy Donin, *To Pray as a Jew*, p. 157.
54. If one forgot to recite the Blessings of the Torah found in the first section of the prayers, one can use this prayer as a substitute.
55. Rabbi Dr. Elie Munk, *The World of Jewish Prayer*, vol. 1 (Feldheim, 1976), p. 108.
56. See chapter 1 of this book, section "Part 1: Finding God from Without," pp. 15–16, where I present the teleological argument.
57. "The history of philosophy is a history of human trial and error. Only God's revealed law, 'the Torah of God,' gives man the guidance which is suited to his innate urges and desires and which leads him to develop in accordance with the Divine plan" (Rabbi Dr. Elie Munk, *The World of Jewish Prayer*, p. 108).
58. Talmud, Berachot 4b, 9b.
59. The end of the first blessing of the *Amidah* concludes with the words "and will bring a Redeemer to their children's children for the sake of His name, in love" (*Koren Shalem Siddur*, p. 108).
60. Rabbi Chaim Soloveitchik's analysis of Maimonides.
61. Although a nineteenth blessing was later added, it continues to be called the *Shemoneh Esrei*.
62. The Men of the Great Assembly included Mordecai (from the Purim story) and the last of the prophets: Haggai, Zechariah, and Malachi.
63. Passover, Sukkot, and Shavuot.
64. Generally, we do not make personal requests on Shabbat or the holidays but instead focus on connecting with the sanctity of the day.

65. "Descendants" can be taken either literally, when referring to someone born Jewish, or figuratively, as in the case of a convert.
66. *Koren Shalem Siddur,* p. 110.
67. *Abudraham HaShalem* (Mossad HaRav Kook, 2003), pp. 39–40.
68. *Koren Shalem Siddur,* p. 110.
69. I Samuel, 12:17–18, with Rashi.
70. *Kuzari* III:17.
71. Rabbi Baruch HaLevi Epstein, *Baruch She'amar* (Am Olam, 2005), p. 120.
72. Maimonides, *Mishneh Torah,* Laws of Repentance 10:6.
73. Rashi on Talmud, Megillah 17b.
74. Donin, *To Pray as a Jew,* p. 82.
75. The source for this practice is Psalms 116:16, where David prayed and said: "I am Your servant, the son of Your maidservant."
76. "Serve God with happiness" (Ps. 100:2) and "And you shall be happy on the holidays" (Deut. 16:14).
77. Donin, *To Pray as a Jew,* p. 88.
78. Mishnah, "Ethics of the Fathers," 4:1.
79. As Hayim Halevy Donin wrote: "Only when the Jewish people are free in their own land is it possible to translate the spiritual yearning to return to Eretz Yisrael into reality" (*To Pray as a Jew,* p. 90).
80. Rabbi David Aaron, *Soul-Powered Prayers* (Targum, 2006), p. 143.
81. Proverbs 24:17.
82. Rabbi David Aaron, *Soul-Powered Prayers,* p. 150.
83. Talmud, Shabbat 31a.
84. Isaiah 56:7.
85. If one forgot to recite the *Yaaleh Veyavo* prayer on any of these special days, Jewish tradition requires one to repeat the *Amidah* since we have not acknowledged the special nature of the day.
86. Rabbi Yehoshua C. Grunstein, *Daven Your Age* (Gefen, 2013), p. 199.
87. Midrash, Numbers Rabbah 11:7.
88. In the Psalms of Praise section, we recite these verses to help rid ourselves of any distracting thoughts so we can be spiritually prepared for the upcoming prayers of the *Shema* and *Amidah.*
89. Talmud, Sukkah 5b.

CHAPTER 4
Kindness and Charity

CHAPTER 4

Kindness and Charity

Building a World of Compassion

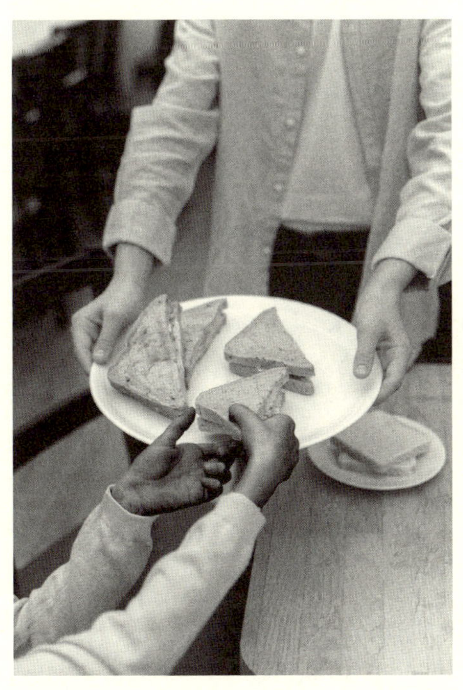

In 1966, an eleven-year-old African American boy moved with his family to an all-white neighborhood in Washington, DC. Sitting with his brothers and sisters on the front stoop of their new house, the boy anxiously waited to see how they would be greeted. People walked by and gave a passing glance in their direction, but no one said hello or welcomed them to the neighborhood. The little boy began to fear they were unwelcome. Suddenly, a white woman coming home from work stopped, turned to the children, and with a broad smile announced: "Welcome!"

She disappeared into her home and soon reemerged with drinks and cream cheese and jelly sandwiches in hand. That seemingly small gesture, the young man later wrote, changed his life forever. For he sensed that although his family was different, they could still find a place in their new home. In that instant, the little boy knew he could belong.

The young man in the story is Stephen Carter, the woman Sara Kestenbaum, an observant Jew. Carter went on to become a Yale professor and to write a book entitled *Civility*. After telling his story, Carter adds that the Hebrew word for "civility" is *chesed*, or kindness, which is rooted in the Jewish belief that all human beings are created in the image of God.

Carter was right. The Jews brought *chesed* as a concept, really a way of life, to the world. Jewish people have been at the forefront of every human and civil rights movement. Equal rights before the law, being kind to the more vulnerable in society – the stranger, the orphan, the widow – all originated in the Torah. Eric Nelson of Harvard[1] demonstrated that more than Greek culture or the Renaissance, it was Hebrew Scripture and Jewish scholarship that inspired modern-day democracy. As a result of the Reformation, when the Hebrew Bible was translated and became accessible to all, seventeenth-century political thinkers started to derive these ideas from the Torah. Political philosophers drew five times more heavily from the Old Testament than from Greek sources in developing the modern ideas of equal rights, checks and balances to avoid abuses of power, and the democratic principle of majority rule. These concepts, commonplace today in all Western democracies, come from the Hebrew Bible – the Torah.

> The world stands on three foundations: Torah, service of God, and acts of kindness. (Mishnah, "Ethics of the Fathers")

But the Jewish commitment to *chesed* did not end with the Bible. The famed Jewish philanthropist Moses Montefiore was once asked what he was worth. He responded: "A few hundred thousand pounds." The questioner challenged the British financier: "A few hundred thousand pounds? We all know you are worth millions!"[2] Montefiore answered: "You asked me what I'm worth, not what I own. We are worth what we are willing to share. The figure I quoted is the amount I gave to charity this year."

We are worth what we are willing to share. This profound idea is reflected in God's own nature. The biblical maxim "The world is built on kindness"[3] teaches us what motivated God to create the world: pure love. God is perfect, so He has no needs. His motivation for creating the universe therefore could not have emerged from an external reason or a desire to receive something in return. Instead, God created the world simply because it is His nature to give. The Torah similarly commands us to give to those in need so that, like God, we too become givers. The concept of *chesed,* giving out of pure love, not only originated in the Torah but actually emerges from the very act of creation.

The Sages of the Midrash[4] give new meaning to the idea that the world is built on kindness. When the angels learned of God's plan to create the world, they divided into two camps. The angels of kindness and righteousness were in favor of creation, asserting that humanity is essentially kind and just. But the angels of truth and peace were opposed, arguing that man is dishonest and prone to quarrels and strife. The Midrash explains that in response to this split, God "took truth and threw it to the ground." In other words, He decided against the angels of truth and chose to create humankind. This midrash is remarkable because it suggests that the very act of creation was only due to God's attribute of kindness – otherwise we wouldn't exist!

> Rabbi Simlai taught: The Torah begins with kindness and ends with kindness. It begins with kindness, as it is written: "God made for Adam and for his wife garments of skins, and clothed them," and it ends with kindness, as it is written: "God buried Moses in the valley." (Talmud, Sotah 14a)

In the Jewish tradition, giving takes place on two levels: acts of kindness and of charity. We will discuss the Jewish approach to both, beginning with acts of kindness.

ACTS OF KINDNESS

Is it no coincidence that the first Jew, Abraham, is known not only for being the first to preach monotheism but also as a paragon of *chesed*.

He shatters his father's idols and challenges the polytheistic status quo while inviting strangers into his home and defending even the corrupt people of Sodom. There are plenty of heroes in the Jewish tradition. One could have easily been the paradigm for belief and another a model for kindness. Yet instead of championing one figure who discovers God and another who embodies kindness, our tradition merges both in the single personality of Abraham. The Torah does this by design: It helps establish a critical link between monotheism and kindness. Believing in a God who creates humanity in His own image (known in Hebrew as *tzelem Elokim*) demands ethical conduct. We must treat one another with respect not only because we are all human but also because we are all created in the image of God.

> KABBALAH CORNER: Abraham personifies the divine attribute of *chesed*, kindness, while his son, Isaac, exemplifies the trait of *gevurah*, inner strength. Abraham introduced unconditional love, while Isaac taught us how to maintain boundaries. On their own, these characteristics can be dangerous because they can lead to extremes. This is why they both had to experience the binding of Isaac together: Abraham needed to learn that sometimes saying "no" is important, while Isaac needed to learn that being overly rigid is also not the best approach. (Rabbi Kalonymus Kalman Epstein)

Think about it this way: If we believe that our natures are merely physical and animalistic, what objective reason is there to treat other people with respect? Simply because we

KABBALAH CORNER:
The phrase *betzelem Elokim,* "in the image of God," has the numerical value of 248, the same as the numerical value of the name Avraham. This number also corresponds to the 248 positive mitzvot, actions that bring Godliness into the world. Jewish tradition further teaches that each human being has 248 limbs, symbolizing our ability to actively perform these mitzvot. Being created in the image of God demands ethical conduct, as our physical bodies are designed to fulfill the mitzvot and spread kindness, just like Abraham. (Rabbi Avraham Arieh Trugman)

have more in common with our fellow humans than with other living creatures? That is a weak argument. Circumstances change, and those feelings of commonality can easily fade, especially when conflicting interests arise. Animals generally disregard the needs of others unless the situation involves their own offspring or they have been trained to behave in a particular way. Why should we expect humans to act any differently? A person who believes that he or she is comprised of more than flesh and blood, who recognizes the divine image within, is more likely to consider the needs of others since they too are created in the image of God.

> "When I was young, I admired clever people. Now that I am old, I admire kind people." (Rabbi Abraham Joshua Heschel)

THE PHILOSOPHY OF KINDNESS

The link between monotheism and morality is powerfully encapsulated in the following rabbinic teaching. According to Jewish tradition, the Ten Commandments Moses brought down from Sinai were engraved on two tablets, each containing five commandments. A further tradition teaches that the first five commandments pertain to our relationship with God and the latter five to our fellow human being. Bearing this in mind, let us turn to the biblical verse which introduces the Ten Commandments: "And God spoke all these words saying."[5] If

God uttered all Ten Commandments, it seems redundant for the verse to emphasize that He "spoke *all* these words." Rashi, the famed medieval French Bible commentator, remarks that the word "all" teaches us "that God spoke the commandments in one utterance, something impossible for a human to do."[6] Is this just a divine magic trick? What is the significance of this synchronized speaking? Rabbi Soloveitchik explained: "We have not ten commandments but one, with ten aspects. The word 'all' in this does not mean all of them, which characterizes a numerical sum total of independent teachings, but rather a totality, an interdependent oneness of all its seeming parts. Faith and morality are integrally one and inseparable."[7]

In other words, the interpersonal commandments are linked to the first set because our belief in and commitment to God is the basis for treating one's fellow human properly. This is the model set forth by Abraham, who promoted both monotheism and ethical conduct. In Judaism, *faith and morality are integrally one and inseparable.*[8]

FROM ACTING TO BECOMING

But Judaism presses us further, urging us to not only *act with kindness* but also to *be kind.* This is reflected in a telling grammatical nuance. The Hebrew term for compassion or mercy is *rachamim,* derived from the Hebrew word *rechem* or womb. (Giving birth is considered one of the greatest acts of compassion in the Jewish tradition.) The term *merachem* is a participle. It therefore places the emphasis on the deed, not the person's nature. In the words of Rabbi Soloveitchik: "[A person] may at times be cold and unfeeling, but he does nonetheless manage to perform many deeds of compassion."[9] By contrast, the word *rachaman,* which derives from the same root as *merachem,* is an adjective that describes a person who feels no choice but to be compassionate. It is not just something they do; it is part of their nature.

"The merciful man benefits his soul, but the cruel person causes harm to himself." (Proverbs 11:17)

Rabbi Soloveitchik explains that through the system of halachah (Jewish law), Judaism directs an individual who is uncertain how to act in the face of human need...to act with compassion and gradually transforms him into a *rachaman* – into a person who spontaneously responds with compassion.[10] The goal of performing acts of kindness is not only to assist others but also to transform ourselves into compassionate, sensitive human beings. This may be helpful to those of us who feel as though it is not in our natures to be thoughtful or kind. Judaism believes that over time, there is a concrete way to not only overcome our inborn natures but even to transform them. The Torah commands us to engage in these acts of kindness on a regular basis so we can change ourselves for the better – to not only act with compassion but also become compassionate.

STOP AND REFLECT:
As long as we *act* kindly, should it really matter whether we also *feel* compassion for others?

KABBALAH CORNER:
A *nekudah tovah*, a point of goodness, exists within everyone and everything. Even if someone has made poor choices his or her entire life, there must be something positive that he or she has done that we can focus on. When we concentrate on this tiny point of goodness, that goodness becomes the person's reality. The same is true for ourselves. (Rabbi Nachman of Breslov)

Biblical Sources for Kindness: Love Your Neighbor Like Yourself

The Torah itself requires us to act with kindness. The best-known relevant passage is "Love your neighbor as yourself."[11]

Maimonides sees this phrase as the biblical source for the Jewish imperative to perform concrete acts of kindness: "It is a positive mitzvah of the Rabbis to visit the sick, to bring comfort to the mourners, to help remove the dead from the home, to help bring the bride to her wedding, to accompany guests into your house, to participate in all aspects of the burial – to carry the casket, walk in honor before it, eulogize the dead, dig the grave, and do the actual burial – and also to bring joy to a bride and groom and to provide them with all their needs. These are physical acts of kindness and there are no limits to what one must do to fill these requirements. Even though these mitzvot are rabbinic in origin, they are included within 'Love your neighbor as yourself.'"[12]

"What is hateful to you, do not do to your fellow. This is the whole Torah; the rest is commentary." (Talmud, Shabbat 31a)

But this raises an obvious problem. Can we really take the phrase "Love your neighbor *as yourself*" literally? Loving others as much as we love ourselves is certainly a wonderful aspiration. But is it really possible to love another person as much as we love ourselves?

Troubled by this question, most commentators on the verse do not take the verse literally. Nachmanides, for example, explains that "Love your neighbor" means that one should not allow oneself to envy another's good fortune, since envy and jealousy result in hatred. Another commentator, Ibn Ezra, suggests that the Torah is instructing that there be no difference between what we want for ourselves and what we wish for our friends, since we are all created by God.

Some medieval scholars[13] resolve the problem differently: "Love your neighbor" means placing yourself in your friend's shoes. In thinking of a friend who is ill, for example, one should ask: If I were in that situation, what blessing would I seek from God? One should then pray that the friend receive that blessing. Yet another commentator[14] proposes that "Love your neighbor" means that one must consider not only the sensitivities of the average person but also the unique sensibilities of each unique individual.

KABBALAH CORNER:
Just as we tend to focus more on our own good qualities than on our faults, so too should we do the same with others. Each of us has many strengths and virtues, as well as areas for improvement. Loving our fellow Jews as we love ourselves does not require us to generate false feelings. Instead, it calls us to shift our focus away from their weaknesses and mistakes and instead emphasize what they are doing right. (Rabbi Mordechai Leiner, the Izhbicer Rebbe)

Rabbi David ben Zimra, who served as chief rabbi of Cairo in the sixteenth century, compares the Jewish community to the body of a single individual: Just as you would never think of deliberately injuring yourself or neglecting a limb of your own body, "Love your neighbor as yourself" commands every Jew to seek the welfare of all members of their people. If we truly saw each other as different organs of the same body, we would be more careful to treat each other with love.

Yet at least one scholar, Maimonides, interprets the biblical command "Love your neighbor as yourself" literally, claiming that there is a mitzvah to love a fellow Jew to the same degree that one loves oneself. In his opinion, one must therefore protect the honor and possessions of a fellow Jew as if he were protecting his own honor or possessions. But is it really possible to love another person as much as one loves their own self? Empathy is one thing, but Maimonides seems to have gone too far.

LOVING THE SPARK WITHIN

Rabbi Richard Mann, one of my esteemed teachers, suggests that to answer this problem, we must address one further question. When the Bible commands us to "love your neighbor" *as yourself*, it assumes that we must love ourselves before we can love someone else. What aspect of ourselves does the Torah ask us to love? The way we look or appear to others? The amount of money we earn? These seem unlikely. But the Torah actually hints to the answer at the end of the verse: "I am the Lord."[15] *I am the Lord* suggests that the part of ourselves the Torah wants us to love is the Godliness within. If we can cultivate an appreciation for and ultimately a love of our spiritual dimension – our own soul – we can also learn to appreciate the spirituality within our friend. Loving your neighbor becomes more realistic when we have learned to love the divine image within.[16]

It is therefore critical to focus on the soul as the essence of a human being. When we view the body as primary, it makes it more difficult to truly love another person. The body and other material dimensions – our cultural backgrounds, our interests, our tastes – separate us from one another. The soul, on the other hand, unites us. Rabbi Shneur Zalman of Liadi writes that since all souls "have one father,"[17] the entire Jewish people are called brothers "due to their [single] source of their souls in the One God."[18] The secret behind "loving your neighbor *like yourself*" is seeing beyond the body to the soul.

IMITATIO DEI

The Sages also point to a less well-known biblical source for kindness. The verse "After the Lord, your God, shall you walk"[19] is explained by the Talmud as follows: "Rabbi Chama son of Rabbi Chanina asks: Is it then possible for a human being to walk after the Shechinah (the Divine Presence)? For has it not been said, 'For the Lord, your God, is a devouring fire'? But the meaning is to walk after the attributes of the Holy One, blessed be He: As He clothes the naked...so you must clothe the naked; as God visited the sick...so should you visit the sick; as God comforted the mourners...so should you comfort the mourners; as God buried the dead...so should you bury the dead."[20]

This passage teaches us a number of fundamental Jewish values. First, it identifies clothing the naked, visiting the sick, comforting mourners, and burying the dead as virtuous deeds. God Himself models the ideal behavior to which human beings should aspire. Second, this passage expresses a fundamental Jewish ideal, famously referred to in Latin as *imitatio Dei* or imitating God: The more we mimic God's behavior, the more Godly we become.[21] Since holiness is achieved by attaching ourselves to God, carrying out the very actions God performs makes us more holy.

> "Jewish ethics is refreshingly down to earth. If someone is in need, give. If someone is lonely, invite them home. If someone you know has recently been bereaved, visit them and give them comfort. If you know of someone

> who has lost their job, do all you can to help them find another. The sages call this imitating God." (Rabbi Jonathan Sacks)

THE "HOW-TOS" OF KINDNESS

We will now delve into the activities identified by the Talmud as *gemilut chasadim* or acts of kindness.

Visiting the Sick

Bikkur cholim or visiting the sick is a classic act of kindness that Jewish tradition considers an important part of the healing process. For this reason, "Rabbi Acha son of Chanina stated: Anyone who visits the sick removes one-sixtieth of the illness."[22] Visiting the sick improves the psychological and emotional state of the patient, which contributes to their overall well-being. A visitor is similarly advised to convey that the patient is not alone and can count on family and friends to help make it through this difficult time.

There are further purposes to paying a sick call. Drawing on Jewish sources, the nineteenth-century German thinker Rabbi Samson Raphael Hirsch identifies three:[23]

- To ensure everything is being done medically for the sake of the patient.
- To see to it that the patient is being adequately attended to and, if not, help obtain proper nursing care, medication, and the like.
- To pray for the patient.

How should one conduct a *bikkur cholim* visit? In contrast to comforting a mourner at a *shivah* call, where the visitor tries to focus the conversation on the deceased, one who pays a sick call should try to cheer up the patient by distracting them from the illness. This distinction between the role of a visitor at a sick visit and a *shivah* call can be understood on a psychological level: Since the purpose of a sick visit is to help the patient recover, their spirits must be lifted, and so dwelling on the illness is counterproductive. On the other hand, one who has lost a close relative must confront the reality of their loss. They therefore do not benefit from being distracted from the loss. Still, when paying a sick visit, one should not completely ignore the patient's illness, just not dwell upon it.

Provided that the ill person wishes to have visitors, Jewish tradition teaches that relatives and close friends should visit promptly, whereas more distant acquaintances should wait at least three days before visiting. It is important to remember that the purpose of visiting is ultimately to help the sick person. Therefore, one is encouraged to visit often, but never so often or for so long as to become a nuisance. When the visitor senses that the sick person has had enough or is tired, he should excuse himself and leave. In addition, one should pay a visit only at a time that it is helpful or convenient for the patient – not just for the visitor. And if a large group or even one extra person is too much for the patient to handle, one should visit alone.

If a sick person is not well enough to receive visitors, it is appropriate to ask the patient's family whether they need anything – in the words of Rabbi Hirsch, to "listen to their complaints, and, of course, pray on their behalf."[24]

In synagogue we recite a prayer called a *Mi Sheberach,* during which the patient's name is inserted. The *Mi Sheberach* is recited whenever the Torah scroll is read in synagogue: Monday, Thursday, Shabbat, and holidays. After any weekday prayer service, the congregation may recite a psalm on behalf of an ill person or group of people, after which the *Mi Sheberach* is also recited.

STOP AND REFLECT: Do you know anyone who is ill and would appreciate a visit? Are there any local hospitals or nursing homes where you can volunteer to visit patients?

ATTENDING TO THE DEAD

Caring for the dead is considered one of the most precious acts of kindness in the Jewish tradition. Since the person performing the kindness can never expect to receive anything in return from the deceased, this is referred to by the Sages as "kindness of truth."

> "The measure of a person is how they treat others, especially those who can do nothing for them in return." (Rabbi Yisrael Meir Kagan)

The *chevra kaddisha,* also known as a Jewish burial society, is a remarkable example of this "kindness of truth." These volunteers, found in nearly every Jewish community, are responsible for the sacred task of preparing the deceased for burial according to Jewish tradition, also called a *taharah.* Members of the *chevra kaddisha* remove the body from the home and immerse it in the mikveh (a Jewish purification bath), recite special prayers, and place the deceased in a simple shroud. If you're not a member of a synagogue with a *chevra kaddisha,* most Jewish funeral parlors offer one upon request. I would strongly urge you to ask for a *taharah.* Besides being traditional Jewish practice for thousands of years, it is also considered a spiritual merit for the soul, helping the soul in its journey to the next world.

There are other ways to honor the dead, including staying with the deceased until the burial is completed. This is called *shemirah* or guarding. It is imperative that a fellow Jew remain with the body from the time of death until interment. This too can and should be requested from the Jewish funeral parlor. It is also a mitzvah to participate in all aspects of the burial, which include carrying the casket, walking in honor before the casket, eulogizing the dead, digging the grave, and performing the actual burial.

Rabbi Hirsch describes the most appropriate mindset for these activities: "seriousness, calm, modesty, and reverence."[25] It goes without saying that attending a funeral is very important, even if one was not close to the deceased. If you ever question whether to inconvenience yourself by attending a funeral, my advice is always to err on the side of attending. I have never regretted attending a funeral or making a *shivah* visit. "Better to go to a house of mourning than a house of feasting,"[26] declared the wise King Solomon. Years ago, I served as a rabbi for a congregation which had a good number of elderly people. As a result, I officiated many funerals and made many *shivah* calls. One of my friends expressed his sympathies that I had to spend so much time around death and bereavement. I told him that although I felt terribly for all the people who lost loved ones, I found that helping others through these challenging moments had a very positive influence on my own spiritual and emotional development. It kept me grateful for the simple blessings of life, like my health – something we all take for granted. And so, although we engage in these activities primarily to show honor and respect for the dead and offer comfort to the bereaved, the benefit to us is also very real.

COMFORTING THE MOURNER

After the burial, the focus shifts from the deceased to the mourners.[27] Immediately after the deceased is buried, the friends and relatives form two rows though which the mourners pass. As the mourners pass by, the friends and relatives say, "May God comfort you among all the mourners of Zion and Jerusalem," the same blessing those who visit during the week of the *shivah* offer the mourner. The phrase "among all the mourners of Zion and Jerusalem" is meant to convey the sentiment that the mourner is not alone: The Jewish community, which remains in mourning over the Temple's destruction, shares this person's loss. That is ultimately the primary purpose of paying a *shivah* call: to help soften the blow of the mourner's loss by demonstrating that they have not been forgotten.

Comforting the mourner

Jewish tradition instructs that when paying a *shivah* call, the visitor should not initiate conversation but wait until the mourner begins to speak. This allows the mourner to determine whether they want to speak and, if so, when. It may feel slightly awkward at times, but it allows the mourner to control the environment. I will never forget an experience when I was sitting *shivah* following the passing of my beloved mother, of blessed memory. At one point during the *shivah,* about six or seven rabbis all showed up at the same time. For some reason, I didn't feel like talking. The rabbis, well aware of this tradition not to initiate conversation at a *shivah* home, remained quiet. The other visitors in the room took their cue from the rabbis, and so, there we were, about thirty of us sitting in a room in absolute silence. It was a powerful moment. I felt the entire room's warm embrace, even though no one hugged me or said a word. Just silence.

It's been twenty-eight years since that experience, and those few minutes of quiet are what I remember bringing me comfort from the whole week of *shivah.* I recall thinking at the time that while there were no words anyone could share to make me feel better about my mother's passing, simply sitting with my friends, colleagues, and teachers made a real difference. It was their *presence* which brought me comfort, not their words. I try to remember this every time I pay a *shivah* call, and I share this story with those who are nervous about what to say in a *shivah* home. What brings comfort to others is not some kitschy phrase or clever line, but simply being there for a loved one or friend.[28]

> "Comforting a mourner is about presence, not eloquence. It is about the simple act of being there, offering your silent support." (Rabbi Maurice Lamm)

BRINGING JOY TO THE BRIDE AND GROOM

Another *chesed* or act of kindness is the mitzvah to make the bride and groom happy. This includes attending a wedding and dancing before the bride and groom. The Talmud relates that some of the greatest rabbis would dance and juggle before the bride, unafraid to "embarrass" themselves, for they were performing a great mitzvah.[29] The mitzvah to make the bride and groom happy can also be fulfilled by helping to provide the couple with financial support or items they might require for their new home.

The author officiating at a chuppah

What ultimately creates the greatest joy for a bride or groom, or for any person celebrating a happy occasion, is being able to share the event with people they love. I know this from my own wedding, when I was able to share the joy of the event by dancing with my family and close friends, and from having had the great merit of doing so for hundreds of others at their joyous occasions.

"The reward for bringing joy to a bride and groom is immeasurable." (Based on Talmud, Berachot 6b)

HOSPITALITY

Extending hospitality to guests, called *hachnasat orchim*, is also considered a classic act of kindness. This is illustrated in the Torah by Abraham and Sarah, who were known for opening their home to strangers passing by their tent. The Sages teach that after Abraham was circumcised, God purposely caused the weather to become extremely hot to prevent people from walking by Abraham's tent so he would not be bothered by having to entertain guests. Ironically, Abraham's inability to extend hospitality distressed him even more. God therefore sent three strangers who, despite Abraham's compromised state, were graciously received by Abraham and Sarah, who went to great lengths to serve a bountiful meal.

The Sages also point out that Abraham oddly interrupts his conversation with God to attend to the passersby. While we might have thought this disrespectful to God, the talmudic Sage Rav actually draws the opposite conclusion: "Hospitality toward guests is greater than receiving the Divine Presence."[30] When I first heard this teaching, I was confused. How dare Abraham interrupt a discussion with God to attend to a stranger? One of my teachers[31] provided a helpful analogy to explain. Imagine you have been hired as a salesman in a store. On a slow day, seeing that there are no customers, you strike up a conversation with the store owner. As you are both engaged in discussion, the door opens and in walks a customer. Would the store owner be insulted if you interrupted to attend to the new customer? Of course not. That is precisely why the store owner hired you in the first place! In the same manner, since God created us to take care of others, to extend hospitality to those in need, it was more than appropriate for Abraham to interrupt his conversation with the Almighty. "Hospitality toward guests is greater than receiving the Divine Presence."[32]

Abraham and Sarah served their guests from their very best,[33] from which the halachah derives that we too should serve our guests on our best china or the like. This also applies to sleepover guests, for whom we are taught to provide the best accommodations possible. Although it is always wonderful to entertain friends and family, the mitzvah of *hachnasat orchim* refers specifically to hosting those in financial need (who require food and/or shelter), or those otherwise in need of a meal on Shabbat or the festivals.[34] Providing hospitality, be it physical or spiritual, is a hallmark of the Jewish faith and a powerful way of expressing Godliness in the world.

"Let your house be open wide, and let the poor be members of your household." (Mishnah, "Ethics of the Fathers")

CARING FOR THE WIDOW, ORPHAN, AND STRANGER

Although Judaism prohibits treating any person in an abusive manner, the Torah singles out the widow, orphan, and stranger (i.e., a convert to Judaism) for special protection. Perhaps it is because each of these individuals lacks a certain *human* protection – the widow a husband, the orphan a parent, and the stranger a tight-knit community – that the Torah commands us to extend them special care and consideration. As the great Indian leader Mahatma Gandhi is often quoted: "The true measure of any society can be found in how it treats its most vulnerable members."

STOP AND REFLECT: Who do you know who might not feel connected with the Jewish community? What can you do to make them feel more welcome?

PURSUING PEACE

Another important act of kindness is pursuing peace. Peace is one of the foundations upon which the world exists: "God created the world on the condition that there be peace among humanity."[35] If there is no peace, it must be pursued, as King David declared: "Seek peace and pursue it."[36]

Although we tend to think of pursuing peace in context of countries in conflict, this mitzvah includes helping create peace among friends, relatives, or colleagues in a dispute. The biblical character best known for this type of activity was Aaron, the brother of Moses. According to rabbinic tradition, Aaron would find individuals in the Jewish community engaged in some dispute and would inform each one separately that the other wished to reconcile. He did this until both were appeased and the two had resumed their relationship. The Torah records that when he died, "the entire House of Israel wept for Aaron for thirty days."[37] Rashi, the biblical commentator, explains that the Torah says "the *entire* House of Israel" to include men and women, since Aaron would walk throughout the camp promoting love between people in dispute, including between husbands and wives.

> "Hillel said: Be a disciple of Aaron: Love peace and pursue peace, love people and bring them closer to the Torah." (Mishnah, "Ethics of the Fathers")

The last mishnah of the entire Mishnah (a foundational work of the Oral Law) records in the name of R. Shimon ben Chalafta: "God has not found a vessel which can bear blessings other than peace, as the verse states: 'God wishes to give strength to His nation; [therefore] God blesses His people with peace.'"[38] In other words, peace is a vessel which can hold many other blessings. It is a prerequisite for so many of the gifts we seek in life. As the Sages of the Midrash teach: "Peace is so great that all the blessings, good things, and consolation that God brings upon Israel are sealed with peace."[39]

STOP AND REFLECT: Are there any relationships in your life that feel strained or lacking? What is one step you can take to bring more peace into that relationship?

KINDNESS TO ANIMALS

It is a mitzvah to save an animal from pain or distress. Conversely, causing undue harm to an animal is a Torah violation. Hunting for sport is frowned upon in the Jewish tradition since it usually involves cruelty to animals. It goes without saying that animal owners are responsible to properly feed and care for their pets. While it is permissible to take an animal's life for food, the animal must be slaughtered in accordance with the laws of *shechitah*, Jewish ritual slaughter, which minimizes the pain to the animal. In addition, the Torah prohibits muzzling an animal while it is being worked in the field,[40] yoking an ox and donkey to the same plow,[41] or removing the eggs or young of a bird in the presence of its mother.[42]

THE SECRET OF GIVING

There was a Jew named Yankel who owned a bakery in Crown Heights, Brooklyn. Yankel had survived the concentration camps and eventually emigrated to the United States. After he settled in America, someone asked him how he had managed to survive the camps when so many others had perished.

Yankel said he attributed his survival to a particular incident which took place on the train to the camps when he was a teenager. The Nazis would transport Jews to the camps in boxcars. Sometimes they would leave the trains unattended overnight, even for days, without providing food or water. And of course, there were no blankets to keep anyone warm.

Yankel found himself in a boxcar filled with fellow Jews being taken to Auschwitz. Night came and it was freezing cold. The Nazis left the train sitting overnight. Next to Yankel was an older Jew, a beloved gentleman whom Yankel recognized from his hometown. The elderly man was shivering from head to toe, and he looked awful. "So I wrapped my arms around him," Yankel described. "I began to warm him up by rubbing his arms, legs, neck, and face. I begged him all night to stay strong and hang on, telling him it would be better in the morning. Somehow, I kept the old man warm, but I was exhausted and I myself was freezing. My fingers were numb, but I didn't stop rubbing heat into this man's body."

Yankel continued to describe what happened: "The

First transport to Auschwitz, Tarnów, Poland, June 14, 1940

hours dragged on slowly, but finally the night passed and morning came. The sun began to shine, and I felt a little warmth in the boxcar. Some sunlight entered and I looked around. To my utter horror, all I could see were frozen bodies. There was a deathly silence. Nobody in the cabin made it through the night. Only two people survived the night – me and the old man. The old man survived because someone kept him warm, and I survived because I was warming someone else."

> KABBALAH CORNER:
> The Hebrew word for "gave," *natan*, is a palindrome. The structure of this word, which is the same forward and backward, symbolizes that the act of giving is circular – what is given flows back to the giver. This palindrome suggests that in the spiritual realm, the act of giving creates a continuous flow of energy. When we give to others, we also receive, whether in emotional fulfillment, spiritual growth, or divine blessings. By meditating on this word, we can appreciate the deeper truth that giving and receiving are intertwined. (Vilna Gaon)

One of the secrets of Judaism is that when you warm another, you remain warm yourself.

We may think that when we go out of our way to help someone else, we are only benefiting the other person. But we're also doing it for ourselves. The Talmud teaches that *ner le'echad ner leme'ah,* "a candle for one is a candle for a hundred people."[43] When we create light for another person, we bring light to ourselves, transforming the lives of everyone around us.

Who do you know that is in need? Who in your orbit can benefit from the warmth you can provide? The love and embrace you offer others will bring you at least as much love and embrace in return. As the Beatles famously concluded one of their greatest albums: "And in the end, the love you take is equal to the love you make."[44]

A SUBLIME VISION

The Jewish people are characterized as a nation consisting of kindhearted individuals: "Three characteristics does this

[Jewish] people possess – they are merciful, modest, and perform deeds of kindness."[45] These qualifications are taken so seriously that Maimonides declares that although Jewish people generally possess an inherent presumption of being Jewish, if one sees someone constantly quarreling with others, or a person is particularly haughty or cruel "and do[es] not perform acts of loving-kindness," we are suspicious of that person's Jewish lineage.[46] *Chesed* is so deeply embedded in Jewish tradition and within the Jewish psyche that if someone is lacking in sensitivity and kindness, their Jewish status could, at least metaphorically speaking, be called into question!

Allow me to conclude our discussion on kindness with Rabbi Samson Raphael Hirsch's magnificent call to action: "If you want to see man as the true image of his Father in heaven, you must behold him as he, filled with pity, with love, with divine spirit, makes bread for the hungry, takes care, as a father, of the infant's well-being and education, nurses the sick, clothes the naked, comforts the suffering, buries the dead, advises the inexperienced, reconciles those at variance, and everywhere strives, by word and deed, to allay suffering, to heal the injured heart, and to dry the flowing tears. And, when roused by such sublime vision, you feel that you are called to the same divine task, then come forward, young man, come forward, young maiden, and, in the sight of God, dedicate yourself, with all that noble, beautiful strength with which He has endowed you, to such work of love for the salvation of His children."[47]

> "Kindness is the language that the deaf can hear and the blind can see." (Rabbi Adin Steinsaltz)

CHARITY

Although there is a tendency to view all good deeds we do for others, particularly for the less fortunate, as kindness or charity, Jewish tradition defines these two terms differently. An act of kindness (*chesed*) refers specifically to activities we perform with the body, whereas charity (*tzedakah*) involves giving money or material items to people or institutions in need. The Talmud[48] tells us that acts of kindness are considered superior to charity in three respects. *Tzedakah* is accomplished with one's money, *chesed* through money and other actions. *Tzedakah* is performed for the poor, *chesed* for the poor and the wealthy. *Tzedakah* is only for the living, *chesed* for the living and the dead. Nevertheless, providing financial support to poor people or worthy organizations is a great mitzvah and a tremendously important part of Jewish life. Little wonder that the Torah declares *tzedakah* greater than all the sacrificial offerings[49] and the means through which the messianic redemption will be ushered in.[50]

Giving tzedakah

Jewish tradition mandates that *every* person is required to give *tzedakah*. That is why I have never been a fan of the term "philanthropist," which implies that this mitzvah is only for the rich. Being a giver is a quality Judaism wants all people to cultivate, whether we are rich or poor or somewhere in between. Jewish law even obligates someone who is a recipient of *tzedakah* to give, even if only a little. Jewish tradition considers that small amount as worthy as larger donations made by the wealthy.[51] Nonetheless, if a person has barely enough to sustain himself, he is exempt from this mitzvah, since taking care of oneself takes precedence over

STOP AND REFLECT: Would you like to give more charity in the coming year? What would help you dig a little deeper so you can give more?

tending to the needs of others. Following the many references in the Torah to tithing one's crops for the poor and to supporting the Temple in Jerusalem,[52] it is common practice to donate a minimum of one-tenth of one's annual earnings (after taxes).

There are two main sources in the Torah for the mitzvah of *tzedakah*, one from the book of Deuteronomy that teaches us priorities in giving, and the other from the book of Leviticus addressing the issue of sensitivity.

PRIORITIES IN GIVING

One of the difficult questions we confront concerns how to prioritize our *tzedakah*. There are so many legitimate needs and only so much money to go around. While the Rabbis do not provide instructions for where to allocate every dollar, one of the Torah's primary sources for the mitzvah to give *tzedakah* addresses this question: "If, however, there is a needy person among you, one of your kin in any of your settlements in the land that your God is giving you, do not harden your heart and shut your hand against your needy kin. Rather, you must open your hand and lend whatever is sufficient to meet the need" (Deut. 15:7–8).

The Talmud explains that this verse helps us prioritize our giving. The opening clause – "If, however, there is a needy person among you" – teaches that the neediest take preference over others,[53] and the phrase "In any of your settlements" implies that the poor of your own city take precedence over the poor of another.[54] The final phrase – "And lend whatever is sufficient to meet the need" – informs us that if the poor person does not want to accept a gift, one should offer the money as a non-interest loan. Lending someone money, although not considered *tzedakah*, is also considered a mitzvah.

KABBALAH CORNER: All beginnings are difficult because they require us to break through barriers. However, *tzedakah* helps us widen the opening. Therefore, one who wants to succeed in something challenging should first give *tzedakah* to create a wider path ahead. (Rabbi Nachman of Breslov)

GIVING WITH SENSITIVITY

A verse in Leviticus underscores the importance of giving *tzedakah* with sensitivity: "And if your brother becomes destitute and his hand falls among you, you shall strengthen him" (Lev. 25:35).

STOP AND REFLECT:
If you had to prioritize one charity in the coming year, what would it be and why?

The language "You shall strengthen him" seems out of place. If the Torah is simply commanding us to donate to someone who is poor, why not just say, "You shall contribute" or "You should give your destitute brother money"? Rashi suggests that the language "You shall strengthen him" is meant to encourage people of means to lend a fellow Jew a helping hand before it is too late. He compares the situation to a donkey carrying a heavy load which causes the donkey to waver: As long as the burden remains on the donkey, one person alone can prevent the donkey from falling. But once the donkey falls to the ground, not even the strength of five people can lift it up. The Torah therefore uses the language of "strengthen him" to encourage others to be supportive as soon as they see their fellow beginning to falter.

Unfortunately, as we see in society today, some people require significant assistance to get back on their feet precisely because no one noticed when they were beginning to waver, when just one person's helping hand could have made all the difference. The Torah is teaching us to be closely attentive to one another, to take notice when someone starts experiencing financial challenge – for example, if they lose their job or fall into debt. That is precisely why the Torah's command "You shall strengthen him" is so urgent: donating money or providing an interest-free loan at a critical juncture can make all the difference.

STOP AND REFLECT:
Is there anyone you know or sense is struggling financially? What can you do to sensitively help get them back on their feet?

There is a well-known story involving the great scholar and community leader Rabbi Chaim Soloveitchik, who, before the holiday of Passover, was approached by a pious Jew with a strange question: "Reb Chaim, is it permissible for one to use milk instead of wine for the four cups at the Seder?" Reb Chaim told the man that milk would not suffice, that he would need to use wine. And then the rabbi gave him a handful of rubles, a relatively large sum of money. The man thanked Reb Chaim profusely and left. Reb Chaim's apprentice, who witnessed the exchange, asked his teacher why he gave the man so much money, to which Reb Chaim answered: "If someone so pious asks if he can use milk instead of wine for the Seder, he probably doesn't have enough money for the meal either. So I gave him enough money to buy fish, chicken, and whatever else he and his family need to enjoy a festive Passover meal."[55]

That is what the Torah means when it says "You shall strengthen him": to be cognizant of the needs of others by providing immediate financial support to someone you sense is in need. It also means speaking to the person in a sensitive manner, giving them the emotional encouragement to help them deal with their financial challenges. Maimonides writes that one of the eight levels of giving *tzedakah* is to give gladly and with a smile. Even if one is unable to provide adequate funding to someone in need, offering a word of encouragement and reassurance can go a long way in helping to restore the dignity that has been lost. That too is part of the mitzvah to give *tzedakah*.

> "Give to the poor generously, without a grudging heart. In return, the Lord your God will bless you in all your work and in everything you do." (Deuteronomy 15:10)

LEVELS OF GIVING

Maimonides identifies eight levels of giving *tzedakah*.[56] Here they are in ascending level of virtue:

When donations are given begrudgingly.
When one gives less than one should but does so cheerfully.
When one gives directly to the poor after being asked.

When one gives directly to the poor without being asked.

When the recipient is aware of the donor's identity, but the donor does not know the identity of the recipient.

When the donor is aware to whom the *tzedakah* is being given, but the recipient is unaware of the source.

When both the giver and recipient are unknown to each other. Communal funds distributed by responsible people also fall in this category.

The highest form of *tzedakah* is helping a person *before* they become impoverished by making a substantial donation in a dignified manner, giving a loan, or helping the person find a job, making it unnecessary for the recipient to become dependent on others in the first place.

WHOSE MONEY IS IT ANYWAY?

Rabbi Samson Raphael Hirsch offers a fascinating explanation of *tzedakah,* which helps explain its centrality to Judaism: The relationship we have to our money is not that of an owner but an administrator. The money is not truly ours. As he puts it: "Why should God give you more than you need unless He intended to make you the administrator of this blessing for the benefit of others?" Why else would we have more money than we need, if "not for the benefit of others"?

This explains why the Jewish term for donating money to the poor is *tzedakah* and not charity. The word "charity" is derived from the Latin word *caritas,* meaning "love" or "benevolence." Charity is something kind we do for others when we are moved or inspired to give. It is not obligatory. *Tzedakah,* on the other hand, means "justice," something we must do. As Rav Hirsch puts it: "*Tzedakah* is the justice which gives every creature that which God allots it."

In other words, we give *tzedakah* irrespective of our feelings *since the money was never ours in the first place.* Money is a gift from God for us to administer, and the Torah mandates that we give some to those in need. This is a radically different way to look at our money, which we have always been taught to see as our own. The Torah views our relationship with our material possessions differently. As such, giving to those in need or to worthy institutions is not just a nice thing to do; it is an obligation. It is *tzedakah* – justice.

> "What does God require of you but to do justice, love kindness, and walk humbly with your God." (Micah 6:8)

THE KABBALAH OF KINDNESS

The Baal HaTanya[57] speaks of the special power of kindness and charity based on a statement in the Mishnah which enumerates these commandments among those whose "fruit a person enjoys in this world and whose principal remains intact for the World to Come."[58] What does this mean? Generally speaking, we believe that the true reward for a mitzvah can only be fully appreciated in the next world.[59] Yet there are some mitzvot, including kindness and charity, whose ultimate reward is reserved for the World to Come, but some of the spiritual benefit can also be experienced in our lives right here and now. On a simple psychological level, we feel good and grow personally when we help others in need. On a deeper spiritual level, the Baal HaTanya explains, when we engage in acts of kindness or *tzedakah,* metaphorically we create gaps or holes in the supernal garment that envelops the physical world. Those gaps or holes, which are created by our acts of kindness and charity, allow for some of God's Infinite Light to descend into the physical realm. Our kindness and charity draw down some of the radiance of God's supernal light from beyond this world into our physical realm and ultimately into our lives.[60] This also helps explain why doing for others feels so wonderful: We are experiencing some spiritual reward in this world.

> "The world is built on kindness." (Psalms 89:3)

PUTTING KINDNESS AND CHARITY INTO PRACTICE

Here are a few ways to make a difference:

- Donate to those in need. There are many excellent organizations that collect for the poor, as well as non-profits that raise money for other vital causes.
- Find a soup kitchen where you can serve food to poor people who do not have the means to purchase meals for themselves. In Brooklyn, New York, for example, Masbia is a wonderful kosher Jewish establishment where you can volunteer to prepare meals for the poor. I went with my family to peel potatoes and chop onions, and you can serve the food as well.

Volunteers at a soup kitchen

- Participate in the mitzvah of *bikkur cholim* by visiting the sick and elderly. In virtually all neighborhoods, there are hospitals and nursing homes filled with people who are alone and in need of greater human contact.
- Join your local synagogue's *chevra kaddisha* or burial society, which involves helping prepare the bodies of the deceased for burial, or volunteer to help mourners during their week of *shivah*.

STOP AND REFLECT: Is there a place nearby where you can volunteer? Who can you invite to come along with you?

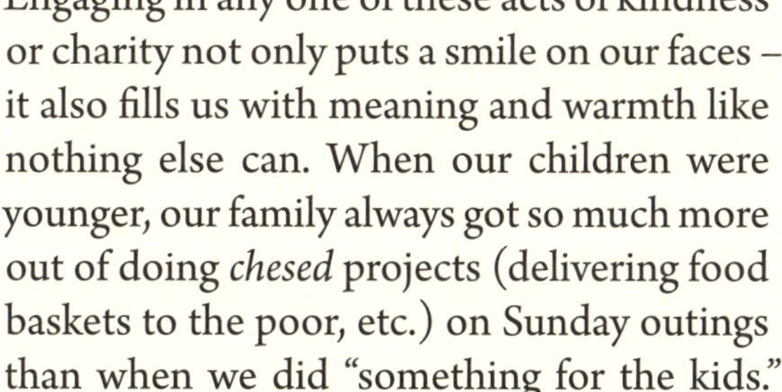

Engaging in any one of these acts of kindness or charity not only puts a smile on our faces – it also fills us with meaning and warmth like nothing else can. When our children were younger, our family always got so much more out of doing *chesed* projects (delivering food baskets to the poor, etc.) on Sunday outings than when we did "something for the kids."

We always returned from those giving experiences so much more fulfilled than after a trip to the zoo or museum.

A PARTING WORD FROM ELVIS

Elvis Presley, I learned, was not just the king of rock and roll but also quite the humanitarian. Upon learning that a young Mexican girl, who had never walked in her life, was in the same hospital ward as someone he was visiting, Elvis sent her gifts, brought her family from Mexico, and paid for their hotel accommodations and for all the little girl's hospital bills. When he learned that a certain Dr. Harry Rosenberg was providing free medical care to people from poor areas, Elvis set up the doctor in his own medical practice, providing him with office equipment and a nurse. He purchased tickets to Disneyland for a small girl dying of leukemia, and he did the same for a poor eighty-seven-year-old man whose lifelong wish was to visit Disneyland. And when you're in Graceland, you can see the many plaques from the fifty local Memphis charities to which Elvis contributed on a regular basis, including the Memphis Jewish Community Center.

At one of his concerts, Elvis strummed his guitar and chanted these beautiful words: "There was a guy who said one time: You never stood in that man's shoes or saw things through his eyes, and watched with helpless hands while the heart inside of you dies. So help your brother along the way, no matter where he starts. For the same God that made you, made him too, these men with broken hearts."

Further Reading

To Heal a Fractured World
Rabbi Jonathan Sacks

Ahavath Chesed: Laws of Charity and Lovingkindness
Chafetz Chaim

The Book of Jewish Values: A Day-by-Day Guide to Ethical Living
Joseph Telushkin

The Jewish Way in Death and Mourning
Rabbi Maurice Lamm

TAKEAWAYS

- Jewish tradition has been a driving force in human rights and civil rights movements, advocating for equality and kindness, principles that originate from the Torah and have helped shape modern democracy.
- The biblical phrase "The world is built on kindness" teaches that in creating the world out of pure love, God set an example of generosity for us to follow.
- Judaism demands that we treat one another with respect since we are all created in the image of God. To "love your neighbor as yourself," we perform acts of kindness such as visiting the sick, comforting mourners, providing hospitality to strangers, bringing joy to the bride and groom, attending to the dead, and pursuing peace – all as a way of expressing the Divine within.
- Giving charity is not just a nice thing but a responsibility. This is why the Hebrew word for charity is *tzedakah*, justice. We are not the true owners of our money but caretakers for God, entrusted to use His blessings to help those in need.
- The way we give *tzedakah* can be as important as how much we give. This is highlighted by Maimonides's eight levels of giving, the highest of which is giving somebody a job so they can have the dignity of being self-sufficient.

Notes

1. In his book *The Hebrew Republic* (Harvard University Press, 2010).
2. Moses Montefiore lived from 1784 to 1885.
3. Psalms 89:3.
4. Genesis Rabbah 8:5.
5. Exodus 20:1.
6. Rashi on Exodus 20:1.
7. Rabbi Soloveitchik, *Reflections of the Rav*, vol. 1, p. 193.
8. Ibid.
9. Ibid., p. 192.
10. Ibid.
11. Leviticus 19:16. For some context, the verse in its entirety reads: "You shall not revenge nor bear a grudge against the children of your people; but you shall love your neighbor as yourself, I am the Lord."
12. Maimonides, *Mishneh Torah*, Laws of Mourning 14:1.
13. This idea is set forward by Chizkuni, a thirteenth-century French scholar, and Sforno, a fifteenth-to-sixteenth-century Italian commentator.
14. This is the interpretation of the Baal HaTurim, a thirteenth-to-fourteenth-century-commentator who also wrote a major code of Jewish law called the *Arbaah Turim*.
15. Leviticus 19:16 reads: "Love your neighbor as yourself, I am God."
16. One qualification of "Love your neighbor," according to some authorities (such as Rashbam), is that this mitzvah only applies to your "neighbor" if he is a good person. However, if he is evil, there is no mitzvah to love him as yourself, as another biblical verse teaches, "Those who fear God hate evil" (Prov. 8:13).
17. Rabbi Shneur Zalman, *The Practical Tanya, Part 1: The Book for Inbetweeners*, p. 362. This phrase is taken from Malachi 2:10.
18. Ibid.
19. Deuteronomy 13:5.
20. Talmud, Sotah 14a.

21. This idea is further conveyed in another biblical verse, "This is my God and I shall glorify Him" (Ex. 15:2). This is explained by the Sage Rabbi Yishmael, who asked: "And is it then possible for a man of flesh and blood to add glory to his Creator?" Another Sage, Abba Shaul, answered: "O, be like Him! Just as He is gracious and merciful, so you also be gracious and merciful."
22. Talmud, Nedarim 39b. One-sixtieth is seen throughout Jewish law as the minimum measure of recognizable significance. For example, Jewish tradition teaches that although meat and milk are prohibited, if less than one-sixtieth of a milk product mixes in with a meat dish, it is permissible to eat. Conversely, if less than one-sixtieth of meat food mixes with a dairy dish, the minority amount is nullified and poses no prohibition of meat and milk. One-sixtieth is thus seen as the minimum measure of recognizability. As such, by saying that visiting an ill person removes one-sixtieth of their illness, the Sages of the Talmud are really saying visiting the ill makes a recognizable difference in the patient's healing process.
23. Rabbi Samson Raphael Hirsch, *Horeb* (Soncino, 1962), p. 432.
24. Ibid, p. 433.
25. Ibid.
26. Ecclesiastes 7:2.
27. Jewish tradition defines mourners as including the husband, wife, father, mother, brother, sister, son, and daughter of the deceased.
28. For more information regarding the *shivah* visit and other related matters of death and bereavement, see Rabbi Maurice Lamm's book *The Jewish Way in Death and Mourning* (Jonathan David, 2000).
29. Talmud, Ketubot 14a.
30. Talmud, Shabbat 127a. When Abraham invited his guests, the Torah tells us: "And he said: 'Lord, if now I have found favor in Your sight, please pass not from Your servant'" (Gen. 18:3). The Sages derive from here that Abraham requested that God, as represented by the Divine Presence, wait for him while he tended to his guests.
31. Rabbi Jonathan Rosenblatt.
32. Talmud, Shabbat 127a.
33. Genesis 18:6–8; Rabbi Yisrael Meir Kagan, *Ahavat Chesed* 3:2.
34. Rema, *Shulchan Aruch, Or HaChayim* 333:1.
35. Midrash, Numbers Rabbah 1:16.
36. Psalms 34:15.
37. Numbers 20:29.
38. Psalms 29:11.
39. Midrash, Leviticus Rabbah 9:9.
40. "You shall not muzzle an ox while it is threshing" (Deut. 25:4).

41. "You shall not plow an ox with a donkey together" (Deut. 22:10). As the language of the verse indicates, this prohibition applies specifically to working the animals together.
42. "Do not take the mother together with her young. Let the mother go" (Deut. 22:6–7).
43. Talmud, Shabbat 122a.
44. "The End," final song on the album *Abbey Road*. Composed by Paul McCartney and credited to Lennon-McCartney.
45. Talmud, Yevamot 79a.
46. Maimonides, *Mishneh Torah,* Laws of Forbidden Sexual Relationships 19:17.
47. Rabbi Hirsch, *Horeb,* p. 432.
48. Talmud, Sukkah 49b.
49. "The doing of righteousness and justice is more preferable to the Lord than the sacrificial offering" (Prov. 21:3).
50. "Zion will be redeemed in justice, and in her returnees with charity" (Is. 1:27).
51. Rabbi Hayim Halevi Donin, *To Be a Jew* (Basic Books, 1991), p. 49.
52. Genesis 14:20, 28:22; Leviticus 27:30; Numbers 18:25; Deuteronomy 14:22; Malachi 3:10; Proverbs 3:9.
53. Rashi, quoting from Midrash, *Sifrei,* Deuteronomy 116:4.
54. Ibid., 116:6.
55. The universally accepted custom of *maot chitim* requires Jewish people to contribute funds to provide for those in need of matzah and other items for the Passover holiday.
56. Maimonides, *Mishneh Torah,* Laws of Gifts to the Poor 10:7–14; Rabbi Donin, *To Be a Jew.*
57. *Tanya, Iggerot HaKodesh,* chapter 3.
58. Mishnah Pe'ah 1:1.
59. According to Jewish tradition, the soul lives on in the World to Come and becomes even more attached to its divine source: God.
60. The Baal HaTanya also teaches that whereas Torah study has the power to draw down God's *shefa* – His endless bounty and light – into the higher worlds of *Beriah* (Creation) and *Yetzirah* (Formation), *chesed* and *tzedakah* are necessary for that light to reach our material world of *Asiyah* (Action).

CHAPTER 5
Shabbat

CHAPTER 5

Shabbat

An Island in Time

It was 6 p.m. on a Friday when a multi-car collision brought traffic grinding to a halt on one of the main roads leading into Jerusalem. Thankfully no one was seriously hurt, but it did not bode well for people's Shabbat plans. The closest community, Geva Binyamin, was half a mile away, and the towns of Psagot and Kochav Yaakov were several kilometers further. And so dozens of Sabbath-observant drivers pulled their cars to the shoulder of the road, grabbed what they could, and started the trek down the road.

As the first wave of travelers arrived in Geva Binyamin, the townspeople were just beginning their Friday night prayers in synagogue. Once the residents understood the situation, they immediately mobilized, sending several runners who swiftly arranged Shabbat meals and places to sleep for stranded families. The same happened in Psagot and Kochav Yaakov. Within an hour, over one hundred families were placed in homes for Shabbat. Remarkably, not one person was left without a place to sleep or eat.

THE MEANING OF SHABBAT

What compels a family to abandon their car with their belongings on the side of the road and spend a weekend with complete strangers? What is it about Shabbat that inspires successful businesspeople to drop the big deal they are about to clinch? What explains the sacrifices and great lengths to which Jews have gone for millennia to observe the day of rest? The answer gets to the heart of the deeper meaning of this holy day.

NOT JUST ANY OLD COMMANDMENT

A cursory review of the Torah and rabbinic literature leads to the overwhelming conclusion that the Sabbath is paramount. Consider:

- Observing the Sabbath is one of the Ten Commandments.[1]
- The Talmud teaches that if every Jew were to observe two Sabbaths, the Messiah would come.[2] Regarding no other mitzvah do the Rabbis make such a suggestion.
- The Kabbalah teaches that "Shabbat is not for the sake of weekdays; the weekdays are for the sake of Shabbat."[3] Or, as Abraham Joshua Heschel puts it: "The Sabbath is the inspirer, the other days the inspired." Shabbat sets the stage for the spirituality of the entire week.
- Only with respect to Shabbat do we use exquisite "descriptions of affection and devotion," even personifying Shabbat as a queen who graces us once a week with her presence.[4]

- More people have found their way back to their Jewish roots through the observance of Shabbat than any other mitzvah. In my own outreach work, I have seen this time and again.

What is it about Shabbat that is so fundamental to being Jewish and so important to have in our lives?

SPIRITUAL SERENITY

The Hebrew Bible makes a bewildering claim. At the end of the creation account, we read: "On the seventh day God completed all of His work."[5] This suggests that God created something on the seventh day. But the Torah also states that God created the world in six days and rested on the seventh. So why does the verse say that God finished His work on the seventh day? It should say He finished on the sixth day!

The Sages answer that God did in fact create something on the seventh day. He created rest.

We generally think of rest as something we refrain from doing. But the Sages teach that the rest God created on Shabbat was a positive act of creation. This is hinted in the very word *Shabbat*. The letters of the Hebrew word *Shabbat* (*shin-bet-tav*) also spell *shevet*, meaning "to sit." The kabbalists teach that all week long there is a tension between the physical and spiritual worlds, but on Shabbat God created harmony between these two realms. The physical and spiritual worlds are able "to sit" together on Shabbat. On the Sabbath, "we cease to struggle with the world, not because the task of perfecting it is on hold, but because on Shabbat, the world is perfect."[6] Through our observance of Shabbat, we are given the opportunity to tap into that perfection and achieve a spiritual state that is unattainable all week long. Many people experience this tranquility on Shabbat. It's hard to explain the feeling. Personally, I find it much deeper than the relaxing feeling I get when I take off from work or go on vacation. It is much more peaceful. Shabbat allows me to connect to myself, my family, my community, and ultimately to God. Shabbat is designed to help us create this kind of space within ourselves to receive God and His blessing.

> "The Sabbath is a sanctuary in time, an island of stillness in the sea of toil." (Rabbi Abraham Joshua Heschel)

TWO TALES OF SHABBAT

The Torah offers two reasons for the command to observe Shabbat, the first expected, the second unexpected.

In the first presentation of the Ten Commandments, which appears in the book of Exodus, the Torah teaches that the purpose of Shabbat is to help us remember creation: "For in six days God made heaven and earth, the sea and all that is in them and rested on the seventh day. Therefore God blessed the Sabbath day, and sanctified it."[7]

This makes good sense, as the verse itself indicates: Just as God rested on the seventh day of creation, so do we. But in Moses's summary of the Ten Commandments in the book of Deuteronomy, another explanation appears: "And remember that you were a slave in the land of Egypt and the Lord your God brought you out from there with a mighty hand and an outstretched arm. Therefore, did the Lord your God command you to observe the Sabbath."[8]

According to this verse, the purpose of Shabbat is to remember the Jews' freedom from Egyptian slavery. This seems strange. What does our emancipation from slavery at the hands of the ancient Egyptians have to do with observing Shabbat?

WHO IS RUNNING THE SHOW?

The great Spanish commentator Nachmanides explains that by freeing the Jews from slavery, God revealed that He not only created the world but continues to remain engaged.[9] Unlike the watchmaker, who makes the watch and then leaves it to run on its own, God remains actively involved in creation. By observing Shabbat, we thus acknowledge that God is not a distant observer but a living ruler who guides the universe, continually maintaining the world by remaining actively involved in its unfolding.[10]

The idea that God's involvement in His world is ongoing is also fundamental to Jewish mysticism. The kabbalists teach that if God were to remove His attention from His creation for even a moment, the world would revert to primordial nothingness.[11] We express this in a prayer we recite each day: "God in His goodness renews every day, continually, the work of creation."[12]

This recognition has never been more important. Most people in the West still believe in God. But as technology advances and we control more and more of our environment, we are increasingly likely to overlook God's vital role in the world. Our success at subduing nature under our domination can easily cause us to forget that we are creatures ourselves. Shabbat reminds us that the very power we wield in our conquest of nature is derived from our Creator, that God remains in charge even as we ourselves play God the rest of the week.[13]

STOP AND REFLECT: Have you ever felt humbled by a stunning mountaintop view or sunset? What made it a spiritual experience?

This is the deeper reason we cease to "work" on Shabbat. By refraining from engaging in certain activities, we "return" the world to God, reminding ourselves that even when we disengage, the world continues to go on. We thus affirm that God not only created the world but remains involved in human affairs, continually pouring His spiritual energy into the universe.

CREATIVE GENIUS

How does refraining from work once a week demonstrate any of this? Because what we refrain from on Shabbat is not simply "going to work." What we refrain from on Shabbat are *creative* activities, specifically thirty-nine activities that were necessary for the construction of the ancient Tabernacle.[14] The Hebrew word for these activities is *melachah,* usually translated simply as "work" but which actually refers specifically to productive and creative work. As Rabbi Dayan Grunfeld explains,[15] each of the thirty-nine categories of work represents another way we exercise mastery over the world using intelligence and skill. Through activities such as plowing, sowing, shearing, baking, building, and creating a fire, along with the other forbidden Sabbath labors, we assert our creative genius over the environment. In keeping with God's command to Adam to "conquer" the world[16] and harness the forces of nature to make the world a better place, we spend six days of the week – really most of our lives – engaged in these creative activities. But one day a week we are commanded to stop, to pull back, to stop asserting control – to surrender.

KABBALAH CORNER: In Kabbalah, Shabbat is connected to the *Sefirah* of *Malchut* (Kingdom), the lowest of the ten divine emanations. *Malchut* is defined by having "nothing of its own," entirely dependent on the six *Sefirot* above it for energy, much like Shabbat depends on the six preceding days. This reflects the humility and surrender we experience on Shabbat, when we stop our labor and recognize that all blessings flow from God. (Zohar)

THE DOCTOR IN HEAVEN

There's an old joke about someone who dies, goes to heaven, and sees a man with a long white coat and stethoscope walking around with a clipboard. The man turns to one of the angels and asks: "Who is that guy with the long white coat, stethoscope, and clipboard?" To which the angel responds: "Oh, that's God. Sometimes He thinks He's a doctor."

With all the wonderful breakthroughs in medicine, science, and technology, and with God's presence so hidden in our world,[17] it is easy to forget God and the essential role He plays in our lives. Ceasing from manipulating and controlling our environment is meant to humble us and prevent us from thinking of ourselves as gods. As technology becomes ever more sophisticated and we control more of our world, we are apt to forget that the very powers we use in our conquest of nature are derived from our Creator. Dayan Grunfeld sums it up well: "We cease from every act of human power in order to proclaim God as the source of all power."[18] Every time we refrain from creative work on the Sabbath, it is a positive expression of our belief in a God who is both Creator and sustainer of the universe.[19]

> "Shabbat is the day we stand still and let all our blessings catch up with us." (Rabbi Jonathan Sacks)

WHAT'S WITH CARRYING?

There is one category of forbidden labor, though, that does not seem to fit this paradigm. Each of the *melachah* activities effects some change in the environment or in the object itself. Plowing, for example, involves turning over topsoil so it can become suitable for seeding. "Cooking" transforms raw food into edible food. The same goes for the rest of the forbidden Shabbat activities. But there is one *melachah* which seems to involve no change at all: "Carrying" prohibits transporting an object in the public sphere or carrying an item from the private to public domain or vice versa. Why is this forbidden on Shabbat? Carrying changes nothing in the object or in our environment! Dayan Grunfeld suggests that carrying represents our activity in the social realm. Carrying is how we conduct business, transferring items from one place in society to the next. "By ceasing from each of the other *melachot*," he explains, "we proclaim God as the source of our power over nature. By ceasing from 'carrying' we acknowledge Him our Master in the sphere of human society."[20] On Shabbat, we relinquish mastery over not only the natural world but even over our ability to control human affairs.

A PERSONAL REFLECTION

Ceasing from creative activities is also why I find Shabbat so deeply relaxing. Knowing that I am prevented from being creatively productive makes me feel free. No matter what is going on in my life, or how much work needs to get done, it will simply have to wait until after Shabbat. Because I so highly value productivity, Shabbat – which teaches us the spiritual value of surrender – is a much-needed drug particularly for ambitious and supermotivated people like me.

STOP AND REFLECT: We live in a world that rewards productivity. What are the pitfalls of being highly productive? What spiritual value do you see in surrendering productivity to God once a week?

DISCONNECT TO RECONNECT

Today, we need Shabbat for another urgent reason: The sheer volume of technology flooding us day and night demands a technology detox. If we want to properly appreciate the blessings and special people in our lives, Shabbat is essential.

Author and radio host Marianne Williamson tells the story of how she was once sitting in her home at her computer answering some emails. Beside her sat her eight-year-old daughter playing a video game on a computer. In the background, some music was playing and a movie was showing on the TV. In short, there was lots of stimulation! Meanwhile, a thunderstorm was raging outside. Suddenly, everything went black. The electricity in Marianne's home went out as a blackout descended on their Detroit suburb. Their desktops shut down, as did the music and TV and, of course, the lights.

STOP AND REFLECT: Is your Shabbat currently unplugged in any way? What can you do to "disconnect to reconnect"?

At first, Marianne's daughter became frightened until they found

Reconnection

some candles and lit them. There was nothing else to do, so they began to talk. Five minutes, ten minutes, twenty minutes flew by as mother and daughter chatted by the small candle that provided a little light. Then, just as quickly as everything had shut down, everything went back on. The lights, computers, music, and TV all roared to life as the electricity was restored. Marianne got back to her emails and her daughter resumed her video-game playing as if nothing had happened. About five minutes later, Marianne's daughter turned to her mother and asked: "Mommy, do you think we'll ever get that chance again?" "What chance?" her mother asked. "The chance to talk like that," answered her daughter. "I don't remember ever speaking with you like that. There's always something else going on."

> "The family that celebrates Shabbat together, stays together." (Rabbi Shlomo Riskin)

An eight-year-old felt the special bond that was forged in those few minutes. The little girl could feel the difference between a conversation with distractions and one where there was perfect focus. We all know when we're really connecting with someone and how challenging it is to bond with others when we are competing with technology. We live in such a distracting world. And that is why Shabbat is so imperative today. It is a kind of self-imposed blackout to ensure that we truly connect with each other, our community, and our spiritual Source. That is why, of all the Torah's observances which I have found young people attracted to today, hands down – it's the Sabbath that wins. Hence the new "unplugged weekend retreats" that have become so popular. These digital detoxing weekends, which first became popular in the United States and then found their way to Europe and Australia, stress mindfulness and begin by having everyone drop their smartphones into a black trunk. People understand that technology, while an indispensable tool for virtually every profession, is also keeping us from deepening our relationships and finding more happiness and meaning.

THE "HOW-TOS" OF SHABBAT

The prohibitions of Shabbat, then, are essential. By keeping them, we create a space in time that ensures we remember our Creator – that we don't become arrogant as we discharge the divine commandment "to conquer" and make the world a better place. Shabbat helps us sanctify time and enables us to stay connected to the people who matter most in our lives. But Shabbat is not just about what we *don't* do, because it's not enough to simply create a vacuum in time. Instead, Judaism calls on us to make Shabbat extraordinary by filling that empty space with the special activities and positive mitzvot of the day. These transform Shabbat from a day of serenity to a day when we can reach spiritual heights. What follows is an overview of those commandments and traditions with which we are charged to "fill" the Shabbat.

WEEKLY PREPARATIONS

Shabbat comes whether we prepare for it or not. But to be transformed by the unique spiritual nature of the day, we need to make a mental shift in order to successfully transition to Shabbat. Our ability to successfully make that mental shift largely depends on the preparations we complete in advance of Shabbat. The term *kevod Shabbat* or the "honor of Shabbat" refers to the activities we perform *before* Shabbat so we can enter the day prepared. These activities include shopping and cooking, bathing, washing, cleaning one's home, dressing in fine clothing, and preparing the table for Shabbat dinner.

STOP AND REFLECT: Which task do you enjoy most when preparing for Shabbat? If you don't currently observe Shabbat, which pre-Shabbat activity do you think you would enjoy most?

Although these tasks may seem mundane, when done to prepare for Shabbat they become quite meaningful. Imagine that the president of the United States is expected at your home for dinner. But when the president arrives at the door, you ask him to wait a few minutes so you can tidy up and prepare something to eat. That would represent a serious lack of respect to any guest, let alone the president! The Jewish Sages teach that God, the King of kings, enters our home every Shabbat. To show proper respect, we prepare before the honored guest arrives.

Preparing our bodies, homes, and minds in advance of Shabbat demonstrates our desire and longing for the Shabbat while helping us appreciate it when the day arrives. We are always more likely to appreciate something for which we have prepared. As Rabbi Soloveitchik remarked: "There can be no holiness without preparation."[21]

> "Preparing for Shabbat infuses our entire week with the radiant glow of divine light." (Zohar)

FRIDAY NIGHT

Now that we have completed our preparations, we are ready to start Shabbat. To do that, first we need to know when Shabbat gets underway.

WHEN SHABBAT BEGINS AND ENDS

Keeping track of Shabbat times can be a bit confusing at first, so here is a basic orientation. Shabbat begins each Friday evening at sunset. Lots of Jewish calendars list eighteen minutes before sunset as "candle-lighting time" to offer us ample opportunity to complete any last-second preparations for Shabbat. Many also have the practice to light the Shabbat candles before that time. (In Jerusalem, candle-lighting time is actually a full forty minutes before sunset!)

The Talmud teaches that Shabbat ends when three medium-sized stars are visible in the sky.[22] Since this is difficult to quantify – especially when it is cloudy! – rabbis have developed standard times for the conclusion of Shabbat. In America, many have the practice to conclude Shabbat between forty and fifty minutes following sunset. Most synagogue websites have calendars which list the exact times each week for candle lighting, sunset, and the end of Shabbat. If you are not affiliated with a particular synagogue or don't have easy access to a calendar, a great resource to know about is myzmanim.com, which provides easy access to the times for Shabbat, prayers, and more.

SHABBAT CANDLES

In my home growing up, all the cooking, cleaning, and prepping – which mostly happened on Fridays – could be quite stressful. It seemed like no matter how much we tried to prepare in advance, there was never enough time to get everything done. It was often nerve-wracking and stressful. But then came that moment every week as the sun was beginning to set. My mother, of blessed memory, would emerge from the chaos in the kitchen into our dining room to light the Shabbat candles.

I watched as she waved her hands over the lights, covered her eyes, and recited the blessing over the candles. Almost like magic, peace and tranquility descended over her and our entire home. For the next twenty-four hours there was no screaming or yelling, no finger pointing or complaining, just great conversation, good food, singing, praying, and peace. And it all started with the candle lighting.

The Jewish Sages instituted that we light two candles[23] in every Jewish home before Shabbat begins. The Sages offer three reasons for candle lighting:

> **KABBALAH CORNER:**
> Kabbalistic teachings explain that in the hours leading up to Shabbat, the forces of impurity (*kelipot*) intensify, attempting to block the incoming light of Shabbat. As the holiness and spiritual elevation of Shabbat approach, the negative forces make their final effort to create obstacles, which often manifest as stress and chaos in our physical preparations. The Zohar describes this spiritual struggle, emphasizing that the *sitra achra* (force of evil) becomes most active just before Shabbat, trying to disturb the serenity that Shabbat brings. (Rabbi Yisrael Sarug)

to bring *kavod* (honor) to Shabbat, to experience *oneg* (joy) on Shabbat, and to foster *shalom bayit* (peace in our home).

All three reasons connect to the very purpose of Shabbat. We show honor to Shabbat by preparing in advance, as the candles are lit *before* Shabbat to prepare for the special divine guest. We experience joy by having our homes lit up on Shabbat itself, since an illuminated home lifts our spirits – it is the opposite of a dark and dreary environment. And the Sages instituted candle lighting to promote *shalom bayit* or "peace in the home." Rashi, the French medieval scholar, writes that the candles bring about *shalom bayit* because "in a place where there is no light there is no peace, since one walks and stumbles, as he walks in darkness."[24] On the literal level, light prevents us from stumbling, but on the metaphorical level it also reflects what we have said about the purpose of Shabbat: to recognize God's hand in directing the world. Life may seem random, lacking purpose or a guiding force; it may feel like we are stumbling in the dark. On Shabbat we exit this state of confusion and uncertainty. We light the candles to dispel the darkness so we can see the world as it truly is: a divine creation guided by a caring Creator. Attaining this awareness brings *shalom bayit* – peace to our home and ultimately to our lives.

> "A single flame of the Shabbat candles can dispel the darkness of the entire week." (Rabbi Shlomo Wolbe)

The power of Shabbat candles is illustrated by a touching story. Inspired by the Lubavitcher Rebbe's message to bring Judaism to all Jews no matter where they live, a certain Rabbi Berkowitz and his friend traveled to some of the remote parts of Alaska in search of Jews. One day they arrived in a small town in northwest Alaska. The mayor told the rabbi and his friend that there were no Jews in the town but invited them to give a talk at the local elementary school about Judaism. The two men addressed the fourth- through eighth-grade students and shared some basic Jewish teachings. The students performed a few Eskimo dances for them, and the rabbi and his friend performed a chasidic dance in turn. Before they left the hall, figuring he had nothing to lose, Rabbi Berkowitz asked the students one final question: "Has any of you ever met a Jew?" One little girl raised her hand. "Who did you met?" asked the rabbi. "My mother," the girl answered. "She's right there," pointing to the school's fifth-grade teacher.

After the assembly, the mother, who was visibly moved by the presentation, came over to thank the rabbi for coming. She explained how she loved nature and moved to Alaska many years earlier, fell in love with a Native American, and together they had this little girl. She said to Rabbi Berkowitz: "I must tell you that living here, I don't know if my daughter will ever meet another Jew again, let alone a rabbi. Can you give my daughter a message so that she will always be proud of her Jewish identity?"

The rabbi began to speak to the girl about the holiness of Shabbat. He told her that it is the Jewish mothers and daughters who usher in the Shabbat every week by lighting the candles. "They are the ones to bring peace and light into the world," he said.

And then the rabbi asked the girl: "Do you know where in the world the sun sets first?" The young girl knew her geography and confidently answered: "Probably New Zealand or Australia." "That's right," said the Rabbi. "Jewish mothers in New Zealand and Australia are first to usher in Shabbat every week. And then Shabbat is ushered in with candles in Asia, then in Israel and in Europe, and then New York, Chicago, Seattle, Anchorage. And even then, there is still one part of the world where the sun has not yet set, where Shabbat has not yet been ushered in: right here in the Yupik territory of Alaska where you live. And so, when mothers and daughters around the globe have welcomed the Shabbat, God and the Jewish people are still waiting for you, the last Jewish girl in the world, to light the Shabbat candles."

Here are practical guidelines for lighting Shabbat candles. Although blessings are usually said before one performs a mitzvah,[25] the Shabbat candles are first kindled. Only afterward is the following blessing recited:

בָּרוּךְ אַתָּה ה׳ אֱ־לֹהֵינוּ מֶלֶךְ הָעוֹלָם, אֲשֶׁר קִדְּשָׁנוּ
בְּמִצְוֹתָיו וְצִוָּנוּ לְהַדְלִיק נֵר שֶׁל שַׁבָּת.

Baruch Attah Ado-nai, Elo-heinu Melech HaOlam,
asher kiddeshanu bemitzvotav vetzivanu lehadlik
ner shel Shabbat.

Blessed are You O God, King of the Universe,
who sanctified us with His commandments and
commanded us to kindle the Shabbat lights.

The blessing is said only after lighting the candles because the blessing ushers in Shabbat, after which "work," which includes kindling a flame, is no longer permitted. However, to remain true to the rabbinic principle of reciting blessings before performing the mitzvah, it is traditional to close one's eyes when saying the blessing. (Most cover their eyes with their hands.) Only after the blessing has been said, we open our eyes to enjoy the light of the candles. In this way, the blessing precedes the mitzvah, which is expressed in the benefit we receive from the light.

The mitzvah to benefit from the light explains two other important details in regard to Shabbat candle lighting. First, the candles should be placed where you will be able to benefit from the light, such as in the dining room or wherever one will be eating Shabbat dinner. Second, since we no longer illuminate our homes with candles, some contemporary rabbinic authorities suggest turning off the electric lights in a room where the candles will be kindled and then turning those lights back on for the sake of Shabbat.[26] That way the blessing is recited not only over the candles but also upon the electric light, which is what technically illuminates our homes today.

STOP AND REFLECT: Candle lighting is one of the most well-observed Shabbat practices. What do you think about when you light the candles?

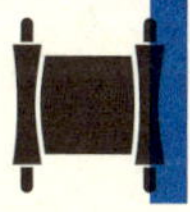

Once Shabbat has begun, it is customary to wish one's fellow Jew either *Shabbat Shalom* or *Good Shabbos*!

FRIDAY NIGHT SERVICES

The Friday night prayer service is referred to as *Kabbalat Shabbat* or the welcoming of Shabbat. This relatively brief prayer service was created by the Jewish mystics of Tzfat, Israel, in the sixteenth century who, dressed in white, would go out to the fields to welcome the incoming Shabbat as an honored guest. These rabbis were building on a much older practice from some one thousand years earlier, when the Jewish Sages would don their finest clothing and say to one another: "Let us go out to welcome the Sabbath Queen."[27]

The *Kabbalat Shabbat* service consists of six psalms[28] capped off by the well-known song *Lecha Dodi* (*Koren Shalem Siddur*, p. 310). Some suggest that each of the six psalms corresponds to another day of the workweek, and *Lecha Dodi* is an ode to Shabbat itself. In this way, we are given the opportunity to briefly reflect on each day of our past week, culminating in a celebration of Shabbat. For the last stanza of the *Lecha Dodi*, the congregation turns

STOP AND REFLECT: Friday night *Kabbalat Shabbat* services can be very inspiring. Given the importance of sharing Judaism with others, which of your friends or colleagues could you invite to one?

KABBALAH CORNER: Kabbalah teaches that everything in life is a result of either an "Awakening from Above" or an "Awakening from Below." This means that God takes the first step, sending us inspiration or spiritual energy "from above." God waits for us to channel that inspiration and create our own spiritual awakening "from below." This in turn inspires God to give us even more – so that we continually inspire each other to give and awaken the other through our receiving. In the *Lecha Dodi* song when we sing to welcome the Shabbat, we respond to the inspiration God sends us during the week by going out to greet the Shabbat Bride, and "awaken" together as a couple. (Rabbi Yosef Yitzchak of Lubavitch)

around to face the back of the synagogue to welcome the Shabbat Queen. This is done because, at this moment, the holiness of Shabbat enters, along with the "additional soul" which the kabbalists teach enables us to appreciate the unique spirituality of the day. After *Lecha Dodi*, psalm 92: *A Song for the Sabbath Day* – the psalm recited by the Levites in the ancient Temple on Shabbat – is then recited.

It has become popular in many synagogues, including my own, to sing many uplifting and soulful melodies for the *Kabbalat Shabbat* service. It is important to note that although it would be hard to create that same kind of energy and inspiration in one's home, the *Kabbalat Shabbat* service may be recited alone at home. The same holds true for the majority of the Maariv or evening service which follows *Kabbalat Shabbat*.

Maariv consists of the *Shema* and its surrounding blessings, and culminates in the Silent Devotion or the *Amidah* (*Koren Shalem Siddur*, p. 334). Just like all the other *Amidah* prayers recited during the week, the opening section of the *Amidah* for Maariv consists of three blessings of praise and a closing section with three blessings of thanksgiving. However, unlike the *Amidah* recited during the week, which contains a series of requests, the Shabbat *Amidah* for Maariv as well as for the next day's Shacharit (morning) and Minchah (afternoon) services consist of a single blessing revolving around the sanctity of the Sabbath day.

It goes without saying that it is important to locate a synagogue service you find meaningful and uplifting. There is no such thing as a perfect synagogue, of course, but the more the rabbi, congregation, and prayer service resonate with you, the more likely you will attend regularly and be moved by the prayers and synagogue experience.

HOSTING GUESTS FOR SHABBAT MEALS

It is meritorious to invite guests to your home for Shabbat meals. Although it is fun to entertain friends and family, the mitzvah of *hachnasat orchim* or providing hospitality to guests refers specifically to hosting those in financial need or who don't have a meal to attend on Shabbat and festivals.[29] Providing hospitality to those in need, be it physical or spiritual, is a hallmark of Judaism and a beautiful way to enhance the Shabbat experience by sharing it with others. For more information on this mitzvah, see pages 180–181 of the "Kindness and Charity" chapter in this book.

STOP AND REFLECT: Do you know anyone who has never experienced Shabbat, or who is alone, that you could invite for a meal?

THE SHABBAT TABLE

Back in high school I could not find an empty seat in a certain classroom, so I sat on the edge of a table in the back of the room. When our teacher, a rabbi, walked in and saw me sitting on the table, I could see he was not happy. "Mark," he said, "you shouldn't sit on a table." "Why?" I asked. He then explained the Jewish concept of a table being likened to an altar. The rabbi said that just as the altar in the ancient Temple served as a means of spiritual connection, the food and even the table on which we place the food is a way to use the physical world to connect with the Divine. The Jewish mystics teach that when food is directed toward a higher spiritual purpose and used in a manner the Torah prescribes, we and the food become spiritually elevated and sanctified in the process. This is even more heightened on Shabbat when the very act of eating is considered a mitzvah referred to as *oneg Shabbat* or "rejoicing in the Shabbat." The Shabbat meal thus offers an opportunity to be

The Shabbat table

spiritually connected through the wonderful sounds, tastes, and smells we experience at the Shabbat table.

In addition to the Shabbat candles, the Shabbat table should have two challot or loaves of bread covered by a cloth, and a cup of wine. The two loaves commemorate the double portion of manna that fell from heaven on the sixth day.[30] God commanded the Jews living in the wilderness not to violate the sanctity of Shabbat by going out and collecting the manna on Shabbat, assuring them a double portion on the sixth day. The double portion of challah on our Shabbat table thus symbolizes our own faith that even though we have one day less to earn our livelihood, God will bless us with enough so we can rest on Shabbat.

> "The manna taught that faith in God is not theoretical, but a practical, lived reality." (Rabbi Eliyahu Dessler)

Also, like the two candles, the challah loaves are also said to commemorate the biblical commands "Remember the Sabbath day"[31] and "Guard the Sabbath day to keep it holy."[32]

SHALOM ALEICHEM: "PEACE UNTO YOU"

Shabbat dinner begins with the singing of "Shalom Aleichem", a prayer composed by the kabbalists of the sixteenth and seventeenth centuries (*Koren Shalem Siddur*, p. 374). The song is based on a talmudic tradition[33] that two angels accompany a person home from synagogue on Friday night and when they see the home prepared for Shabbat, they bless the family.

ESHET CHAYIL: "WOMAN OF VALOR"

After singing *Shalom Aleichem*, it is customary to sing "Eshet Chayil" or "Woman of Valor" (*Koren Shalem Siddur*, p. 378). Taken from the biblical book of Proverbs, this stirring poem was written by King Solomon, who describes the ideal woman as both a deeply spiritual person who carries out acts of kindness on behalf of strangers and, at the same time, someone practical-minded who raises her family and takes care of what is needed for her household. Some commentators see the woman in the passage as a metaphor for the Divine Presence or the Shabbat itself, which is personified as a bride. Either way, singing "Eshet Chayil" at Shabbat dinner on Friday night is a poetic way for a husband and children to give thanks to their wife and mother for all she does for her family.

KIDDUSH

We Jews love to eat, so it comes as something of a surprise that we don't start the Shabbat meal with food. Instead, we begin with Kiddush. This is derived from the biblical mandate to "remember the Sabbath day to sanctify it,"[34] which requires a declaration of Shabbat's uniqueness at both the beginning and conclusion of Shabbat. These declarations are our opportunity to express and ultimately feel the uniqueness and holiness of the day. The opening declaration is called the *Kiddush*, and the concluding one *Havdalah* or "Separation."

> "*Kiddush* reminds us that time is a gift from God, and Shabbat is His invitation for us to use that time wisely and spiritually. (Rabbi Yitzchak Berkovits)

The Jewish Sages added the requirement that the *Kiddush* declaration be recited over a cup of wine (or grape juice), a distinguished beverage associated with joy and festivity. Wine may also have been chosen since it helps alter our consciousness: On Shabbat our souls enter a different state of being, one of "inner tranquility"[35] and "spiritual receptivity."[36]

> "The peace of Shabbat penetrates into the depths of the soul, subduing its strivings and reminding the soul of its higher purpose." (Rabbi Samson Raphael Hirsch)

If no wine or grape juice is available, one can even recite the *Kiddush* over the two Shabbat loaves. Using a silver or other decorative cup is also preferable since that also enhances the mitzvah, although any cup that holds a minimum of 3.3 fluid ounces will suffice. It is preferable for one person, usually the head of the household, to recite the *Kiddush* on behalf of all those present, rather than each person saying it for themselves.[37] Only the person reciting the *Kiddush* technically needs to drink (a mouthful) from the wine, but it is customary for all those present to have a taste.

Most have the practice to stand for *Kiddush*, at least during the opening paragraph, which recounts God's creation of the world. The Sages teach that reciting these words is akin to bearing testimony to God as the Creator. Since Jewish law requires witnesses to stand while testifying, we stand for the *Kiddush* or at least for that part.

The *Kiddush* contains three parts:

1. *Biblical excerpt on creation:*

(Quietly: There was evening, and there was morning –)

The sixth day.

Then the heavens and the earth were finished,
and all their vast array.

On the seventh day God finished the work that
He had done,

and on the seventh day He rested from all the
work that He had done.

God blessed the seventh day and sanctified it,

He rested from all His work, from all that God
had created and done.

2. *The blessing over wine*

בָּרוּךְ אַתָּה ה׳ אֱ־לֹהֵינוּ מֶלֶךְ הָעוֹלָם, בּוֹרֵא פְּרִי הַגָּפֶן.

Baruch Attah Ado-nai, Elo-heinu Melech HaOlam,
borei peri hagafen.

Blessed are You, Lord our God, King of the Universe,
who creates the fruit of the vine.

3. Blessing of sanctification

Blessed are You, Lord our God,
King of the Universe,
who has made us holy through
His commandments,
who has favored us,
and in love and favor gave us His holy
Sabbath as a heritage,
a remembrance of the work of creation.
It is the first among the holy days
of assembly,
a remembrance of the Exodus
from Egypt.
For You chose us and sanctified us from
all the peoples,
and in love and favor gave us
Your holy Sabbath as a heritage.
Blessed are You, Lord, who sanctifies
the Sabbath.

The custom is to begin the *Kiddush* by first reciting the last two words of the previous verse in the Torah, namely *yom hashishi* or "the sixth day." The first Hebrew letters of these two words (the letters *yod* and *heh*), taken together with the first two letters of the next verse (*vav* and *heh*), the opening verse of the *Kiddush*, form God's Ineffable Name, otherwise known as the tetragrammaton. Based on this tradition, the great scholar Rabbi Adin Steinsaltz explained that the first part of *Kiddush* speaks of Shabbat from God's transcendent point of view – the divine aspect of Shabbat – whereas the last paragraph of the *Kiddush* expresses the sanctity of Shabbat from the point of view of the Jewish people, highlighting the special relationship between Shabbat and the Jewish people.

BLESSING THE CHILDREN

The Shabbat evening meal continues with the custom to bless one's children, a moving experience for parents and children alike. It is my personal favorite part of the Shabbat meal, and I look forward to it each week. The parents place their hands on top of the child's head and bless their sons to be like the biblical Joseph's two sons Ephraim and Menashe, and their daughters to be like the matriarchs Sarah, Rebecca, Rachel, and Leah. Both declarations are followed by the Priestly Blessing. One of my teachers, Rabbi Shlomo Riskin, suggests that boys are blessed to be like Ephraim and Menashe and not like the patriarchs, because there was always strife between the sons of the patriarchs, whereas Ephraim and Menashe are the first siblings in the Torah between whom there is no rivalry. Others suggest that it is because Ephraim and Menashe were the first children to be raised in exile. Despite their foreign surroundings, they remained true to the traditions of their people, an aspiration we have for our own children. Girls are similarly blessed to be like the matriarchs, who were also raised in spiritually alien surroundings and nonetheless went on to become our people's greatest heroines.

Senator Joseph Lieberman, of blessed memory, in his book on the Sabbath, has this to say about blessing one's children on Shabbat: "It is a priceless moment of connection that no matter what has happened during the week, the parent feels blessed to have that child and asks God's blessing on that son or daughter. As a parent, you know that weeks can go by when you think of your children less as blessings and more as problems to be solved.... Stopping to bless your children once a week makes us pause to appreciate how blessed we are to have them in the first place and reminds them of the love we feel for them."[38]

> "A parent's blessing on Shabbat is a protective shield, surrounding the children with divine grace and mercy." (Rabbi Yosef Yitzchak of Lubavitch)

Blessing for a boy:

May God make you like Ephraim and Menashe.
May the Lord bless you and protect you.
May the Lord make His face shine on you
and be gracious to you.
May the Lord turn His face toward you
and grant you peace.

Blessing for a girl:

May God make you like Sarah, Rebecca, Rachel
and Leah.
May the Lord bless you and protect you.
May the Lord make His face shine on you
and be gracious to you.
May the Lord turn His face toward you
and grant you peace.

WASHING HANDS

After *Kiddush*, everyone washes for the meal using a cup, pouring water over each hand twice. Before the hands are dried, the following blessing is recited:

בָּרוּךְ אַתָּה ה׳ אֱ־לֹהֵינוּ מֶלֶךְ הָעוֹלָם, אֲשֶׁר קִדְּשָׁנוּ
בְּמִצְוֹתָיו וְצִוָּנוּ עַל נְטִילַת יָדָיִם.

Baruch Attah Ado-nai, Elo-heinu Melech HaOlam, asher kiddeshanu bemitzvotav vetzivanu al netilat yadayim.

Blessed are You, Lord our God, King of the Universe,

who has made us holy through His commandments,
and has commanded us about washing hands.

We do not interrupt between washing our hands and eating bread.

What is the significance of the hand-washing tradition? In the days of the Temple in Jerusalem, the Jewish priests or *kohanim* ate what was called *terumah,* the tithed crops donated by fellow Jews. The *terumah* was considered pure and holy, as it represented the people's support for the priests and the Temple service. The Sages therefore required the priests to eat the *terumah* only after they had washed their hands. Although our priests today no longer consume *terumah,* we continue this tradition of hand washing before starting a meal with bread[39] because *terumah* represents the uniquely Jewish attitude toward food, which continues to this very day. Food does not merely provide us with nourishment. It is also necessary for leading a spiritual life. The Kabbalah teaches that when we prepare and consume food in the precise manner the Torah instructs, both we and the food are spiritually elevated and sanctified. Washing our hands before breaking bread as we start our meal reminds us that we eat not simply to survive but as a means for greater divine connection. Since the food possesses this potential for holiness, we wash our hands, as did the priests before eating their sanctified food.

BREAKING BREAD

After everyone has washed their hands, one person uncovers the two loaves of bread[40] called challot and recites the following blessing on behalf of everyone seated:

בָּרוּךְ אַתָּה ה׳ אֱ־לֹהֵינוּ מֶלֶךְ הָעוֹלָם, הַמּוֹצִיא לֶחֶם מִן הָאָרֶץ.

Baruch Attah Ado-nai, Elo-heinu Melech HaOlam,
hamotzi lechem min ha'aretz.

Blessed are You, Lord our God, King of the
Universe, who brings forth bread from the earth.

Whoever recites the blessing over the bread should then cut himself a piece and distribute a piece to each person at the table.

With that, the meal begins!

KABBALAH CORNER: Sharing bread in unity at the Shabbat table fosters peace. The word *shalom* (peace) comes from *shalem* (wholeness), reminding us that true peace is found in tranquility and completeness.

TABLE TORAH AND DISCUSSION

It is customary for someone at the table to share some words of Torah, either about the weekly Torah portion that is read that Shabbat, or anything else they find interesting to discuss. At my family's Shabbat table, since we have many guests and newcomers, we like to pose a question which helps us get to know our guests and which spurs further conversation. Questions like "What is one thing you are grateful for?" or "Who is your favorite biblical personality and why?" are helpful for inspiring deeper discussion at the Shabbat table.

SINGING SONGS

It is also customary to sing Shabbat songs, called *zemirot,* at the Shabbat table, something my family really enjoys. A good number of these songs were written by great Sages specifically to be sung at the Shabbat table. Many of them appear in *bentchers,* small books that contain the special prayers we recite at Shabbat meals. In the back of the popular NCSY *bentcher,* there are also some shorter and easier-to-follow melodies that can be sung at the Shabbat table. Or one can simply sing what is called a *niggun,* a tune without words. The chasidic masters teach that music, even a simple

The author at his bar mitzvah reading from the Torah

STOP AND REFLECT: What do you think is special about singing a melody without words?

tune, can open our hearts and help us become more spiritually connected. Singing can truly transform a Shabbat table. I highly recommend it!

KABBALAH CORNER:

Music permeates the very foundation of creation. The *Tikkunei Zohar*, a foundational kabbalistic text, interprets the first word of the Torah, *Bereshit* (Genesis), as an anagram for *Shirat Av*, meaning both "The Song of the Father" and "The Song of the Alphabet." This alludes to the tradition that God created and continues to create the world through speech and the vibrations of the Hebrew letters. From a scientific perspective, the universe is built on vibrations and harmonic frequencies – sound pulsating in harmony. This parallels the role of music in our lives, as music is the fusion of chaos and order. Although each musician in a band or orchestra may seem to be playing independently, they unite to form a harmonious whole. This is why singing *zemirot* or even a tune at the Shabbat table can be transformative: It connects us to the divine harmony of creation. (Rabbi Avraham Arieh Trugman)

GRACE AFTER MEALS

We tend to forget God, or even other people who have helped us, *after* we have gotten what we needed. The blessings we recite *before* eating are there to help us acknowledge God as the source of what we are *about* to enjoy. But to express our gratitude for we have *already* enjoyed, we recite the Grace After Meals or *Birkat HaMazon* (*Koren Shalem Siddur,* p. 974). So important is this value that *bentching* is actually a biblical obligation that is derived from the biblical verse "And you shall eat, be satisfied, and bless."[41]

The *Birkat HaMazon* contains four blessings:

1. *God who sustains all.* This was composed by Moses in gratitude for the falling of the manna in the wilderness.
2. *On the land and on the food.* This was composed by Joshua

upon bringing the Jewish people into the Land of Israel. 3. *Rebuilding Jerusalem.* This was composed by David and Solomon over the city of Jerusalem and the building of the Temple. 4. *God who is good and does good.* This was written by the Sages of Yavneh in the aftermath of the Bar Kochba rebellion in 135 CE. After destroying the city of Beitar, the Romans left the Jewish corpses strewn across the battlefield to rot, preventing the Jewish community from giving the troops a proper burial. Miraculously, even though the bodies lay across the hot field for seven years, the bodies did not decompose, allowing the Jews to bury their dead and inspiring the Rabbis to compose this blessing.

It is important to note that the Grace After Meals is meant to be recited after any meal containing bread, whether on Shabbat, a festival, or a regular weekday. However, it is often on Shabbat that newcomers are introduced to this biblical tradition and take the time to recite the various blessings outlined above.

Some time after the meal, it will be time to go to sleep. Resting and sleeping well on Shabbat is actually a mitzvah – so enjoy!

SHABBAT DAY

Shabbat day offers a new range of prayers and opportunities to connect to the holiness of the day. Here are some of the most important.

SHABBAT MORNING SERVICES AND KIDDUSH

While one may recite the Shabbat morning prayers at home, there is a special value to attending synagogue on Shabbat mornings. The Shabbat morning prayers follow the same format as the daily prayers, but with three major differences. The first difference can be found in the *Amidah*, the Silent

Devotion. As on weekdays, the opening section of the Shabbat *Amidah* consists of three blessings of praise and a closing section with three blessings of thanksgiving. But unlike the weekday *Amidah,* whose middle section contains a series of requests, the Shabbat *Amidah* consists of just one blessing revolving around the sanctity of the Shabbat day (*Koren Shalem Siddur,* p. 480).

Music and prayers

The second difference is the addition of the Torah Reading. The Torah scroll is taken out of the ark and handed to the cantor, also referred to as the *chazan.* The *chazan* sings special prayers and brings the Torah to the *bimah,* the special table from which the Torah is read. The Five Books of Moses are split up into what are called *parashot* or Torah portions, each one to be read on a different Shabbat. (You may be familiar with this from your bar or bat mitzvah.) Each Torah portion contains seven *aliyot,* sections of the reading; a different person is called to recite a blessing before and after the reading of each section. In many synagogues, there is also an opportunity to recite a special *Mi Sheberach* or prayer for the ill, during which we recite the names of those in need of a *refuah sheleimah,* or recovery from illness. After the *parashah* of the week is read, a small section of the Prophets called the *haftarah* is read as well.[42]

Lastly, on Shabbat and festivals there is an additional prayer service called Musaf, which literally means additional or extra (*Koren Shalem Siddur,* p. 536). The Musaf service, which consists of an additional *Amidah,* takes the place of the additional offering brought in the Temple on Shabbat and festivals. Shortly before Musaf, many synagogues recite special prayers for Israel and the Israel Defense Forces, and many communities outside of Israel include prayers for the government and armed forces.

At that point, the Torah is returned to the ark. In many synagogues the rabbi shares a *devar Torah,* a Torah insight that is often related to the Torah portion of the week. The Musaf *Amidah* begins immediately afterward.

STOP AND REFLECT: Who do you know currently serving in the armed forces in Israel or elsewhere that you can keep in your prayers for a safe return?

In most synagogues, Shabbat morning services are followed by a *Kiddush* consisting of wine, grape juice, or whiskey, over which *Kiddush* is recited. This *Kiddush* is different from the one recited on Friday night since it was instituted by the Sages, in contrast to the Friday night *Kiddush,* whose source is biblical.[43] The Saturday morning *Kiddush* is also shorter, consisting primarily of the blessing over the drink, although many have the custom of also reciting some Shabbat-related verses from the Torah before the blessing:

(When saying *Kiddush* on wine or grape juice:)

בָּרוּךְ אַתָּה ה׳ אֱ-לֹהֵינוּ מֶלֶךְ הָעוֹלָם, בּוֹרֵא פְּרִי הַגָּפֶן.

Baruch Attah Ado-nai, Elo-heinu Melech HaOlam,
borei peri hagafen.

Blessed are You, Lord our God, King of the Universe,
who creates the fruit of the vine.

Most synagogues also serve refreshments at the *Kiddush* following services. This is done both because *Kiddush* must be accompanied by a meal[44] and because it promotes community building. The *Kiddush* has become a wonderful time for members of the community to check in with each other, stay connected, and build new relationships. In Jewish communities which have many singles, the *Kiddush* following services often serves as an important meeting place. Of the 382 couples who have met and married though the Manhattan Jewish Experience (MJE), the organization I am privileged to direct, many have met at the *Kiddush* following our services.

SHABBAT LUNCH

Shabbat lunch begins with the recitation of the Shabbat morning *Kiddush*, unless one has already heard the *Kiddush* in synagogue and eaten some food containing grain.[45]

Just like Friday night dinner, *Kiddush* is followed by hand washing and the recitation of the *HaMotzi* blessing over two loaves of bread. It is again customary to sing songs and share words of Torah, and the meal concludes with the *Birkat HaMazon*, the Grace After Meals.

ENJOYING THE AFTERNOON

In the afternoon, some like to take a leisurely walk, take a nap, read a book, study Torah, or play board games. These activities are all considered part of the mitzvah of *oneg Shabbat*, rejoicing on Shabbat.

THE THIRD MEAL: AS SHABBAT EBBS AWAY...

It is also considered part of the mitzvah of *oneg Shabbat*, "rejoicing on Shabbat," to eat a third meal or *Seudah Shelishit*. Since the first meal is on Friday night and the second is Saturday lunch, the third meal is usually eaten later in the afternoon before sundown.

It is not as elaborate as the first two, but should also include hand washing, two loaves of bread, and the Grace After Meals. *Kiddush* is not recited. The third meal is also a time to sing soulful songs as Shabbat begins to ebb away.

Rabbi Soloveitchik once recounted that when he was younger, there was a small chasidic synagogue

KABBALAH CORNER:
When God first created the finite universe, He created a great light that He hid away for the righteous in the future. The Torah refers to this light as "day," while also using the word "day" three times in regard to celebrating Shabbat. This is because when we celebrate Shabbat by eating three meals, we experience a taste of the great light that will once again shine in the World to Come. (Rabbi Yehudah Aryeh Leib Alter)

where he would occasionally go for *Seudah Shelishit*. As a child he would join with the Chasidim as they would sing the traditional songs for the third meal, about which he noted, "It occurred to me that they weren't singing because they wanted to sing; they were singing because they did not want to allow Shabbos to leave." He went on to share another experience he had in that small synagogue: "One of the men who had been singing most enthusiastically, wearing a *kapoteh* (chasidic robe) consisting of more holes than material, approached me and asked if I recognized him. I told him that I did not, and he introduced himself as Yankel the Porter. Now during the week, I knew Yankel the Porter as someone very ordinary, wearing shabby clothes and walking around with a rope. I could not imagine that this individual of such regal bearing could be the same person. Yet on Shabbos he wore a *kapoteh* and *shtreimel* – the long black jacket and ornate hat made of fur worn by chasidic Jews on Shabbat. That is because his soul wasn't Yankel the Porter, but Yankel the Prince. Well, after nightfall I naively asked him, 'When do we daven Maariv (the concluding service of Shabbat)?' He replied: 'Do you miss weekdays that much [that you cannot wait to daven Maariv]?'"

KABBALAH CORNER:
The Shabbat meals correspond to the three stages of a Jewish wedding: betrothal, marriage, and unity/seclusion. The Friday night meal separates Shabbat from the rest of the week, as we are still usually thinking about the past week even after Shabbat begins. By Shabbat lunch, we are already comfortably in Shabbat mode and feel a different connection than we felt the previous evening. Finally, at the third meal, as Shabbat ebbs away, we reach a unity that is higher than any connection we have felt until then on Shabbat: We become one with the Shabbat Queen.
(Rabbi Shalom Noach Berezovsky, the Slonimer Rebbe)

Rabbi Soloveitchik was recalling the warm emotions this man and the other Chasidim had for Shabbat – a feeling he could sense at the third meal. For those who are truly in love with Shabbat, the third meal is a sad time since it begins to mark the end of Shabbat. This feeling of melancholy can be sensed in the soulful and even sad songs sung at the third meal. The songs we sing at the three meals of Shabbat express the emotions Shabbat engenders within us. Getting into that headspace allows us a respite from the difficulties we face during the week and enables us to create an island in time to reconnect with our Creator and the most important people in our lives.

HAVDALAH: ESCORTING THE SHABBAT QUEEN

Just as we inaugurate Shabbat with the *Kiddush,* we mark the conclusion of Shabbat with *Havdalah.*[46] The *Havdalah* is our way of escorting the Shabbat Queen with dignity and grace. The word *Havdalah* means "separation." As we take leave of Shabbat with this prayer, we acknowledge our ability to distinguish – to tell the difference between holy times like Shabbat and the festivals and more mundane periods like the workweek. The ability to distinguish, to know that there is a time and place for everything, is uniquely human.

Havdala at MJE

Distinguishing between Shabbat and weekdays is part of Judaism's larger philosophy. While we live in a world that often intentionally seeks to blur differences, Judaism maintains that we must draw distinctions between roles (i.e., parent and child, male and female, etc.) and categories, such as sacred and profane. For this reason, the *Havdalah* also acknowledges our ability to tell the difference between "light and darkness,"[47] a metaphor for good and evil. We are held responsible for our moral choices precisely because we possess the ability to tell the difference between right and wrong.

> "Woe to those who call evil good and good evil, who turn darkness into light and light into darkness, who make the bitter sweet and the sweet bitter." (Isaiah 5:20)

The *Havdalah* prayer is recited over a flame, which means that the *Havdalah* candle must consist of at least two wicks or candles. This halachah (law) is based on the following rabbinic tradition. Due to Adam and Eve's sin of eating from the forbidden fruit, God wished to hide the primordial light He created for the world on the first day of creation and to expel Adam and Eve from the Garden of Eden. However, due to the sanctity of Shabbat, God stayed the sentence and left the light to shine until the end of Shabbat. When the sun began to set at the end of the very first Shabbat, at the end of the seventh day of creation, Adam became terrified of the darkness. God taught Adam how to create his own light by directing him to rub two stones together, creating fire for the first time. At that moment, Adam praised God and recited a blessing: "Blessed are You, Lord our God, who creates the lights of the fire" – the blessing we say as part of *Havdalah*.[48] To commemorate this creation of fire by human beings, we conclude the Shabbat by creating a flame and we then enjoy its light.

Former chief rabbi of Great Britain Rabbi Jonathan Sacks, of blessed memory, shared a profound idea on this last point: "The light of the first day was created by God. The light of the eighth day is what God taught us to create. It symbolizes our 'partnership with God in the work of creation.' There is no more beautiful image than this of how God empowers us to join Him in bringing light to the world. On Shabbat we remember God's creation. On the eighth day (Motza'ei Shabbat) we celebrate our creativity as the image and partner of God."[49]

This brings us full circle in our exploration of Shabbat. As I noted in the beginning of the chapter, by ceasing from creative activity each Shabbat we turn the world back to God, demonstrating our belief that God is both Creator and Sustainer of the world and an ever-present force in our lives. *Havdalah,* which transitions us back into the workweek, acknowledges humanity's special role in partnering with God to be creators in making the world a better place.

> "God created the world incomplete and tasked man to perfect it, making him a partner in the unfolding of the heavenly design." (Rabbi Moshe Chaim Luzzatto)

HOW TO RECITE HAVDALAH

The items needed for *Havdalah* are a glass of wine, grape juice, whiskey, or beer, a *Havdalah* candle[50] (consisting of two or more wicks), and spices. The *Havdalah* ceremony begins with the recitation of a selection of verses from the Hebrew Bible.[51] They are usually sung but can simply be recited or chanted in Hebrew or English.

Behold God is my salvation; I will trust and not be afraid.

The Lord, the Lord, is my strength and my song.

He has become my salvation.

With joy you will draw water from the springs of salvation.

Salvation is the Lord's; on Your people is Your blessing, Selah.

The Lord of hosts is with us, the God of Jacob is our stronghold, Selah.

Lord of hosts: happy is the one who trusts in You.

Lord, save! May the King answer us on the day we call.

For the Jews there was light and gladness, joy and honor – so may it be for us.

I will lift the cup of salvation and call on the name of the Lord.

Afterward, we recite the following blessing over the wine (or grape juice, whiskey, or beer) [52] but we don't drink the wine or other beverage until the conclusion of *Havdalah*:

בָּרוּךְ אַתָּה ה׳ אֱ־לֹהֵינוּ מֶלֶךְ הָעוֹלָם, בּוֹרֵא פְּרִי הַגָּפֶן.

Baruch Attah Ado-nai, Elo-heinu Melech HaOlam, borei peri hagafen.

Blessed are You, Lord our God, King of the Universe, who creates the fruit of the vine.

We then recite the following blessing over spices and smell them:

בָּרוּךְ אַתָּה ה׳ אֱ־לֹהֵינוּ מֶלֶךְ הָעוֹלָם, בּוֹרֵא מִינֵי בְשָׂמִים.

Baruch Attah Ado-nai, Elo-heinu Melech HaOlam, borei minei vesamim.

Blessed are You, Lord our God, King of the Universe, who creates the various spices.

We smell spices during *Havdalah* to help revive the soul, which is saddened by the departure of the "additional soul," which the Sages teach enters as Shabbat begins. This additional soul enables us to be more disposed to peace and tranquility throughout Shabbat. Some suggest that we use a fragrance to ease the pain of the soul because smell was the only sense Adam and Eve did not use in committing the sin of eating from the Tree of Knowledge. Smell is therefore seen as the most refined of the senses and the one most enjoyed by the soul.[53]

After smelling the spices, we recite the following blessing over the flame:

בָּרוּךְ אַתָּה ה׳ אֱ־לֹהֵינוּ מֶלֶךְ הָעוֹלָם, בּוֹרֵא מְאוֹרֵי הָאֵשׁ.

Baruch Attah Ado-nai, Elo-heinu Melech HaOlam, borei meorei ha'esh.

Blessed are You, Lord our God, King of the Universe, who creates the lights of fire.

We then make use of the light by looking at the fingernails and palm of our hand. We do this because the flame must be bright enough to see the difference between coins of one country and another,[54] which can be determined by seeing the difference between nail and flesh. Nails are also a symbol of blessing in that they constantly grow. Some also explain that as we leave the peace and harmony of Shabbat and we enter the workweek, we are forced to confront challenge and conflict. Such negative spiritual forces are associated with the nails.[55] When we gaze at the fingernails in the light of the *Havdalah* candle, we symbolically weaken their energy.[56] Some also gaze at their palms since according to Jewish mysticism, there is a sign leading to blessing in the creases of one's palms.[57] The custom is therefore to clench the four fingers over the thumb so the nails and palm can be viewed at once.

After the blessing over the flame, we recite the concluding blessing of *Havdalah,* which expresses our ability to distinguish between the holy and mundane, the Jewish people and rest of nations of the world, light and darkness, and the seventh day from the first six days of creation.

> "*Havdalah* is not just a farewell to Shabbat, but a call to infuse the mundane with the sacred light we have absorbed." (Rabbi Asher Weiss)

בָּרוּךְ אַתָּה ה׳ אֱ־לֹהֵינוּ מֶלֶךְ הָעוֹלָם, הַמַּבְדִּיל בֵּין
קֹדֶשׁ לְחוֹל, בֵּין אוֹר לְחֹשֶׁךְ,
בֵּין יִשְׂרָאֵל לָעַמִּים, בֵּין יוֹם הַשְּׁבִיעִי לְשֵׁשֶׁת יְמֵי הַמַּעֲשֶׂה.
בָּרוּךְ אַתָּה ה׳, הַמַּבְדִּיל בֵּין קֹדֶשׁ לְחוֹל.

Baruch Attah Ado-nai, Elo-heinu Melech HaOlam, hamavdil bein kodesh lechol, bein or lechoshech, bein Yisrael laamim, bein yom hashevi'i lesheshet yemei hamaaseh. Baruch Attah Ado-nai, hamavdil bein kodesh lechol.

> Blessed are You, Lord our God, King of the Universe, who distinguishes between sacred and secular, between light and darkness, between Israel and the nations, between the seventh day and the six days of work. Blessed are You, Lord, who distinguishes between sacred and secular.

The person reciting *Havdalah* then drinks the wine (at least 3.3 fluid ounces) and extinguishes the flame. Upon the completion of Shabbat, it is customary to wish each other *Shavua tov* or *Gut voch*, the Hebrew and Yiddish terms for "Have a good week!"

THE KABBALAH OF SHABBAT

Earlier, we mentioned that Shabbat is derived from the same root as *shevet* or sit – meaning that the physical and spiritual worlds sit in a state of harmony. The Kabbalah takes this a step further, explaining that Shabbat is a day of unity between God – as symbolized by the Sabbath – and humanity. Kabbalists thus compare Shabbat to a wedding ceremony: Just as seven blessings are recited under the *chuppah* (wedding canopy) at a Jewish wedding, so do we recite seven blessings in each *Amidah* (Silent Devotion) of Shabbat. The *Lecha Dodi* prayer, recited each Friday night, emphasizes this theme, urging the groom (representing the Jewish people) to welcome his beloved bride (representing the Sabbath).

This sense of unity we experience on Shabbat extends beyond the relationship between God and the Jewish people: Each person can experience an inner tranquility that cannot be captured in human language, and, at the same time, the entire universe is said to be in perfect harmony. On Shabbat, a spiritual wholeness permeates all of creation.

> "Shabbat is the secret of the world's inner harmony, the day when the entire universe recognizes its source in the Divine." (Rabbi Abraham Isaac Kook)

SAYING NO TO ONE THING IS SAYING YES TO ANOTHER

In my outreach work over the years, I have generally emphasized the things we *do* on Shabbat – the candle lighting, the *Kiddush,* time with family, community, and friends. But as we discussed earlier in the chapter, it is also what we *don't do* that makes Shabbat special. It is ultimately refraining from the *melachot,* the creative thirty-nine activities that we don't do on Shabbat, that create the special sanctity of the day. By setting aside our phones, we introduce a certain peace and tranquility into our lives. We stop manipulating and exercising our dominion over the physical world. In doing so, we create a vacuum, a space. We then fill that space with Shabbat candles, *Kiddush,* singing, time spent with community, and family. Of course, we can observe all these positive Shabbat activities without the space, without pulling back from the *melachot,* but it's not the same. We need that vacuum. The *Kiddush* and double portion of bread are just not the same when the craziness of the week prevails. I remember watching a skit put on by some Jewish high school kids who were playing a Jewish family at a mock Shabbat table. The young man portraying the father of the household was making *Kiddush,* but while he was doing so his son was playing a video game on his phone, his daughter was texting a friend, and his wife was answering an email. The high schoolers were trying to show how the Shabbat restrictions were necessary to create the kind of space needed to properly enjoy and appreciate the positive aspects of Shabbat.

It is difficult to say no to something to which we have become accustomed. But we know that if we want to get the most out of any activity, or from any relationship, we need to be restricted in some manner. In a romantic relationship or marriage, restricting oneself from others ultimately makes the relationship with our significant other special. Infidelity is not just unethical; it also robs the relationship of what is special, of the exclusive bond between two people. When someone else is in the mix, the intimacy is broken. There are many other examples in the physical world of the necessity of restriction. If on the first day of your vacation in the Caribbean you go out to sit in the sun without sunscreen, what happens? The sun feels good on your body, but you burn and end up in pain and have to stay inside the rest of time. (I know this from personal experience!) But if you apply sunscreen – if you create a barrier, a restriction – you can enjoy the sun without getting burned.

Ironically, it's the absence of a barrier which creates a restriction. Imagine playing soccer on a roof of a fifty-story building and there's no fence. You'll end up having to restrict yourself to the middle of the court because you're in constant fear the ball will roll off. The fence is necessary for us to feel comfortable playing. We see this with children. Everyone acknowledges children need parameters and boundaries. When we get older, we imagine we can do whatever we want and there won't be a negative impact. But it's simply not true.

Rabbi Lord Jonathan Sacks, told the following story when he spoke at MJE. He had been producing a documentary on the state of the family in Britain for the British Broadcasting Company (BBC), and he brought Britain's leading childcare expert Penelope Leach to a Jewish kindergarten in London. It happened to be a Friday morning, and the rabbi and Penelope Leach walked in on a class of five-year-old children preparing for Shabbat. They were having one of those pre-Shabbat meals you may remember from Hebrew school. One little boy was dressed as the *abba,* the daddy, wearing a white shirt and a tie. A little girl on the other side of the table was dressed like the *imma,* the mommy. There was a

Shabbat kindergarten party

five-year-old *bubby* (grandmother) and a five-year-old *zadie* (grandfather). Penelope Leach turned to a random five-year-old boy and asked him: "What do you like about the Sabbath and what don't you like?" The little boy immediately yelled back: "On Shabbos I can't watch TV. It's terrible!" "Okay," Penelope responded. "But what do you like?" The little boy answered: "I like Shabbos because it's the only time Daddy doesn't have to rush off." As Rabbi Sacks was leaving the school, Penelope Leach turned to him and said: "You know, Chief Rabbi, Shabbat is saving their parents' marriages."[58]

But observing Shabbat in this way requires discipline. It demands that at times we say no and restrict ourselves. To help us make that change, it is important to remember that when we say no to one thing, we are saying yes to something else which may be more important in the long run. The little boy in London was upset because he couldn't watch TV on Shabbat. But look what he got instead – a better relationship with his father!

STOP AND REFLECT: What role would you want Judaism to play in the lives of your current or future children?

Of course, if presented with that kind of choice, we would all opt for what is more important in the long term. The problem is that we get wrapped up in the here and now, in what is right before us. Stanford University ran what has become famously known as the Marshmallow Test. They placed one marshmallow before children aged four to six and told them they could eat the marshmallow now, or, if they wait fifteen minutes, they would get two. The study, which spanned many years, concluded that the kids who waited, and were able to display "delayed gratification," turned out to be significantly better suited for success in the world.

STOP AND REFLECT: How can Shabbat strengthen our marriages and relationships?

Spending more quality time with our family and community, doing some praying and learning more about our Judaism, are all great things in the long run, but our jobs and need for instant gratification tend to hijack us. We're just trying to get through the day, pay the bills, and have a little fun on the weekends. There's nothing wrong with that, but Judaism reminds us to stay focused on our long-term goals. If we hold off on that marshmallow, we will have something much better down the road. Saying no to something on Shabbat is saying yes to something far greater.

DEVELOPING YOUR OWN SHABBAT EXPERIENCE

Having said all this, I have always taught my students that Jewish observance is *not* an all-or-nothing proposition. So if you're just starting out, my suggestion is to find something about Shabbat which resonates with you and build from there. It could be the candle lighting before Shabbat or enjoying a Shabbat dinner with friends or family. It could be attending Friday night or Saturday morning services, saying *Havdalah* at the end of Shabbat, or shutting off your laptop and phone to create that empty space. Whatever it is you feel inspired to observe, make it consistent so you can build on it and have some Shabbat in your life.

KEEPING SHABBAT FOR THOSE WHO CAN'T

As Israel was attacked on October 7, 2023, Israeli soldiers were called up for emergency military service en masse. Three weeks later, Israeli ground troops entered Gaza, and many soldiers were no longer able to safely observe the Sabbath.

Meanwhile, countless people around the world scrambled to do everything they could to support the soldiers. There was an urgent call for prayers, rations, and military supplies. But when supporters asked if there was anything else they could do to help, many soldiers asked if others could keep Shabbat on their behalf.

IDF soldiers on duty

Two rabbis, one from Detroit and another from Toronto, offered their community members the opportunity to be paired with Israeli soldiers on whose behalf they would observe the Sabbath. Within a month, eighty-five volunteers observed Shabbat for the first time on behalf of soldiers who no longer could.

One couple, Lauren and Randy Lesson from Detroit, started observing Shabbat on behalf of soldier Steve Gar. When Gar heard that Shabbat had been observed on his behalf, he said: "Knowing I'm not able to be in shul (synagogue) with my family or wear my Shabbat clothes and eat the delicious Shabbat food – but that Jews thousands of miles away were lighting their candles, blessing their children, and sitting down to a nice Shabbat meal...it made me feel the Shabbat wasn't wasted."[59]

On Shabbat, we disconnect from technology and reconnect with our families, our communities, ourselves, and God.

> "The Sabbath is the heart of Jewish time, the stillness at the center of a turning world." (Rabbi Jonathan Sacks)

No wonder so many Jewish soldiers feel something is missing when they are unable to keep the Sabbath, and they also feel a sense of comfort when discovering that a fellow Jew is observing it for them. As the Sages beautifully remarked: "A precious jewel have I in my possession, which I wish to give to Israel, and Shabbat is its name."[60]

Further Reading

The Sabbath
Aryeh Kaplan

The Sabbath: A Guide to Its Understanding and Observance
Dayan Dr. I. Grunfeld

The Sabbath
Abraham Joshua Heschel

The Radiance of Shabbos
Rabbi Simcha Bunim Cohen

The 39 Avoth Melacha of Shabbath
Baruch Chait

TAKEAWAYS

- When a multi-car collision blocked Highway 1 leading into Jerusalem, nearby communities quickly mobilized to host stranded travelers for Shabbat, showcasing Jewish devotion to and love for Shabbat.
- The Shabbat is not just any commandment but a revolutionary spiritual practice that Judaism brought to the world.
- All week long there is a tension between the physical and spiritual worlds, but on Shabbat these two realms coexist in harmony and enjoy spiritual serenity.
- Observing Shabbat helps us remember two fundamental principles of Jewish faith, God's creation of the world and His continued involvement in our lives.
- By refraining from creative work on Shabbat, we relinquish control over the world and hand it back to God, the ultimate Creator.
- Shabbat provides a much-needed break from technology, allowing us to disconnect from digital distractions and reconnect with family, community, and our Judaism.

- By reciting *Kiddush* at the beginning of Shabbat and *Havdalah* at the end, we mark the transition between the sacred time of Shabbat and ordinary weekday.
- Other mitzvot of Shabbat include preparing for Shabbat, lighting Shabbat candles, reciting special prayers in synagogue and at home, blessing the children, washing our hands and eating bread, discussing Torah ideas at the Shabbat table, hosting guests, singing songs, and reciting the Grace After Meals.

Notes

1. Although the Jewish Sages generally did not consider the Ten Commandments to be more important than the other biblical commandments, the medieval sage Saadia Gaon viewed them as ten categories under which all other commandments fall. In that sense, the Ten Commandments take on a significant role in the rabbinic tradition.
2. Talmud, Shabbat 118b.
3. Zohar II, 63b.
4. Rabbi Donin, *To Be a Jew,* p. 61. Rabbi Donin goes on to compare explaining the Sabbath to someone unaware of its beauty to describing a sunset to a blind person: Until you experience it yourself, it is impossible to appreciate it.
5. Genesis 2:2.
6. Rabbi Menachem Mendel Schneerson, the Lubavitcher Rebbe, cited in Senator Joseph Lieberman, *The Gift of Rest* (Howard Books, 2011), p. 4.
7. Exodus 20:11
8. Deuteronomy 5:15
9. Nachmanides on Exodus 20:11.
10. Nachmanides on Deuteronomy 5:14.
11. This idea recurs throughout the *Tanya's Shaar HaYichud veHaEmunah.* See Ariel Evan Mayse, "The Sacred Writ of Hasidism: Tanya and the Spiritual Vision of Rabbi Shneur Zalman of Liady," in Stuart W. Halpern, ed., *Books of the People* (Maggid Books, 2017), pp. 109–56; and especially p. 135 in *Books of the People: Revisiting Classics of Jewish Thought,* ed. Stuart Halpern (Maggid Books/Straus Center, 2017).
12. See *Koren Shalem Siddur,* p. 90.
13. Dayan Dr. I. Grunfeld, *The Sabbath* (Feldheim, 1959), pp. 16–17.
14. The Tabernacle was essentially a portable Temple. The Jewish people served God in the Tabernacle throughout their forty years in the desert and for hundreds of years in Israel before the permanent Temple was built by Solomon.
15. Dayan Grunfeld, *The Sabbath,* pp. 12–19.
16. Genesis 1:28.

17. The Hebrew word for world is *olam,* which also means hidden. The reason for this, the kabbalists teach, is that God is hidden in the world.
18. Dayan Grunfeld, *The Sabbath,* pp. 17–18.
19. Rabbi Hirsch, *Horeb,* pp. 62–64.
20. Dayan Grunfeld, *The Sabbath,* p. 28.
21. Rabbi Soloveitchik, *Divrei Hashkafah,* p. 146, quoted in Dayan Grunfeld, The Sabbath, p. 28.
22. Talmud, Shabbat 35b.
23. One candle corresponds to the biblical term *zachor* or "remember," referring to the command to fulfill the positive aspects of Shabbat, such as *Kiddush.* The other denotes *shamor* or "guard," referring to the command to not violate the sanctity of Shabbat by engaging in the *melachot.*
24. Rashi on Talmud, Shabbat 25b.
25. The blessing typically precedes the mitzvah in order to help us focus on the mitzvah we are about to perform.
26. Rabbi Moshe Feinstein, cited by Rabbi Simcha Bunim Cohen, *The Radiance of Shabbat* (Mesorah, 1998), p. 20.
27. Talmud, Shabbat 119a.
28. A psalm is taken from the section of the Hebrew Bible called Psalms, composed by King David.
29. Rema, *Orach Chayim* 333:1.
30. Like the two candles, the challah loaves are also said to commemorate the biblical phrases "Remember the Sabbath day" and "Observe the Sabbath day to keep it holy.
31. Exodus 20:8.
32. Deuteronomy 5:12.
33. Talmud, Shabbat 119b.
34. Exodus 20:8.
35. Rabbi Adin Steinsaltz, *The Miracle of the Seventh Day* (Maggid Books, 2007), p. 38.
36. Ibid.
37. This is in keeping with the biblical adage "In the multitude of the nation will the King be more honored" (Prov. 14:28), which teaches that the King (i.e., God) receives more honor when people join together in the performance of a mitzvah than when they perform the mitzvah individually.
38. Senator Joseph Lieberman, *The Gift of Rest,* p. 56.
39. A meal in Jewish tradition is defined as including bread.
40. The two loaves of bread (challot) are covered with a cloth for the following reason: Jewish law forbids one to pass over a mitzvah. Since there are two mitzvot before us at the Shabbat table, namely *Kiddush* and challah, by definition, we will be passing up one mitzvah to engage in the other. We therefore cover the challah, so that in a sense that mitzvah is "not there," allowing us to engage in the mitzvah of *Kiddush* which is before us without passing over the challah. Another reason offered is to not

embarrass the challah, by which we really mean to use the challah as a way to impart the important Jewish teaching of sensitivity.

41. Deuteronomy 8:10.
42. The Sages chose the sections of the Prophets to be read, based on some thematic connection between that part of the Prophets and the parashah of the week.
43. The Friday night *Kiddush* is derived from Exodus 20:8: "Remember the Sabbath to make it holy."
44. The idea that *Kiddush* should be recited in the place where we have a meal is explained by the medieval commentator the Rashbam, who offers two possible reasons: The first is based on a verse from the prophet Isaiah (58:13), which states: "And you shall call the Shabbat a delight." The verse means that the "calling" of the day, which we achieve through the *Kiddush*, should be done in a place of "delight," which is accomplished through the meals of Shabbat. The other possibility is not from a verse but from a logical inference: since the best way to recite the *Kiddush* is over wine, and on Shabbat wine is an essential part of our meals, the two thus become linked.
45. Food containing one of the biblical grains, such as wheat, barley, and spelt, constitutes "a meal," thereby fulfilling the rabbinic requirement of reciting the *Kiddush* where we eat our meal. Therefore, if one merely hears *Kiddush* in synagogue but does not eat something of substance, they should begin their Shabbat lunch with *Kiddush*. One should also recite the *Kiddush* even if they heard it at synagogue (and ate food constituting "a meal") if there are people at the table who have not heard *Kiddush*.
46. According to Maimonides, the *Havdalah* is also based on the same verse: "Remember the Sabbath to make it holy" (Ex. 20:8).
47. From the text of the *Havdalah* prayer.
48. Talmud, Pesachim 54a; Midrash, Genesis Rabbah 11:2.
49. https://www.rabbisacks.org/covenant-conversation/shemini/the-light-we-make/.
50. If you don't have a *Havdalah* candle, you can simply use two candles and hold them together so that the flame on the two wicks join.
51. From the biblical books of Isaiah, Psalms, and the book of Esther.
52. If one is reciting *Havdalah* over whiskey or beer, the wine blessing should be replaced with the following blessing, said over general beverages: "Blessed are You O God, whose word brought everything into being."
53. *Bnei Yissaschar*, Chodesh Adar I.
54. Talmud, Berachot 51b and 53b.
55. This explains why according to Jewish tradition, nail clippings should not be left around and why one must ritually wash one's hands after cutting one's nails.
56. *Sefer Taamei HaMinhagim* 415.
57. Rav Hai Gaon, quoted by the Tur, *Orach Chayim* 298.
58. Lecture delivered at MJE in 2012.
59. https://www.jns.org/those-who-can-keeping-the-day-for-those-who-cant-shabbat-4-soldiers/.
60. Talmud, Shabbat 10b.

CHAPTER 6
Tikkun Olam

CHAPTER 6

Tikkun Olam

Jewish Social Justice

In April 2015, Nepal was hit by one of the most devastating earthquakes in history. Almost immediately, Israel sent an IDF relief team to help save people trapped under the rubble and to set up a field hospital for the wounded. In just ten days of operation, its 150 medical personnel treated at least 1,472 victims, including ninety life-saving surgeries, six caesarean sections, and two natural births. The hospital offered operating rooms, imaging facilities, advanced labs, and an intensive care section. It even had a synagogue and kosher kitchen.[1]

IDF soldier volunteering in Turkey, 1999

When the Israeli medical team returned to Israel, Prime Minister Benjamin Netanyahu personally greeted the team, proclaiming: "You have shown the true face of Israel – a country that values life."

This was not an isolated event. Israel is consistently one of the first countries to respond to disasters all over the world. The IDF has sent relief medical teams to countries hit by earthquakes in all corners of the globe, including Mexico, Armenia, Turkey, El Salvador, India, Peru, and Indonesia. In 1994, during the Rwandan refugee crisis, Israel initiated operation Interns for Hope, establishing a field hospital in neighboring Zaire to deliver medical aid to refugees. Israel sent aid supplies to Sri Lanka in response to the devastating flood of 2003 and was among the first three countries to provide aid to victims of the 2004 tsunami that ravaged parts of Southeast Asia. In 2010, when Haiti was devastated by a 7.0-level earthquake, Israel sent an emergency team of 250 doctors, nurses, and rescue workers. Newspapers reported that the mother of the first Haitian child the Israeli team delivered named her son "Israel" because of the extraordinary care she was given by the Israeli team.[2]

My friend Rabbi Yosie Levine told a story about an Israeli named Meir, who traveled each year to the United States to raise money for a worthy cause in Israel. On one of his trips, Meir forgot to fill the tank of the car he had rented. Sure enough, as he was driving down a New Jersey highway, he ran out of gas. Meir pulled the car onto the shoulder and got out. As he was trying to figure out what to do, a jeep driving by pulled over. The driver, a black man, spotted Meir, an unmistakably Orthodox-looking Jew. Meir shared that he was visiting from Israel. The driver immediately became emotional and began to cry. Tears rolling down his eyes, the driver stepped forward and hugged Meir. Taken back, Meir asked: "Are you alright? Why are you hugging me?" Composing himself, the driver answered: "I am from Haiti. My entire neighborhood was devastated in the earthquake. Most of my family was killed. We thought the world was coming to an end and there was no one to help. No one seemed to care. And then Israel came. They cared. I have never since met anyone from Israel, so I pulled over my car to help you – and really to thank you."

For such a small country, Israel has successfully shared its considerable know-how with many other nations – creating, innovating, and making an impact far beyond its numbers. Consider these impressive accomplishments:

- Per capita, Israel leads the world in the number of scientists and technology professionals in the workforce.
- Back in the day, Israelis developed the technology for voicemail and AOL Instant Messenger.
- Israel developed the cell phone and most of the Windows operating systems.
- Israel designed the Pentium MMX chip technology and the Pentium microprocessor used in most computers.
- Israeli scientists developed the first fully computerized, no-radiation diagnostic technology to detect breast cancer.
- Israel developed the first ingestible video camera. Small enough to fit inside a pill, it is used to view the small intestine from the inside to detect disease.

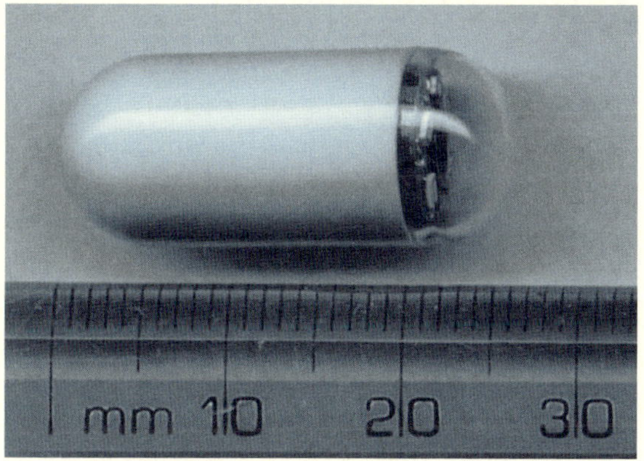

Endoscopic capsule

Globally, Jews are at the forefront of virtually every field. The most prestigious law firms, the most prominent universities, and the best hospitals have disproportionate numbers of Jewish partners, professors, and physicians. Most human rights and civil rights movements have been led by Jews.

Jews are also recognized for their disproportionate contributions to society. The Jewish people constitute less than one-fifth of 1 percent of the world's population, yet they have won 20 percent of the Nobel Prizes in chemistry, 26 percent in physics, 27 percent in medicine, and 41 percent in economics.

When I relate these statistics to my students, they are duly impressed, and always ask: How do we explain this statistical anomaly? Are Jews simply an especially industrious and ambitious people, discovering numerous cures for disease and winning so many Nobel Prizes? Or was this God's plan all along? Put differently, is making the world a better place something Jews were commanded to do or is it simply something Jews *have* been doing? And if this is our mission from on High, what does that mean for us as individuals – do we need to quit our jobs and join the peace corps? Finally, it's not clear how ritual mitzvot that do not seem to be improving the world, such as praying or keeping kosher, fit into the bigger picture. Are these mitzvot important even though they do not seem to improve the world?

These questions are anything but theoretical. Despite how far we have advanced in the modern era, millions still suffer from hunger, disease, poverty, war, and human trafficking. Depression and suicide rates have skyrocketed in the West; the United States, the most prosperous country in the world, consumes more than 75 percent of the world's antidepressants. Our world seems shattered and fragmented. At the same time, for many of us, fixing our own personal lives feels overwhelming, let alone tackling the larger problems of society. Figuring out what Judaism teaches about our responsibility to improve the world is too urgent to overlook.

> "The world stands on three things: justice, truth, and peace." (Mishnah, "Ethics of the Fathers")

A Metavalue: Four Sources from the Torah

Although there is no mitzvah per se to fix the world,[3] *tikkun olam* or bettering the world is a fundamental religious imperative that is expressed throughout the Written and Oral tradition – so much so, that I would call it a meta-ethic in Judaism, an overarching value of Torah. It should not replace or dwarf other parts of Judaism,[4] but it remains a divine mission that the Torah lays out for us to follow. The foundational nature of *tikkun olam* is evident in the following teachings found in the Bible, which we will consider one at a time:

- A Light unto the Nations
- A Kingdom of Priests

- Fill the World and Subdue It
- Remember That You Were a Slave in Egypt

1. "A LIGHT UNTO THE NATIONS"

The term "light unto the nations" appears in three verses in the Bible, all from the prophet Isaiah: "I am the Lord; I have called you with righteousness, I will hold your hand; I will protect you and I will form you and make you a covenant people, for a light unto the nations.[5] And He said: It is not enough that you be a servant for Me [only] to raise up the tribes of Jacob and to restore the ruins of Israel, I made you a light unto the nations, so that My salvation may extend to the ends of the earth."[6] And: "And nations shall go by your light and kings by the brilliance you shine forth."[7]

While the imagery of being a light to the nations is uplifting, if you think about it, it's not so clear what it actually means. The Radak, one of the great biblical commentators, explains these verses to mean that through the seven Noahide laws of ethics and morality[8] – which, according to the Torah, are incumbent upon *all* people to observe – peace and justice will be achieved in the world. This heightened level of peace and justice will in turn cause others to view the Jewish people, who brought these laws to humanity, as "a light to the nations." The Radak also understands these verses to teach that when the nations of the world see the return of the Jewish people to Israel and the fulfillment of other biblical prophecies, they will look to the Jewish people for truth and moral guidance. This is the first way we make a larger impact: Through the wisdom of the Torah, the Jewish people inspire and illuminate the world.

2. "A KINGDOM OF PRIESTS"

As the Jews stood at the foot at Mount Sinai preparing to receive the Ten Commandments, God charged them to become a kingdom of priests: "And now, if you listen well to Me and observe My covenant, you shall be to Me the most beloved treasure of all peoples, for Mine is the entire world. You shall be to Me a kingdom of priests and a holy nation. These are the words that you shall speak to the children of Israel" (Ex. 19:5–6).

But what does it mean to be a "kingdom of priests"? After all, not all Jews were priests (in Hebrew, *kohanim*) – only those descended from Aaron were to be Jewish priests! All other Jews were Levites or simply Israelites. How is it possible for all Jews to be considered priests?

The answer lies in the fact that the priests performed the sacrificial service in the Temple, serving as teachers and role models for the Jewish community.[9] Just as there was a group of priests *within* the Jewish community responsible for educating and uplifting the Jewish nation, so too are the Jewish people charged to be teachers and role models for all of humanity, with the goal of bringing all humankind to the service of God.[10]

A number of Jewish scholars across the generations address this question. According to Rabbi Avraham son of Maimonides (thirteenth century), God was telling the Jewish people: "Become leaders of the world by keeping My Torah, so that your relationship to [humanity] becomes that of a priest to his congregation, so that the world follows in your path, imitates your deeds, and walks in your ways." Rabbi Ovadia Sforno (fifteenth–sixteenth century) similarly explains that to be a "kingdom of priests" means that it is the Jewish mission to bring humanity closer to God – "to teach the entire human race to call on the name of God and serve Him with one accord." And the Netziv, Rabbi Naftali Tzvi Yehudah Berlin (nineteenth century), writes that "kingdom of priests" instructs the Jewish mission "to be an illumination to the nations to cause them to arrive at knowledge of the God of the universe."[11]

Scholars debate how this mission is meant to be carried out. According to some, there is a Jewish obligation to proactively influence people to follow the seven Noahide laws.[12] Others argue that by simply observing the laws of the Torah, the Jewish people model an ethical lifestyle, inspiring others to lead more virtuous lives. Either way, as "the people of the book," the Jewish people are charged with carrying out God's will and, in doing so, serving as His ambassadors in inspiring all people to follow the ways of the Lord.

> "Let justice flow like water, righteousness like an unceasing stream." (Amos 5:24)

THE $100,000 QUESTION

Rabbi Noach Muroff, 2013

Imagine the following scenario. You purchase an item for $250. When you open the package, you are shocked to find $100,000 along with the object. Do you return the money? In 2013, almost precisely this scenario occurred. Rabbi Noach Muroff purchased a desk on Craig's List for $250. The desk didn't fit through his office door in New Haven, Connecticut, so he had it dismantled. To his surprise, Rabbi Muroff discovered $98,000 in cash hidden inside the drawer. Instead of keeping the money, he returned it to its original owner – even though one could argue that by buying the desk and whatever was inside, he was fully entitled to keep the money. Rabbi Muroff was featured on ABC, CNN, and other major news outlets, and his story went viral. This is a classic example of what is known as a *kiddush Hashem*, when one sanctifies God's name by acting in an ethically refined manner.

STOP AND REFLECT: If you were in Rabbi Muroff's shoes, would you have returned the money?

Since Jews are charged to inspire humanity by being a kingdom of priests, the way the Jewish people conduct themselves ultimately reflects on the way God is viewed in this world. This is why one can create a *kiddush Hashem* or a "sanctification of God's name" by acting in a morally upright manner, whether it is by being careful not to speak ill of others or maintaining one's integrity in their business dealings.[13]

The Talmud[14] tells a story of a Jewish man by the name of Shimon ben Shetach who had purchased a donkey from an Arab merchant. When his servants brought the donkey home, they discovered a valuable jewel in its harness. Shimon immediately ordered them to return the jewel, instructing his disciples: "I would prefer that a gentile say 'Blessed be the God of the Jews' than for me to have all the money in the world." The way we act is meant to inspire other people in their own ethical behavior. When people understand that this refined ethical activity is a direct result of our following God's word as expressed in the Torah, it creates a *kiddush Hashem.*

KABBALAH CORNER:
When God desired to create the finite universe, He "contracted" His infinite essence to create an empty space, known as a *chalal,* from which He could create finitude. A *chilul Hashem,* popularly translated as "a desecration of God's name," is therefore caused when one could have revealed God's presence but does not, creating a void. In contrast, a *kiddush Hashem* occurs when God's presence is revealed through human activity.
(Rabbi Isaac Luria, the Arizal)

Inspector Kowalchick

The power of creating a *kiddush Hashem* is especially significant for me on a personal level. Years back, a prominent businessman called my father, of blessed memory, who was an immigration attorney, to see if his grandchildren could get sworn in as citizens while they were visiting the United States for the holiday of Passover. My father explained that getting such an appointment with the INS (Immigration Nationality Service) usually takes months. My father called a colleague in Ohio, where the swearing-in was to take place, who confirmed that it simply could not be done: "The mayor, congressman, and senator all tried," he said. "Don't waste your time." In a last-ditch effort, my father called the INS and was put in touch with an Inspector Kowalchick, who reiterated the message: "Doesn't sound like anything can be done in this time frame. In any case, I'm a deportation officer, so I don't handle citizenship." Before hanging up the phone, though, my father told him: "I'm from a small town in Pennsylvania called Olyphant, and I remember a Kowalchick family that had a store in Olyphant that sold. . . ." Before my father could finish his sentence, Inspector Kowalchick interrupted: "Furniture! How do you know my family's store?" "I grew up there," my father answered. "My father had a store there too." "Let me see what I can do," said Kowalchick.

The author's father working at his immigration law firm

A few days later Kowalchick phoned my father: "Who is Harry Wildes?" he asked. "That's my dad," answered my father. Kowalchick continued: "My mother is in her nineties. When I asked her if she ever heard the name 'Wildes,' she responded: 'Sure, Harry Wildes, I know him. He's the honest Jew.'"

> "Honesty is the first chapter in the book of wisdom." (Rabbi Moshe Chaim Luzzatto)

Kowalchick continued: "Your father Harry came as a peddler to my mother's house. She bought a housedress from him and gave your father a twenty-dollar bill, but Harry gave her change as though she had only given him ten dollars. Your father only realized he had given her the wrong amount after he got home, which was quite a distance from where my mother lives. Around midnight there was a knock at my mother's door.

Harry had traveled all the way to my mother's home to return the ten dollars. She never forgot that." Kowalchick continued: "Look, there's not much I can do about your case, but the least I can do for Harry Wildes's son is to try."

Sure enough, Kowalchick got the INS appointment and swore in my father's client's grandchildren himself as citizens of the United States.

That is a *kiddush Hashem* – when a Jewish person exhibits morally upright behavior which reflects positively on God and the Torah because they are seen as the sources for the ethical conduct.

A few years ago, a woman who attended MJE programs said that what inspired her to pursue a more religiously observant lifestyle was an experience she had in medical school. When the school brought out the cadavers for the students to learn from, at first, all the students were respectful. However, as time went on and the students became more comfortable in the presence of a corpse, the students became more cavalier, some even disrespectful. But there was one student in the class, a young man wearing a yarmulke, who was careful to never speak idly or casually in the presence of the cadavers. He was very strict not to crack any jokes or do anything that could compromise the dignity of the dead. When the woman learned that the young man's more sensitive behavior was based on the Torah's laws concerning *kevod hamet,* the respect Jewish law requires that we give to the dead, it inspired her to look more deeply into her own Jewish roots. This is another example of fulfilling the Jewish mission of being a kingdom of priests: to model the ethical behavior laid out in the Torah.

STOP AND REFLECT: Think of a time you or someone else made a *kiddush Hashem.* What change would you make in your workday or personal life to give God a good name?

GIVING GOD A GOOD NAME

The Talmud similarly describes that the very commandment to love God involves not only a personal affirmation of our love for God but also an external expression so that those around us can also come to love God through our actions. As the Talmud[15] teaches in a remarkable passage: "Abaye said: As it was taught [in a *baraita*]: 'And you shall love the Lord your God' (Deut. 6:5), [which means] that you shall make the name of Heaven beloved. [How should one do so?] [One should do so] in that he [should] read [Torah], and learn [Mishnah], and serve Torah scholars, and he should be pleasant with people in his business transactions. What do people say about [such a person]? Fortunate is his father who taught him Torah, fortunate is his teacher who taught him Torah, woe to the people who have not studied Torah. So-and-so, who taught him Torah, see how pleasant are his ways, how proper are his deeds. The verse states about him [and others like him]: 'You are My servant, Israel, in whom I will be glorified' (Is. 49:3). But one who reads [Torah], and learns [Mishnah], and serves Torah scholars, but his business practices are not [performed] faithfully, and he does not speak pleasantly with other people, what do people say about him? Woe to so-and-so who studied Torah, woe to his father who taught him Torah, woe to his teacher who taught him Torah. So-and-so who studied Torah, see how destructive are his deeds, and how ugly are his ways. About him [and others like him] the verse states [that the gentiles will say]: 'Men said of them: These are the people of the Lord, yet they had to leave His land' (Ezek. 36:20). [Through their sins and subsequent exile, such people have desecrated the name of God.]"

According to this passage, our actions do not only reflect on ourselves. By acting with simple decency and integrity, we can also transform other people's perceptions of Judaism and even of God Himself.

BUSINESS ETHICS: MORE THAN AN AFTERTHOUGHT

Honesty in business practices is an underappreciated but essential part of the Torah. In fact, these laws make up the entirety of *Choshen Mishpat,* one of just four sections in the major code of Jewish law, the *Shulchan Aruch.* In Judaism, keeping honest weights and measures is no less important than keeping kosher.

> "Better a poor man with integrity than a rich man crooked in his ways." (Proverbs 28:6)

And, as we mentioned earlier in this chapter, the two sides of the Ten Commandants are equally divided between mitzvot between man and God and interpersonal mitzvot, to teach us that faith and morality go hand in hand.

In fact, there is a whole series of tractates in the Talmud, known as the "Bavas," entitled Bava Kama, Bava Metzia, and Bava Batra, that are dedicated to our financial responsibilities to one another. While many people tend to draw a line between their religious and professional worlds, the Torah sees them as part of a seamless whole: a complete dedication to infusing holiness into all dimensions of our lives, sacred and mundane alike.

Here are just a few examples, among many, of how the Torah seeks to make integrity in business dealings and interpersonal relationships not just a theoretical ideal but a very concrete, specific set of legal obligations:

STOP AND REFLECT: Most people separate their religious and business lives. What is one way you can introduce Jewish values into your professional life?

- ***Hashavat Avedah*** – This refers to the mitzvah to return a lost object. The Torah teaches that if we find such an object, *lo tuchal lehitalem,*[16] we may not ignore the item. Instead, *hashev teshivem le'achicha*[17] – we have an obligation to return the object to our friend. There are myriad details in the Talmud and later codes about the precise circumstances under which one must return a lost object and how one goes about identifying the owner – all because of the importance of ensuring that property is restored to its rightful owner.

- **Fraud** – The Torah outlines a series of laws that outlaw dishonest business practices. For example, one may not falsify measurements[18] or misrepresent an item one is selling.[19] If one does so, the sale is voided. There are also detailed rules banning price gouging[20] and unfair competition.[21]
- **Mistreating Employees** – There are strict laws governing the treatment of workers, especially servants. For example, one may not mistreat a servant by demanding that he or she perform menial tasks.[22] One must pay workers in a timely fashion.[23] Under certain circumstances, one is even obligated to pay a worker on the very same day the task is completed.[24]

"When a person is brought before God for the final judgment, he is asked: Did you conduct your business dealings with faithfulness and integrity?" (Talmud, Shabbat 31a)

- **Verbal Abuse** – The term *onaat devarim* teaches that just as one may not mistreat an employee, one should not mistreat others even outside a business context. It is therefore strictly prohibited to speak in a manner that is harmful to another person.[25] For example, if someone discovered Judaism later in life, one may not remind him or her of that earlier period in their lives if it might cause them pain.[26] The Talmud goes so far as to declare that it would be better to throw oneself into a fiery furnace than embarrass another person in public.[27] While this is not meant to be taken literally, it demonstrates the seriousness with which the Rabbis related to this law. Similarly, the Torah strictly prohibits spreading negative stories about other people, whether true (*lashon hara*) or untrue (*motzi shem ra*). Gossiping (*rechilut*) is outlawed as well.[28] Ultimately, while we tend to think of laws between humanity and God, such as keeping kosher, as most important in Judaism, but what comes out of our mouths is no less important than what goes into it.

CHRISTIANITY AND ISLAM

When discussing the idea that Jews are meant to be priests to the world, inspiring others to embrace God and ethical monotheism, my students often ask: Have we really accomplished this? After all, there are so few Jews in the world, and most rabbis focus on educating their own flocks. One of my answers is that the Jewish people have fulfilled their role as a kingdom of priests by inspiring the creation of the other great monotheistic world religions. Maimonides makes the point that Christianity and Islam, which both grew out of Judaism, have spread many of the basic concepts of ethical monotheism globally in a way that Judaism could not accomplish on its own. Even though these faith systems contain views that are theologically problematic to Jews, Maimonides writes that thanks to both of these religions, "the world has become full of the ideas of the Messiah, the ideas of the Torah, and the ideas of the commandments, so that these have spread to faraway islands and to many hard-hearted nations, and they now discuss these ideas and the commandments of the Torah."[29]

3. "FILL THE WORLD AND SUBDUE IT"

There is a third biblical dimension of *tikkun olam*. Not only are we bidden to inspire the nations through the Torah and our ethical actions, but we are also urged to *directly contribute to the betterment of the world.*

> "It is through the toil of our hands – building homes, engaging in honest work, creating a just society – that we fulfill our duty to perfect the world." (Rabbi Samson Raphael Hirsch)

The imperative to fix the world appears in God's command to the first man, Adam: "Be fruitful and multiply, fill the earth and subdue it; and rule over the fish and the sea" (Gen. 1:28). According to Nachmanides, this verse obliges humanity to rule over the physical and animal world, "to build, to uproot that which is planted, and to mine copper from the mountains, and the like."[30]

The notion that God created an imperfect world and charged His highest form of creation to work alongside Him to help perfect it is a very Jewish one indeed. In his masterpiece *The Lonely Man of Faith,* Rabbi Joseph B. Soloveitchik speaks of the Jewish value of achieving dignity in our lives: "Dignity is unobtainable as long as man has not reclaimed himself from co-existence with nature and has not risen from a non-reflective, degradingly helpless instinctive life to an intelligent, planned, and majestic one.... [The dignity of man] cannot be realized as long as he has not gained mastery over his environment."[31] Our ability to live lives of dignity, Rabbi Soloveitchik explains, is dependent on our ability to successfully master the physical world in which we live: "Man of old who could not fight disease and succumbed in multitudes to yellow fever or any other plague with degrading helplessness could not lay claim to dignity. Only the man who builds hospitals, discovers therapeutic techniques, and saves lives is blessed with dignity. Man of the seventeenth and eighteenth centuries, who needed several days to travel from Boston to New York, was less dignified than modern man who attempts to conquer space, boards a plane at the New York Airport at midnight, and takes several hours later a leisurely walk along the streets of London."[32]

Rabbi Joseph B. Soloveitchik, circa 1958

Besides making the world a more suitable and pleasant place to live, building a better world is also how we imitate God, another important religious principle. The God of the Hebrew Bible is a Creator. By engaging in the creative process, by manipulating and trying to perfect the physical world, we mimic God. In so doing, we express an important aspect of our Godliness within.

FINISHING WHAT GOD STARTED

Jewish tradition directs us to take this a step further: to improve the world not only so we can reflect our Godliness as creators, but also to complete God's work of creation. The Talmud tells us that the great Sage Rabbi Akiva was once engaged in dialogue with the Roman leader Turnus Rufus, who asked the great rabbi: "If your God loves the poor, why does He not support them Himself?" Rabbi Akiva responded: "He commands us to save the poor so that through them we will be saved from the judgment of *Gehinom* (Hell)." The judgment of *Gehinom* is given to those who fail to fulfill the very purpose for their creation. God can certainly care for the poor. He could, of course, heal anyone who is sick and provide for all of our needs. But then what would be the point of our creation? God purposely created an imperfect world to give us the opportunity to partner with Him in improving that world and helping others – to finish what God began.

4. "REMEMBER THAT YOU WERE A SLAVE IN EGYPT"

There is a fourth and final biblical source for the obligation to improve the world: "You shall not pervert the justice due to a stranger or to the fatherless; nor take a widow's garment in pawn. Remember that you were a slave in Egypt, and the Lord your God redeemed you; therefore I command you to observe this commandment" (Deut. 24:17–18).

The Torah here connects the command to act morally toward a convert, orphan, and widow with the Jewish enslavement in Egypt. What is the relationship between the two?

Rabbi Soloveitchik answers: "Whenever the Torah wants to impress upon us the mitzvah of having compassion for the oppressed in society, it reminds us of our similar helplessness and lowly status during our bondage in Egypt."[33] Thousands of years later, the oppression to which the Jewish people were subject as slaves in Egypt remains a fundamental reason for the Jewish obligation to extend special care and sensitivity toward

"Remember that you were a slave"

the more vulnerable in society. The "stranger," referring to the convert to Judaism, "personifies the helpless one who has no family or friends to intercede on his behalf. For this reason, as the Talmud indicates, the Torah exhorts us in thirty-six scriptural references to treat the stranger kindly."[34] The Jewish teaching of compassion, which appears throughout biblical and rabbinic literature, was established on the foundation of Jewish historical memory: "The Egyptian bondage was of great value for us, since it served to implant within us the qualities of kindness and mercy."[35] It "sharpened the Jews' ethical sensitivity and moral awareness."[36]

"Pursue goodness, seek justice, right the wrongs of the oppressed, defend the orphan, champion the widow." (Isaiah 1:17)

KABBALAH CORNER:

The kabbalistic concept of *yeridah letzorech aliyah,* "descent for the sake of ascent," is deeply woven into the fabric of creation. A physical or spiritual decline is often necessary to achieve an elevation that otherwise would not have been possible. For example, while the Jews suffered immensely in Egypt, their slavery also sharpened their ethical sensitivity, implanting within them the quality of compassion and preparing them to receive the Torah. The same is true for us as individuals: Every descent carries within it the seeds of our future elevation. (Rabbi Moshe Chaim Luzzatto)

Rabbi Soloveitchik adds that this emphasis on kindness helps explain why Jews, even those alienated from religious practice, tend to be highly responsive to causes affecting mankind and are less involved in crimes involving murder or physical violence. He writes that "embezzlement and cheating in financial matters may entice Jews vulnerable to the temptations of money and riches; but rarely homicide, which occurs so frequently in other cultures." Rabbi Soloveitchik maintains that this has something to do with the fact the Jewish people began as an enslaved people. Compassion is something all humans have the capacity for since all mankind was created in God's image, but it can be suppressed. This is why the Torah urges time and again that we must learn the lessons of the Exodus. "The Egyptian experience sought to transform the Jews into a people to whom compassion would be a necessity, not merely a capacity."[37]

STOP AND REFLECT: What *tikkun olam* cause most inspires you?

This, then, is the fourth dimension of *tikkun olam*: We must utilize our experience in Egypt as a catalyst to care for the impoverished and the downtrodden, Jew and non-Jew alike.

JEWISH RESPONSIBILITY TO SOCIETY

Some claim that this Jewish responsibility to act kindly to care for the downtrodden is limited to caring for other Jews. But Maimonides makes it clear that this is not true: "Even with respect to gentiles, our Sages required us to visit their sick, bury their dead along with the dead of Israel, and maintain their poor as well as the Jewish poor in the interests of peace. Behold it is written, 'The Lord is good to all, and His mercies are over all His works' (Ps. 145:9). It is also written, 'Its ways are ways of pleasantness, and all its paths are peace' (Prov. 3:17)."[38]

My teacher Rabbi Dr. Jacob Schacter points out that the latter verse Maimonides quotes – "Its ways are ways of pleasantness and all of its paths are peace" – is a "blanket statement about the ethical sensitivity of Torah in general."[39] This makes it clear that our responsibilities extend to all humankind. Following similar logic, the eighteenth-century German scholar Rabbi Yaakov Emden applies the tradition of burying the gentile dead, comforting their mourners, and supporting their poor "in the interests of peace" even to times when the Jewish community has authority over gentiles and does not fear reprisals or anti-Semitism. Ultimately, it is simply the right thing to do for Jews and non-Jews alike.

This also explains the Jewish tradition to read the book of Ruth on the holiday of Shavuot. The central theme in the book of Ruth is kindness: the kindness shown by Ruth to her widowed mother-in-law Naomi and the kindness shown by the aristocratic landowner Boaz to Ruth – a convert and newcomer to the Land of Israel.

This kindness, Rabbi Soloveitchik teaches, was always meant to be extended beyond the Jewish community. While circumstances did not always permit us to performs acts of kindness for our non-Jewish neighbors, there is a fundamental Jewish responsibility to be concerned for all humankind.

> "To heal a fractured world, we must be true to our faith and a blessing to others regardless of their faith." (Rabbi Jonathan Sacks)

KABBALAH CORNER:

At a certain point, God sends every soul from the heavenly realm to the finite universe to inhabit a physical body. Because of the coarseness and temptations of the lower realm, a soul will often become distracted from its Godly mission of elevating its encasing body. Eventually, after sleeping through the storms of this lower reality for long enough, the soul will "wake up" and reconnect with its Godly mission, once again striving to inspire its encasing body so that it may continue elevating the world around it. (Zohar)

This point is powerfully driven home by the fact that we read from the book of Jonah on the holy day of Yom Kippur. This book of the Hebrew Bible tells the story of the Jewish prophet Jonah, who was commanded to travel to the non-Jewish city of Nineveh to motivate its people to repent of their wicked ways.

In the words of Rabbi Soloveitchik: "During the Yom Kippur services, our prayerful concerns are almost exclusively with our own people.... But this self-involvement is not hermetically exclusionary. The universal emphasis is prominent in all our prayers, in Scripture, the Talmud, and the Midrash; and when opportunities were benign and conditions propitious, we have contributed far more than our proportionate share to the welfare of humanity.... It is, therefore, characteristic of the universal embrace of our faith that as the shadows of dusk descend on Yom Kippur day, after almost twenty-four hours of prayer for Israel, the Jew is alerted through the book of Jonah, prior to the closing of the "heavenly gates" (*Ne'ilah*) that all humanity is God's children. We need to restate the universal dimension of our faith."[40]

Depiction of Jonah on a boat

The four biblical sources, then, point to four key ways we are charged to contribute to the world:

- *A light unto the nations* indicates that the nations learn about God from the Torah, which the Jews bring to the world.
- *A kingdom of priests* teaches that by modeling ethical behavior, Jews inspire other nations to embrace our God.
- *Fill the world and subdue it* charges us to partner with God and help complete His creation by advancing civilization for the better.
- *Remember that you were a slave in Egypt* teaches that we have a unique obligation to care for all needy people, Jew and non-Jew alike.

SPIRITUAL TIKKUN OLAM

When we look beyond the biblical sources, *tikkun olam* takes on even more meaning in the Jewish tradition. For one, bringing the world to a higher state of God-consciousness is also a *tikkun olam* imperative. Every Jewish prayer service concludes with a prayer called the *Aleinu,* which contains the phrase "when all of humanity will call upon Your name."[41] This expresses the prophetic vision that at the end of days, all of humanity will acknowledge the existence of God. This will not happen on its own but through the Jewish people modeling Godly behavior. Ultimately, it is the Jewish responsibility to inspire all people, not only people of the Jewish faith, to acknowledge God as the source of all existence.

YOU CAN RUN BUT YOU CAN'T HIDE

The great Sage Rabbi Shimon bar Yochai told of a parable involving a boat that is beginning to sink. The men and women aboard the boat are frantically scurrying about, looking for the cause of the sinking ship. Finally, they find one of the passengers drilling a hole in the floor under his seat! The other passengers begin screaming at the man, demanding that he stop drilling. The man responds: "Why do you care? I'm only drilling under my seat – not yours!"[42]

> "The pain of one Jew is the pain of all Jews." (Rabbi Nachman of Breslov)

KABBALAH CORNER:

The kabbalistic concept of *Adam Kadmon* represents the primordial human – a cosmic, all-encompassing spiritual form that contains the root of all souls. The idea is that we are all spiritually interconnected as part of a single, unified body. The *Sefirot* (divine emanations) within *Adam Kadmon* flow through each of us, and when one part of the body is affected, the entire body feels the impact. Our individual choices therefore do not just affect us personally but influence the spiritual and material reality of those around us. We are not isolated individuals but parts of a greater whole, each one essential to the well-being of the entire spiritual structure. (Arizal, based on the Zohar)

The lesson of the parable is clear. We are all in the same boat and must see our lives as inexorably connected with one another.

As a result, we are responsible for each other not only in the material realm but also when it comes to another person's spiritual journey. The book of Jonah teaches our responsibility to all people, but it also emphasizes that Jonah was not interested in accepting that mission. He did not want to help improve the behavior of the people of Nineveh. And so Jonah boards a ship to flee across the Mediterranean Sea to the city of Tarshish, in the exact opposite direction. Yet God keeps following Jonah, persistently reminding him of his responsibility to improve the conduct of the people of Nineveh. The prophet gets thrown overboard and is swallowed by a giant fish, but he still refuses to get involved. Jonah remains stubborn, but God keeps trailing after him, teaching him – and all of us – that we can never escape our mission to help others.

At times, we all feel the urge to escape, to flee from our obligations and retreat into our own needs. Deep down, though, I believe many of us sense a responsibility to others, that we were created for a higher purpose beyond ourselves. We must start by working on ourselves, on our own character and our own flaws. But Jewish tradition teaches us to also be concerned with the spiritual and ethical growth of others. We can't simply attend to our own spiritual development while ignoring that of everyone else.

This is a difficult concept to accept in our modern society. In Western culture particularly, we are taught to stay out of other people's business, especially when it comes to religion and ethics. We generally take a *laissez-faire* attitude when it comes to other people's lifestyles. "Live and let live" has become our mantra. Religion, values, and ethics are personal matters, and it is not our place to interfere in other people's lives. And in any case, as outsiders, we can never truly know where someone else stands in their spiritual connection and devotion.

At the same time, though, if we truly felt connected to other people – if we really cared about other people's welfare, Jewish or not – it should bother us that someone is spiritually disconnected or is not living up to their God-given potential. We never want to come off as judgmental or as "holier than thou," but we are meant to inspire our fellow human beings in a positive way, not by self-righteous preaching but through leading by example. Every parent knows that children pay more attention to parents' actions than their words. The same is true for people of any age. If we want to inspire greater ethical conduct in the people around us, we need to demonstrate that same dedication in our own behavior. What we say matters far less than what we do. And what we do can motivate other people, whose lives *should* matter to us. We are all, after all, in the same boat.

> "The covenantal community is one of shared responsibility, where the destiny of the individual is tied to that of the entire people, and no one is left to stand alone." (Rabbi Joseph B. Soloveitchik)

TIKKUN OLAM AS A LEGAL FORCE

While there is no mitzvah per se to perform *tikkun olam,* the term is mentioned in a few parts of the Mishnah[43] in reference to rabbinic enactments created to ameliorate certain difficult legal situations in the areas of divorce, freeing slaves, and redemption of captives. For example, the Talmud[44] employs the term *tikkun olam* when warning against paying exorbitant amounts of money to ransom a kidnapped Jew because of the fear that other unfriendly non-Jews will get in the habit of regularly kidnapping others.

A particularly telling example of a *tikkun olam* legal enactment is called a *pruzbul.* Hillel the Sage saw that the rich were refraining from lending to the poor because of a fear that their loans would be canceled by *Shemittah,* the Sabbatical year, during which the Torah cancels all outstanding loans between Jews. Hillel therefore devised this legal instrument which would, in effect, circumvent the Torah's loan cancellation while, at the same time, maintain technical adherence to its laws. This innovation was also intended to help the poor by alleviating the difficulty they had in obtaining loans. Hillel called this new innovation *pruzbul,* a shortened form of the Aramaic expression *pruzbulti,* "an enactment for the rich and the poor."

Rabbi Michael Rosensweig of Yeshiva University explains that the *pruzbul* is not simply a loophole for convenience, but a mechanism to ensure the intended outcome of the Torah's imperative to loan money to those in need. To ensure that the wealthy loan to the poor and not be deterred by the remission of those loans during the Sabbatical year, Hillel instituted this device, not as a simple workaround, but to carry out Judaism's original intention to help the poor. Jewish law, then, uses *tikkun olam* to ensure that the poor continue to receive the loans they need to carry on.

THE KABBALAH OF TIKKUN OLAM

The sixteenth-century kabbalist Rabbi Isaac Luria, otherwise known as the Arizal, uses the term *tikkun olam* in a much more metaphysical manner. In describing the creation of the world, Lurianic Kabbalah sets out the doctrine of *shevirat hakelim* or the "breaking of the vessels." It was God's will to bring a material world into existence – a world which was physical and finite but which could also contain some of God's spirituality. To

create this kind of world, God operated through what are called *Sefirot* or emanations of the Divine. These emanations first existed as ten undifferentiated lights, but then were divided into ten distinct entities or vessels which could receive God's light.[45] God sent out rays of His light to be held in these vessels so the physical world could partake of His spirituality.

The Arizal goes on to teach that God's rays of light were too intense for the vessels to contain them, so they burst, sending forth fragments of God's spiritual light into the world. *Tikkun olam* is a term used to refer to our spiritual task of gathering up those fragments and sparks of God's Infinite Light and restoring them to their proper place.[46] The world is filled with these broken vessels and sparks, and the Torah's mitzvot are our means of restoring the broken vessels so they can once again contain the divine light. Every mitzvah we perform enables us to harness the spiritual forces necessary to "fix" the spiritual explosion which ensued shortly after creation. That is the Jew's unique spiritual task in this world: utilizing the mitzvot to elevate the physical world by releasing the sparks of holiness inherent in all things.

KABBALAH CORNER:

In Rabbi Nachman of Breslov's story "The Holy Fixer," the protagonist finds deep fulfillment by repairing broken objects. Despite constant challenges and obstacles, he continues to fix what is broken, symbolizing our spiritual task of repairing the world. Each repair brings him a sense of joy and completion. When we engage in *tikkun olam* by fulfilling our unique purpose in the world, we too feel the most fulfilled and spiritually connected. And just as the fixer derives joy from his work, so do we experience the deepest satisfaction when we participate in the divine task of repairing the brokenness in creation.

In this sense, *tikkun olam* refers to the spiritual impact we can have on the world and on humanity. It has nothing to do with physically saving another person, curing a disease, or making some physical improvement in the world. This mystical variety of *tikkun olam* explains how religious observance, specifically carrying out the mitzvot, impacts the world and not just the person observing the mitzvah. This is also why some Orthodox Jews who lead more insular lives believe that they are nonetheless making a difference in the world and fulfilling the Torah's imperative of *tikkun olam*: By performing mitzvot which repair the broken vessels, they thereby enable the physical world to partake of God's spirituality.

> "If you believe that breaking is possible, believe that fixing is also possible." (Rabbi Nachman of Breslov)

MY OWN TAKE

Which of these two perspectives on *tikkun olam* is correct – the physical or spiritual interpretation? In my view, the ideal is to engage in activities which help repair the world *both physically and spiritually*. The world, after all, is a physical place with much work to be done. God created an imperfect world with many challenges – disease, poverty, and natural disasters, to name just a few – and charged us to fix what we can. Any attempt on humanity's part to repair that brokenness is a fulfillment of God's command to Adam of *vekivshuha* – to conquer the forces of nature and make the world a better place. But that is only on a physical level. Spiritually speaking, because of the shattering of vessels at the beginning of creation, the world lacks much of God's spirituality. We are thus charged to take part in a more spiritual *tikkun* or fixing – bringing more of God's presence into the world through the observance of the mitzvot. Each mitzvah of the Torah, in its own unique way, allows more of God's light to be felt in the physical realm, enabling us to restore the broken vessels so they can recapture the divine light. In elevating an otherwise physical world through our spiritual acts, we partner with God to complete His creation of the world.

NOT A RELIGION OF ITS OWN

I have tried to demonstrate how bettering the world, both physically and spiritually, is central to living a Jewish life. But it's equally important to emphasize that *tikkun olam* is part of the larger structure of Judaism and should not be viewed as an end unto itself. What we do to make the world a better place must be consistent with other Jewish values. The 1960s' sexual revolution is an excellent case in point. Inspired in part by the civil rights movement of the late 1950s, the feminist movement pushed for more equality in the lives of women. They advocated for equal rights under the law and in the workplace – admirable and positive goals. At the same time, the movement promoted the value of sex outside of marriage. While there were some noble intentions and even some positive results, that dramatic change brought an avalanche of social and health problems resulting from uncommitted sexual relationships such as sexually transmitted diseases, unplanned pregnancies, anxiety, low self-esteem, suicidal tendencies, divorce, and the breakdown of the family. In seeking to make the world a better place, we dare not discard other Jewish values along the way. The feminist and other social movements of the twentieth century have accomplished many great things for society, but the sexual revolution went too far. The road to hell, as they say, is paved with good intentions.

In addition, if we promote one value of the Torah while negating another, we run the risk of behaving immorally and distorting Jewish ideals. The book of Genesis offers a powerful example, when Abraham's nephew Lot, in his attempt to protect his guests from being sexually assaulted by the wicked residents of Sodom, offered up his daughters instead: "I have two daughters who have never known a man. I shall bring them out to you and do to them as you please; but to these men do nothing as they have come under the shelter of my roof."[47] Lot's devotion to his guests demonstrated the great value he placed on the Torah's mitzvah of *hachnasat orchim* (hospitality to guests). But since it came at the expense of another fundamental Jewish principle, his act was anything but *tikkun olam*.

THE DAWNING OF REDEMPTION

As we have discussed, curing disease and innovating technology are expressions of *tikkun olam*. But since making the world a better place is ultimately a spiritual imperative expressed in the Torah, *tikkun olam* must also be directed at bringing humanity to greater God-consciousness and the world to a higher moral standard. The phrase we recite at the end of every Jewish prayer service – *letaken olam bemalchut Shadai*, "to fix the world within the kingdom of God"[48] – speaks of improving society in relation to God. This popular expression is a reference to the Messianic Age when, as the Jewish prophets teach, all of humanity will acknowledge the God of Israel and live by the values of the Torah. Since it is ultimately the Jewish people who are charged to bring about the messianic redemption, it becomes their mission to help the rest of humanity find spiritual enlightenment through the Torah. The metric, value, and aspiration of repairing the world is to create an environment suffused with Jewish spiritual values.

As such, embracing only the material component of *tikkun olam* – of improving the world physically but not spiritually – misses much of the point. Being a *light unto the nations* means that the Jewish people are improving the world both technologically and spiritually. And on the micro level, it means producing balanced Jewish individuals who are committed to traditions such as Shabbat or *kashrut* while acting ethically in the workplace and performing acts of kindness for others – Jew and non-Jew alike. Such a person demonstrates that their willingness to help others is rooted in something greater than themselves. Seeing religiously committed individuals who truly care about other people and the world around them inspires others not only to perform acts of kindness themselves but also to be connected to the Source of kindness. We become a light unto others by shining a light onto God.

I can think of no greater privilege than being God's partner in making the world a better place, endeavoring to improve things both physically and spiritually. Living up to that challenge will, no doubt, bring great meaning to our personal lives and make us worthy of being a *light unto the nations.*

Further Reading

The Lonely Man of Faith
Rabbi Joseph B. Soloveitchik

Inner Light
Aryeh Kaplan

TAKEAWAYS

- The four biblical sources for *tikkun olam* – "A Light unto the Nations," "A Kingdom of Priests," "Fill the World and Subdue It," and "Remember That You Were a Slave in Egypt" – call on Jews to be moral guides to humanity, models of ethical integrity, and active contributors to the betterment of the world.
- Israel has consistently responded to global disasters, sending aid to countries like Mexico, Armenia, Turkey, El Salvador, India, Peru, and Indonesia. These are examples of *kiddush Hashem,* sanctifying God's name through acts of *tikkun olam.*
- Israel has made dramatic contributions to technology, including the development of the cell phone, Pentium microprocessors, and ingestible cameras for medical diagnostics, and boasts a disproportionate number of Nobel Prize winners.
- Jewish tradition teaches that we have a unique responsibility to first care for the needs of our fellow Jews. At

the same time, as Maimonides emphasizes, the Jewish responsibility to act kindly extends to all humankind.

- *Tikkun olam* is not just about repairing the world physically; it is also about repairing the spiritual vessels shattered during creation. Every mitzvah we perform brings God's light into the world, helping complete His creation and bring us to the ultimate redemption.

Notes

1. https://www.thejc.com/news/world/idf-hospital-giving-hope-to-nepal-ixhzce3y.
2. https://www.australianjewishnews.com/miracle-birth-of-baby-israel-in-haiti-video/.
3. *Tikkun olam* is not listed as one of the 613 commandments of the Torah.
4. This has unfortunately taken place in some segments of the Jewish community.
5. Isaiah 42:6.
6. Ibid. 49:6.
7. Ibid. 60:3.
8. The seven Noahide laws are a set of universal moral laws, which, according to the Talmud (Sanhedrin 56a), were given by God as a covenant with Noah and his descendants to be observed by all humankind. The seven laws comprise the commandments to belief in God and to establish a judicial system, and the prohibitions against idolatry, theft, cursing God, ripping a limb off a living animal, and sexual immorality.
9. The following verse from the Bible serves as a source: "For the lips of the kohen should safeguard knowledge and people should seek teaching from his mouth, for he is an agent of God, Master of legions" (Malachi 2:7). It also derives from the following passage in Maimonides: "Why did the Levites not receive a portion in the inheritance of Eretz Yisrael and in the spoils of war like their brethren? Because they were set aside to serve God and minister unto Him and to instruct people at large in His just paths and righteous judgments, as it states (Deut. 33:10): 'They will teach Your judgments to Jacob and Your Torah to Israel.' Therefore, they were set apart from the ways of the world. They do not wage war like the remainder of the Jewish people, nor do they receive an inheritance, nor do they acquire for themselves through their physical power. Instead, they are God's legion, as it states (Deut. 33:11): 'God has blessed His legion,' and He provides for them, as Numbers 18:20 states: 'I am your portion and your inheritance'" (*Mishneh Torah*, Laws of the Sabbatical Year and Jubilee 13:12).
10. Rabbi Avraham ben HaRambam (on Ex. 19:6) explains that the priest of a congregation is its most honored member, through whom the community learn to follow the right path. As Rabbi Samson Raphael Hirsch puts it: "As the priest among the

people, so should [Israel] among mankind uphold the vision of God and humanity and by so doing be a holy nation" (*Horeb*, vol. 2, pp. 465–67).

11. Introduction to *Haamek Davar*.
12. The Lubavitcher Rebbe Rabbi Menachem Mendel Schneerson, for example, actively encouraged Jews to exert their influence to persuade non-Jews to follow the Noahide laws.
13. For example, the Talmud (Sotah 10b) says that by resisting Potiphar's wife's advances and remaining loyal to his master, Joseph also made a *kiddush Hashem*.
14. Jerusalem Talmud, Bava Metzia 2:5.
15. Talmud, Yoma 86a.
16. Deuteronomy 22:3.
17. Ibid. 22:1.
18. Leviticus 19:36.
19. *Shulchan Aruch, Choshen Mishpat* 228:6.
20. Leviticus 25:17.
21. Talmud, Bava Batra 20b.
22. Talmud, Kiddushin 20a.
23. Talmud, Bava Metzia 112a.
24. Leviticus 19:13; Deuteronomy 24:19.
25. Leviticus 25:17.
26. Talmud, Bava Metzia 58b.
27. Talmud, Berachot 43b.
28. Leviticus 19:16.
29. Maimonides, *Mishneh Torah*, Laws of Kings 11:7–9.
30. Nachmanides on Genesis 1:28.
31. Rabbi Joseph B. Soloveitchik, *The Lonely Man of Faith*, pp. 14–15.
32. Ibid.
33. Rabbi Soloveitchik, *Reflections of the Rav*, vol. 1, p. 190.
34. Ibid., based on Bava Metzia 59b.
35. Midrash, *Mechilta DeRabbi Shimon ben Yochai*, Exodus 13:3.
36. Rabbi Soloveitchik, *Reflections of the Rav*, vol. 1, p. 190.
37. Ibid., p. 191.
38. Maimonides, *Mishneh Torah*, Laws of Kings 10:12.
39. "Tikkun Olam: Defining the Jewish Obligation," p. 194, in *Rav Chesed: Essays in Honor of Rabbi Dr. Haskel Lookstein*, vol. 2, ed. Rafael Medoff (Ktav, 2009).
40. Rabbi Soloveitchik, *Reflections of the Rav*, vol. 2, pp. 142–43.
41. *Aleinu* prayer, *Koren Shalem Siddur*, p. 180.
42. Midrash, Leviticus Rabbah 4:6.
43. Mishnah Gittin 4:2, 4:9, 5:3, 9:4; Eduyot 1:13.
44. Mishnah Gittin, chapter 4.
45. Rabbi Aryeh Kaplan, *Inner Light* (Mesorah, 1991), p. 79.

46. According to Kabbalah, God Himself began this rectification but purposely did not complete the process. In this way, humanity would have a purpose, namely to reveal some of God's light and, in so doing, complete the fixing of a broken world. Humanity thus becomes God's partner in filling the world with holiness. According to the Ramchal, if God Himself were to fix any more of the broken vessels, there would be nothing left to fix and no purpose to man's creation.
47. Genesis 19:8.
48. This phrase is found in the second paragraph of the *Aleinu* prayer (p. 180 of the *Koren Shalem Siddur*).

Image Credits

All images are the property of Koren Publishers (Jerusalem) LTD, apart from:

Chapter 1 – Finding God

Page 9, © GPO/David Rubinger - This is available from National Photo Collection of Israel, Photography dept. Government Press Office (link), under the digital ID D327-047, Public Domain, via Wikimedia Commons; page 12, Sodabottle - Own work, CC BY-SA 3.0, via Wikimedia commons; page 17, Designed by Freepik; macrovector; page 19, New York Zoological Society – Picture on Early Office Museum, Public Domain, via Wikimedia Commons; page 21, © Designed by Freepik; kliveroo; page 25, Leonardo da Vinci, Public Domain, via Wikimedia Commons; page 29, Designed by Freepik; Racool_studio; page 38, © Mark Wildes/MJE; page 45, © Designed by Freepik; erstudio (adapted)

Chapter 2 – Torah

Page 60, © Designed by Freepik; kriserdmann; page 63, The Providence Lithograph Company – http://thebiblerevival.com/clipart/1907/ex20-1.jpg, Public Domain, via Wikimedia Commons; page 71, Designed by Freepik; page 80, Ovedc – Own work, CC BY-SA 4.0, via Wikimedia Commons (adapted); page 82, User:Black Stripe, CC BY-SA 3.0, via Wikimedia Commons (adapted); page 85, Eliyak – this PNG graphic was created with GIMP, Public Domain, via Wikimedia Commons (adapted); page 90, Unattributed – This image is available from the United States Library of Congress's Prints and Photographs divisionunder the digital ID npcc.25595. This tag does not indicate the copyright status of the attached work. A normal copyright tag is still required. See Commons:Licensing., Public Domain, Via Wikimedia Commons

Chapter 3 – Prayer

Page 102, © Mark Wildes / MJE; page 103, Designed by Freepik; Racool_studio; page 112, Asturio Cantabrio – own work, CC BY-SA 4.0, Via Wikimedia Commons; pages 119 - 288,

© Designed by Freepik; EyeEm; page 127, BuickCenturyDriver – Picture of Mezuzah or Tefillin, Public Domain, Via Wikimedia Commons; page 140, Designed by Freepik; stocking; page 143, North Charleston, SC, United States – Scales of Justice, CC BY-SA 2.0, Via Wikimedia Commons; page 151, Designed by Freepik; nikapeshkov

Chapter 4 – Kindness and Charity

Page 165, © Designed by Freepik; Guzov Ruslan; page 180, © Mark Wildes /MJE; page 184, Unknown author – Aleksandra Pietrzykowa, "Region tarnowski w okresie okupacji hitlerowskiej. Polityka okupanta i ruch oporu", Warszawa-Kraków: Państwowe Wydawnictwo Naukowe, 1984, Public Domain, Via Wikimedia Commons; page 187, © The Jewish Life Photo Bank; David Khabinsky; page 193, © Designed by Freepik; EyeEm

Chapter 5 – Shabbat

Page 203, epSos.de, CC BY 2.0, Via Wikimedia Commons; page 210, © Designed by Freepik; Terra.Incognita; page 225, © The Jewish Life Photo Bank; Sarah Raanan; page 228, © Mark Wildes/MJE; page 231, © Designed by Freepik; starline; page 235, © Mark Wildes/MJE; page 242, By permission of Rav Tzvi Ron and Midreshet Moriah, Jerusalem; page 245, ©GPO/Moshe Millner

Chapter 6 – Tikkun Olam

Page 255, © GPO/IDF Spokesperson; page 257, Euchiasmus assumed (based on copyright claims – no machine-readable source provided), Public Domain, via Wikimedia Commons; page 261, Courtesy of Rabbi Noach Muroff; page 263, © Mark Wildes/MJE; page 269, Courtesy of Yeshiva University; page 271, © Designed by Freepik; rawpixel.com; page274, © Designed by Freepik; resdikarawaty75; page 278, © Designed by Freepik; estha

The fonts used in this book are from the Arno family

Maggid Books
The best of contemporary Jewish thought
from Koren Jerusalem